DATELINE — PEKING

A man from Harbin.

DATELINE— PEKING

•

FREDERICK NOSSAL

HARCOURT BRACE & WORLD, INC.
NEW YORK

PRINTED IN GREAT BRITAIN

FOREWORD

This foreword to *Dateline — Peking* is written with some diffidence. Prefaces can be tedious—even misleading—things which sour the taste for what is to come. The only justification of this one is as a note of explanation of how the book came to be written by Frederick Nossal instead of any one of several hundred newspapermen who would have sacrificed a great deal for his assignment.

It is the policy of the *Globe and Mail* to try to locate its correspondents in the often neglected areas, those from which the news coverage is not equal to the importance which the paper's editors believe the country or region to have in world affairs—the Far East, the Indian sub-continent, Africa, the Middle East.

When Nossal went to China there were really only two sources of news to the West—Reuters and the French Agency, both of which seemed to be having difficulty in maintaining continuity in their service—and not always for reasons attributable to the Chinese.

As an advocate of recognition of China once the Communist régime was established, the *Globe and Mail* naturally was anxious for representation there. In 1958, having planned a trip to the Soviet Union with some Canadian businessmen, I decided it would be a good idea to continue on to Peking (then only eight and a half hours by jet from Moscow) and negotiate directly for a Bureau.

The necessary visa had not been approved when I passed through London on my way to Moscow. However, the Chinese Chargé d'Affaires assured me that all the necessary documents had been sent to the embassy in Moscow, and the visa almost certainly would be issued there.

It was not. Significantly, the Soviet ministers who had been most friendly and helpful during my Russian visit, who were willing to assist in obtaining visas for any of the satellite countries, could not—or would not—do anything about a visa to China. Their reluctance stirred an already considerable curiosity about the relations between these Communist partners and increased my determination to visit Peking.

On my return to London I pressed my case and finally the visa arrived. This meant travelling back across the Atlantic, across Canada and the Pacific to Hongkong, then overland to Canton, and by air to Peking—more than fifty-four hours of travel time instead of eight and a half.

The delays in negotiating in Peking were almost as frustrating as those in obtaining the visa. Finally, Foreign Minister Chen Yi gave me assurance that a *Globe and Mail* correspondent would be acceptable. Frederick Nossal, a former member of the *Globe and Mail* staff but then working in Australia with the Melbourne *Herald*, was our third nominee. Approval of him required almost fourteen months of negotiations, during which time we learned that anyone who had experience in China (pre- or post-revolutionary), anyone with knowledge of the language (unless a Party nominee), was unlikely to be welcome.

Faced with these unstated qualifications, the *Globe and Mail* chose Nossal because of his familiarity with the newspaper and its standards, his established integrity and proven objectivity. He had also a considerable, if unpublicized, awareness of the new China.

What Frederick Nossal has written here is essentially a documentary of his time and experiences in revolutionary China. He has written in retrospect with the same objectivity, I believe, as his reports from the scene. Moreover, he had the good fortune to share his experiences and to rationalize his impressions with a young family completely unprepared, or in any way "conditioned" by previous experience or indoctrination, for the migration from democratic Australia to authoritarian China.

Unquestionably, the "collective" impressions have helped to shape Mr. Nossal's opinions and influence some of his conclusions. But acceptance of any or all of these is in no sense important to the value the reader can obtain from his book in assessing, as all of us must, the significance and place of this new-old force in our world.

OAKLEY DALGLEISH
Editor and Publisher, *The Globe and Mail*,
Toronto, Canada

CONTENTS

ILLUSTRATIONS

I

THE MOUNTAIN-MAKERS

The men laughed as they built their mountain.

I tried the sentence first silently, then scribbled it into my notebook. It ran easily and, more important, it was true. I was at Miyun, where the Chinese were building a series of dams out in the hills forty miles north of Peking. And the dam builders were laughing.

They ran wildly with their loads of earth and stone, as if this were a weird unending novelty race. They sprinted along with their barrows, joking with each other, slithering—some of them —over the soft earth and tumbling to the ground as they emptied their loads.

Our car had come upon the main dam suddenly, after rounding a bend in the road. The toiling dam builders were a vast blue-clad army, complete with red banners and rumbling drums to lead them into action. They carried shovels on their shoulders as though they were rifles. Tens of thousands were trudging, toiling, lifting, laughing. For twenty-four hours a day and seven days a week, work on the Miyun Reservoir went ahead without a halt. This was the largest water-storage project in North China. At the height of the drive to get the reservoir under way, 200,000 workers had manned the various dam sites. In the past, the flooded Chao and Pai rivers had regularly washed away villages and livestock, and sometimes people. Each year from the bare, rocky hills, the river water had rushed down into the valleys, inundating farms in the Tungchou, Shunyi, Chihsien, Wuching and Paotie counties. To control this summer flood peak, armies of workers were linking various hills to form a vast reservoir. There would be two large dams and nine smaller ones. In two or three years many of the grey hills would disappear beneath a lake. An interpreter explained that with winter coming much had still to be done on the land. There were now only 60,000 workers on the job. We gaped. Only 60,000! The Russian and eastern European

correspondents were as impressed as I was. This was my introduction to China's power through weight of population.

The trip to Miyun was the first venture out of Peking the
Chinese Foreign Ministry had allowed me, and as the months
passed I was to find such excursions from the capital becoming increasingly rare. We had reached the construction area after a
dusty ride through ageless villages, with houses the colour of mud.
The languid peasants of the countryside seemed not in the slightest
degree concerned about Peking's command that they must
"Build Socialism" more rapidly, but the busy dam sites offered a
fantastic contrast. These containing walls were not smooth,
concrete structures but man-made mountains. When work first
began, the labourers carried the earth and stone in baskets. Later
on they were supplied with quaint bicycle-wheeled barrows,
which made the hauling a little easier. As the dams grew, lines and
pulleys were rigged, and the filling was hauled up by rope. Later
still, both manpower and machines were used, and now finally the
filling was being brought to the bottom of the dams by rail.
Thousands of workers in blue off-loaded the earth from the
freight cars on to conveyor belts which carried it to the top of the
dam, and there the men with the bicycle barrows took over. The
stones and dirt clattered in the wooden barrows, as the men
rushed to empty them.

"Why do they run?" I asked one of the Chinese guides.

"Time is precious," he said; "they want to finish the reservoir
before next summer to stop the floods. Already this year they
have built the dams high enough to save many thousands of
acres from flooding."

Then, seemingly for no reason at all, he mentioned forced
labour. The Chinese are very touchy about this question. They
are genuinely hurt at the way the term is often used in the
West.

"You can call it forced labour if you like," he said, not looking
into my eyes, "but it is the threat of flooding and nothing else
which forces these men to work as they do. You see those people
over there?" He pointed to the spot where the dam was highest
and where the men seemed to be running faster than elsewhere.
"Those men are from the villages that will benefit most by the
dams. Previously when the river flooded, it carried away their
food and their homes. They're eager to work here."

It was certainly not a forced labour camp. I saw no armed

14

soldiers with rifles, no police, no barbed wire. Troop-loads of men arrived by train, tramping in long lines from the terminal each with bedding and a few personal belongings in a neat soldier-like pack. They marched in single file to their new homes —low mud huts with straw matting covering doors and windows. That night or the following morning they would go to the dams, and they would see engraved in the mountain side, in red Chinese characters twenty feet high, the messages which told them whose idea the Miyun Reservoir was.

"Long live the People's Republic of China! Long Live the Party's General Line! Long Live our Beloved Chairman Mao Tse-tung!"

And then to the blare of martial music—coming from loudspeakers or bands—they would march to work with banners flying. Every day each man would add several tons of earth and stone, and by the next year the artificial mountains he had helped to make would stem back more than four thousand million cubic yards of water.

"This is the force that is building China!" said the Chinese standing next to me. Suddenly the small man seemed much taller. He stood very erect, his eyes burning with pride.

The day after visiting the reservoir, I saw a film about the Miyun project which had been shot earlier in the year. Short and dramatic, it showed how the main dams grew from nothing; how at first men (and at that time women also) built them with their bare hands by sheer weight of numbers; how everyone battled with the flood peak during the summer of 1959. On the screen workers toiled in torrential rain, catching the water in huge canvas sheets where the earth was soft, to prevent the flood from breaking through the growing dam.

Endless lines of men with heavy stones on their backs trudged to the site, dropping the stones where the dam was weakest. The Communists in China have one advantage many countries lack. If one man can't do the job, they get two; if five hundred can't finish a building in the planned time, they put on another thousand. Set hundreds of millions of people to work for low wages, and there must be development.

To see for the first time a well-drilled wall of Chinese workers tackling a construction job was highly alarming. I asked myself what hidden force moved these men? Gradually, I came to understand. It was a combination of pressures—political, social and economic. China's war of labour is a frantic, nation-wide battle to blot out the poverty and backwardness that has been the nation's cross for centuries. The great incentive is the physical progress; factories, canals, dams, railways, new cities are rising, as China's millions can see for themselves. It is necessary to remember recent Chinese history when viewing Peking's work armies. China is a giant awakening from a nightmare of hunger and civil war. Not so long ago new-born girl babies could be left in the streets to die, or put into the dustbin. Their destitute parents thought this a kindness—for life in China was simply not worth living.

When I first arrived in China in the autumn of 1959 it seemed as if right across the country people were working in the same way as the mountain-makers of Miyun. The pace was not always as fast but the motive was the same. *You must work to build the new China!* By propaganda, by pleading, and by persuasion, the Communist Party had harnessed an inexhaustible labour force of seven hundred millions. But in the months ahead I came to realise that weight of numbers was not enough. The party leaders had turned this unbelievable army of workers loose without any controlled planning, and with a completely unrealistic insistance on progress, progress, progress. The coming years were to bring disastrous shocks to the national economy.

Just over two weeks before the Miyun visit I had walked jauntily across the short steel bridge at the Shumchun border station into China. A Western newspaperman going into China might justifiably feel jaunty, for very few are admitted these days.

It was September 30, 1959, the eve of the tenth anniversary of the People's Republic. Despite flags, decorations and patriotic slogans, I found Shumchun a grim place. Hundreds of poorly-dressed Chinese travellers were shuffling to and fro across the border, loaded with sacks of rice, cooking oil, sugar, and bread. At one time China-bound travellers from Hong Kong were lucky if the Chinese Customs men let them through with their ragged baggage. Usually each article was examined minutely and all foodstuffs rejected with a curt, "You know there's plenty of food in China now." Towards the end of 1960, and in 1961, however, famine conditions became so acute that the Chinese were only too glad to allow as much food across the border as people could carry.

Students of Peking Petroleum Institute doing their morning exercises typify China's disciplined society.

Devout grandmother with children praying at a shrine outside a church in Peking.

My own Customs examination passed quickly and soon I was on the train to Canton with an entire carriage to myself. There were forty comfortable leather armchairs in the airy observation car at the end of the train, all of them empty. As the train gathered speed, I began tinkering with my cameras and immediately a pig-tailed girl attendant, smart in white blouse, blue skirt, black shoes and white bobbysocks, appeared from nowhere, pointing frantically at the cameras. It was clear that I wasn't to use them in any circumstances. For the rest of the journey to Canton she sat far away at the other end of the carriage, never once taking her eyes off me.

For two blurred hours I waited between trains at Canton, but had time only to note a grey, ugly, miserably poor city. All the people looked thin in their shiny black cotton clothes. Bony women were lugging fantastic burdens. I remember seeing six people around a cart with tiny metal wheels. It was piled high with rusty machinery and scrap metal. The load was so heavy the only way the six could move the vehicle at all was by two of them pulling in the front like horses, two pushing at the back and two using iron levers. They edged the cart along the street inch by inch, panting and sweating.

It was late afternoon when my train left for Peking. This time I had, although not a carriage, at least an entire compartment to myself. The bunks were hard but very clean. By the window stood a pot with a flowering white geranium, and on the table were four Chinese tea mugs. I spent my first night in China sleeping lightly, being awakened regularly by the fearful blaring of loudspeakers at all the stations.

On the journey northward I had a couple of days and nights to think about the assignment. Mine was an opportunity such as few newspapermen get these days. It was a very open reporting mission. The only specific instructions I had were to send, upon my arrival, my newspaper's compliments to the Foreign Minister, Chen Yi, and the deputy-director of the Ministry's Information Department, Hsu Huang. My Canadian editors had asked me not to write interpretive pieces early during my stay. In the first weeks the Peking assignment would be a straight look-see reporting mission. Later on, I hoped it might become something more.

The one message I had with me from Oakley Dalgleish, the editor and publisher of my paper, the Toronto *Globe and Mail*, was hopeful and encouraging. The last two words symbolised the newspaper's attitude toward the Peking operation. "Good hunting," Dalgleish had cabled.

The *Globe and Mail* had originally approached me in Melbourne where I was reporting for *The Herald*, Australia's largest evening paper. Would I be interested in an experiment, the Canadians inquired. They wanted me to work four months, possibly longer, in Peking. I had spent twelve months with the *Globe* in Toronto seven years earlier and had lately been their Australian correspondent. I jumped at the opportunity of a trip to China, obtained leave from *The Herald* and within two months had my Chinese visa. George Bain, then the *Globe's* London man, had trekked back and forth between his bureau and the office of the Chinese Chargé d' Affaires in London repeatedly pleading on the newspaper's behalf and on mine, and at last here I was writing to my wife as the train rushed northward. After finishing this letter I began typing notes on my first impressions of China. There were the train attendants with their fly-swatters, the station food stalls, the reasonably well-dressed travellers, the new brick buildings rising amid clusters of crumbling mud houses, the innumerable huge black locomotives which my children would have loved. Never have I seen so many hulking steam locomotives, pulling freight and passenger trains, shunting at goods yards, taking on the coal which China has in hundreds of millions of tons. I noted that most people in the dining car ate twice as much as I did. The furniture and fittings in the diner as in my compartment were old but clean. In this land of no flies, I had spied one or two of the brutes on the stations. From the train window I glimpsed thousands of overcrowded hovels, and people pulling ploughs and carts loaded with crops. But I saw no beggars, no one in rags. I was startled by the sharp contrasts. Great blocks of modern, multi-storied flats were rising next to fields where water carriers with two heavy buckets across their shoulders on a bamboo stick jogged along, bent low under the weight. In the distance were factories belching smoke, and along the tracks women were scrounging through heaps of black dust looking for bits of coal. As an Australian used to journeying through endless tracts of empty, dry land, I was amazed at the intensive cultivation. When there weren't cities and towns, there were fields of rice and vegetables. Rice and other grain grew on terraces resembling giant steps leading to the hilltops. Even along the railway embankments food was being grown.

Ancient wood and bamboo wheels raised water to the higher ground. Peasants, men and women, were treading the wheels in teams of two or three, or were using blindfolded donkeys and oxen which plodded around in circles.

There was too much to take in during these first days on the train. It was like racing through a museum too fast, with the past and the present jumbled around me. The ancient and traditional, then the new, strident China came and went in an instant. The train from Canton to Peking travels through only five of China's twenty-two provinces, and I sensed the vastness of this land of which I was getting just a glimpse. The train impressions were very incomplete, but my first image of China, as an ancient land with primitive backward habits trying desperately to pull itself into the twentieth century, has never altered.

In any other country in the world, trains become dirtier as they near their destination. In China they grow cleaner. On the last day, I wondered why at each station attendants now busied themselves sweeping, cleaning windows, washing down the sides of the train. The attendant on my carriage showed increasing concern about my cabin. Towards dusk, the cleansing activity inside the train became quite frenzied. I am not a tidy person by nature. The cabin boy kept looking into my compartment, at first hopefully, and later with great alarm. My baggage had crumpled each one of the four bunks. There seemed to be pillows everywhere, pillows I had slept on, typed on, sat on. A pillow under a typewriter is ideal for taking out the jolts during a train journey. Strewn about were bits of paper, notes, letters, newspapers, books, pieces of camera. The compartment reminded me of a news room at edition time—an unholy mess. Being the only European on the train, I felt I must make a special effort to get the cabin into some kind of reasonable shape after I had packed, but when the train clanked to a stop in Peking the train guard was still far from satisfied.

In China's countryside night brings mostly darkness, more so than in other countries. Electric light is a luxury, and even in towns and cities lights glow only faintly because power is used mainly for industrial enterprises. And so to come into the Chinese capital and find it festooned with a million fairy lights for the tenth anniversary celebrations was a truly memorable experience. On the black horizon had suddenly appeared tall city buildings and ancient tilted roofs, outlined brilliantly against the night sky.

It was like passing from a dingy unlit entrance hall into a room bright with Christmas trees.

At last I understood what all the cleaning had been about. The moment the train halted, inspectors marched through it, from one end to the other, as if through an Army barracks. Everything had to be clean and tidy. Several inspectors who arrived outside my compartment barked at the miserable guard. He looked very downcast but I was determined not to be intimidated by these two bullies, the first unpleasant Chinese officials I had met. With some appearance of annoyance I had indicated to them that since no other passengers had occupied the compartment, I had made myself comfortable. Then I thrust out my hand at the guard, who grinned shyly, and stalked down the corridor leaving the startled inspectors gaping.

It was about 10 p.m. and the China International Travel Service interpreter who was to meet me was late. I found myself the only foreigner on a large, very new platform. I hadn't the faintest idea which hotel I had been booked into. I didn't even know the names of the hotels. Nobody around me could speak English. A girl porter put my bags on a trolley and led the way to a cab rank in the large square outside the station. As I was getting into the cab, out of the night appeared a man with spectacles, and asked in excellent English, "Are you Mr. Nossal from the Toronto *Globe and Mail?*" He apologised for being late. I was wondering how on earth he had found me in the darkness, but soon I learned that a European's movements anywhere in China are closely watched, and evidently also recorded.

As we drove to the hotel we made small talk. He told me a room was ready for me. The city was very crowded, of course, because of the celebrations. He was pleasant, but non-committal, and I sensed that he wanted to get on with celebrating the national day. Since I didn't want anything special, he said, he would see me again in the morning, and he left me at the hotel. After a quick brush-up—even in my hurry I made a mental note that my room was very like any other in hotels the world over—I went alone into the streets. It was now well past eleven but Peking was still wide awake with crowds of people around. Everybody seemed to be heading for one spot and I followed. The crowds led me to a great square jammed with people. Below, the blazing street lamps made it as light as day, and above, the sky was burning in a million colours. How much the Chinese had spent on fireworks is anybody's guess, but for hours the thunder of crackers and rockets shook the square. Stars and flowers of light cascaded out of the sky. I walked through the singing, dancing crowds, feeling very much of an outsider. Among all these thousands, I did not recognise a single European. Most foreigners in Peking were watching the fireworks from special positions, but I had arrived in Peking too late for any invitations, and I preferred it that way. I tramped on alone, across Tien An Men square, through the very heart of Peking.

On this night, I experienced for the first time a feeling that was frequently to recur—a sense of fear and foreboding generated by the dynamism and appeal of this nationalistic Communism which the Peking Government had created during its decade of government. Groups of young people looked at me proudly as if to say, "You white people are no longer the bosses of the world. Soon it will be us."

Since I spent two days and two nights on the train, I was late for some of the Peking festivities, but the handful of Western reporters who had been allowed in by the Chinese assured me I had not missed much. The Chinese had kept the most distinguished of their visitors, Nikita Khrushchev, well in the background to stop him stealing the limelight. The night after my arrival Khrushchev was the guest of honour at a Chinese concert show. I was invited with other reporters to the palatial National People's Congress Hall, a vast stone and marble palace seating ten thousand people in its main auditorium. We reporters were put right at the back of the hall downstairs—so that we could not see where Khrushchev was sitting up in the balcony. Against the advice of some old Peking hands, a correspondent from D.P.A., the West German News Agency, moved down the hall to see how the Russian guest was faring. He was immediately ordered back by an official.

When Khrushchev left on the morning of October 4, 1959, he gave a speech at the airport. It was, of course, in Russian, but the D.P.A. correspondent, who lived in Moscow, gave me a couple of sentences here and there, though it was by no means an exact translation. A Chinese Foreign Ministry man with whom I'd had brief dealings soon after my arrival, was standing near me at the airport. Hundreds of Chinese had heard Khrushchev's public address translated into Chinese as it proceeded. I asked the official whether he would help me with the translation.

"We will translate speeches for you given by our side," he said, and turned away. Here was the first hint, to be followed by many in the coming months, that all the hidden tensions between the Russians and the Chinese would simply have to burst into the open before long.

The following morning all the newspapers carried an officially approved Chinese translation of the speech.

2

THREE WAS A CROWD

Ronnie Farquhar marched into the dining-room in his rather crumpled trousers and very tweedy jacket, and sat down at my table. Several of the waitresses immediately rushed across to him with menus. He was very popular. After eighteen months in Peking he had learned a good deal of Chinese and could carry on a passable conversation. As the representative of Reuters News Agency in London, he must have been one of the Hsin Chiao's best customers. He occupied two rooms. One was his bedroom, the other his office, which he shared with two interpreters.

"What did you have?" he asked me.

"Wiener Schnitzel. It wasn't bad."

Then Farquhar played his daily farce. He had picked up a stomach ailment while serving in tanks in North Africa and had the bad luck to suffer a new attack not long after reaching Peking. The nurse of the British Chargé d'Affaire's office had put him on a strict non-fatty diet.

Now, months afterwards, he was still sticking to it. He told me on several occasions when I wasn't feeling too well, that in all his time in China his health had never been completely up to scratch.

"I'll order your meal for you," I said.

"No, don't, they might have something else." His very clear blue eyes looked almost pathetic.

For a full minute he studied the menu, which we both knew off by heart, grinned in his delightful sheepish manner and said quietly to the waitress: "Chicken Stroganoff—no onions, no mushrooms."

I had countless meals with Ronnie, but I can't recall more than one or two occasions when he ate anything else but his eternal shredded chicken.

Ronnie was the perfect man for the Peking job. He was calm and unruffled, and nothing surprised him. He lived the Peking

23

story day and night, and was genuinely interested in all aspects of Chinese affairs. He was one of the few people who knew many of the top leaders by sight, although this kind of interest was never in any way rewarded by the Foreign Ministry. They gave him none of the chances a top correspondent always hopes for, such as an interview with one of the leaders. We Westerners knew we could not get in to see Mao, his off-sider Chairman Liu Shao-chi or Premier Chou En-lai. Even Foreign Minister Chen Yi was inaccessible. Ronnie and I would always hold a brief protest meeting, just the two of us, after some visiting correspondent, either from Scandinavia or from Latin America, had been granted interviews with Chen Yi. None of the others was admitted to Mao or Chou during my term—except delegation members who merely shook hands—and therefore Chen Yi was a bit of a plum. We thought so at the time, anyhow, although probably our editors would not have considered him as important.

Farquhar's predecessors had created all kinds of legends about the Reuter man in Peking. David Chipp, the first Reuter representative to be allowed in on a permanent basis after the Communist take-over in China, used to sleep with the Hsinhua (New China News Agency) teleprinter next to his bed. They say he had a good number of nightmares during his term in Peking. The next Reuter man had a wife. She objected to sharing her husband's affections with a teleprinter, and that was when Reuter branched out into two rooms at the Hsin Chiao. This was Ronnie's predecessor who had been banished from China for alleged misreporting rather in the same way as I was to be eased out in due course. Ronnie had also drawn the line at sleeping with his teleprinter. He kept on the two rooms but he had banished the teleprinter to his bathroom. The dusty bath was filled to the brim with old reports by the official Chinese news agency—great heaps of them. The teleprinter was sitting fair and square above the toilet bowl. And, as Tommy Munns, the Executive Editor of the *Globe and Mail* put it when he heard this, "I can't think of a better place for a teleprinter."

Farquhar was the dean of the Western Press corps in Peking during my time, and was hoping to be replaced by another Reuter man sometime in 1960. The second Western Press man was Bernard Ullmann of Agence France-Presse. I was the junior member of the trio. Farquhar had had considerable experience reporting from Communist countries, as head of the Reuter office in Budapest during the 1956 revolution, and at posts in Moscow, Prague, East Berlin and Warsaw. Ullmann had reported wars in North Africa and Korea.

We ran a kind of informal Three-man Press club and met often over lunch, or at the drab bar of the Hsin Chiao. We sat together at Press conferences, strange affairs at which the Chinese reporters invariably asked no questions. It would be up to the foreign correspondents to fire all the curly ones. At Press briefings the Communist correspondents from Russia and Eastern Germany were often as cynical and acrid as we Westerners in their questioning of Foreign Ministry officials.

The Chinese idea of reporting was quite comical. There was little attempt to condense the material to be published—especially important statements. It was simply sent to the various newspaper, radio and news agency offices, and was printed or transmitted in full. The weirdest journalistic experience I had in China was at the opening session of the 1960 National People's Congress, the Parliamentary meeting of a Government supposed to represent the views of almost seven hundred million people. The only correspondents left about half an hour after the main speeches were finished were an East German, Farquhar and myself. There were no Chinese reporters around—possibly they were segregated from the foreign correspondents. In any other country there is always a great hustle to catch editions and radio bulletins at the end of an important Parliamentary session, but here in Peking, the question of what was to be published and broadcast had clearly been decided beforehand. I almost burst out laughing when a Foreign Ministry woman official walked up to us as we were banging away on our typewriters in a large reception hall which had been converted into the Press room. "How long will you be?" she asked. "The cleaners want to tidy up." We left and finished our cables at the main telegraph office.

The Foreign Ministry made a habit of telephoning correspondents with mysterious messages about special Government announcements. There would never be any hint of the topic. The non-committal Chinese voice at the other end of the line would merely say, "This is the Information Department. We have a statement to release. You may come to the Foreign Office and collect it."

"Could you tell me what it's about?" I always asked—mainly on principle.

"It is ready for you right here," the cold voice would reply.

Once or twice, when the phone call to my hotel room came at two or even three o'clock in the morning, I just said, "Thank you very much," and went back to sleep. My paper did not expect me to compete with the news agency boys like Farquhar who was the most conscientious of us all. He would struggle out of bed, long after midnight, to get one of these typical dull propaganda statements, and cable a few paragraphs based upon it. Sometimes after three or four hours' sleep, he would race to the airport very early in the morning to see some Communist Government delegation arriving or departing.

When I did make the trip from the hotel to the Foreign Ministry it was in a variety of ways, depending on the time of day and the mood of the taxi attendant at the front of the hotel. On a sunny morning, with my edition time half a day away, I walked along Hatamen, across the wide boulevard called Changan and up to the corner where there was a huge red star on a building that looked like a garage. At first it was the only landmark by which I could locate the tiny street which led to the grey, staid Foreign Ministry building, for, of course, street names were in Chinese characters, and at first they all looked alike to me. If the little man at the front of the hotel was in a good humour and there was a cab available, the ride would take only five minutes, but in mid-winter, when it was too cold for the half-hour walk there and back and there was no cab, I would hire a pedicab. I never minded driving up in a taxi, past the armed guard at the gate of the compound right into the grounds, but I drew the line at pulling up to the forbidding Foreign Ministry portals in a tatty pedicab. Instead I would ask the man to wait, march inside, pick up my propaganda piece and would then be pedalled back to the warmth of the Hsin Chiao Hotel whose central heating system worked superbly—when it was turned on.

It was vital for a correspondent to make a token appearance at the Foreign Ministry every so often. We were utterly dependent in the Information Department. To incur the wrath of the department could easily mean the end of the Peking assignment, because searching for news independently in China was a near impossibility. In addition the Western reporter was hamstrung by any number of difficulties, the main ones being his European appearance and usually his lack of the language. His face meant that almost nobody would speak to him, even though he might be a Russian or a Communist from Eastern Europe. This didn't alter things in the slightest. The Chinese people are trained to be suspicious of all foreigners.

The Peking citizen was always on the lookout for party spies, and was therefore of little use to the foreign reporter. Shopkeepers were polite but careful not to speak of anything beyond business. Political conversation anywhere was out of the question. Several Communist and Western reporters who spoke Chinese told me that when addressed in the street people would either smile politely and say nothing or would simply walk away. This meant that most of the time you were confined to taking wordless strolls through Peking, or you could sit in the hotel room reading translations of the Communist Press.

There was a time in Peking when Western reporters had to ring the Foreign Ministry even when they wanted a taxi. Today there are not these extremes, but all the same I was almost totally beholden to my coldly smiling hosts for everything from a talk with a railway official to travel permits, interpreters and accommodation. Occasionally, the Information Department arranged one of the many interviews I had requested.

The Wai Chiao Pu, as the Foreign Ministry was called, had an attitude toward the working journalist I simply could not fathom. Why did they allow reporters in at all? They seemed to regard us as a quite unnecessary evil which had been imposed on them by sheer misfortune. Farquhar insisted that he and Ullmann were allowed to remain in Peking purely because the Chinese had reciprocity arrangements whereby the New China News Agency had representatives in London and Paris. I was not in this lucky position. The External Affairs Department in Ottawa offered a Canadian visa to a Chinese newspaperman but nothing ever came of it. During various interviews with the Information Department, I asked several times whether the visa to a Hsinhua correspondent had been granted by Canada. On each occasion the Chinese told me nobody had applied.

Even on such simple matters as picture captions, the Chinese refused to co-operate. Very early during my stay I went with a large party of correspondents to visit a new museum built on Tien An Men Square opposite the National People's Congress Hall. When the *Globe and Mail* returned a set of pictures I had taken to be identified, I rang the Foreign Ministry to ask whether I might take them to the museum with an interpreter and collect

27

material for the captions. I was told that the museum was not open to the public. Very few buildings are.

"But I want to be sure to write correct captions for the museum exhibits," I protested. As usual, the voice was polite, and noncommittal. "The museum is closed at present. But we will let you know."

They never did.

My general relations with the Foreign Ministry could be summed up as being icily polite. When I realised that there was no possible point of contact between the Western reporter and the Chinese Communist officials, I too fell back on distant courtesy as the only language the Chinese understood and respected. There was never any warmth or humanity about the Foreign Ministry's staff members, and I came to realise after a time that they simply could not afford to be too friendly to a representative of the enemy imperialist class. Their jobs might have been imperilled.

Once I told Tommy Munns, to whom most of my mail from Peking was addressed, that I thought "the thaw had begun". It was after I had talked for two hours through interpreters, with Hsu Huang, the Information Department's Deputy Director, the day before my first visa expired. I told him frankly about my problems, and he listened sympathetically. He and the two English-speaking members of the Foreign Ministry's Information Department present were so interested in my complaints that we all had only one cup of tea, instead of the usual dozen served at such interviews.

I told Hsu Huang it would be invaluable if there were somebody —anybody—in the Information Department whom I could contact quickly by phone for queries that might arise. He readily agreed and ever afterwards there was, in fact, somebody I could contact fairly rapidly.

But I never got a single worth-while answer to any of my many questions.

3

"WE'RE THE PRISONERS OF PEKING!"

In Peking, the British are still the leaders of the Western diplomatic community. In most other world capitals they have been replaced by the Americans but not in China where resident Americans are either in prison, or working for the Communists. The British, I think, enjoy their rôle, but I often felt the entire Western community could have done much more to improve the morale of the diplomats, their wives and the embassy staffs as a whole. There were, of course, the endless parties, but for a community of Western islanders in a Chinese ocean, there might have been better and more varied arrangements to make life more pleasant. The British led the Westerners mainly because of their larger numbers, since the Danes, Norwegians, Swiss and Sweden had small missions with only a handful of people in each embassy. The British staff, with their wives and children, numbered about fifty or sixty. I was so busy writing during October there was little time to visit the diplomats. I had spent several pleasant evenings at the British Club, but because I hadn't made contact with the Queen's representative immediately upon arrival in Peking, my first official meeting with the British Minister was somewhat strained. His name was Michael Stewart. He was an elegant man with a magnificent mane of white hair whom I had seen at several dances. I had paid an official call on the Commercial Secretary, Ken Ritchie, but had not visited Stewart, who held the appointment of Her Britannic Majesty's Chargé d'Affaires. The *Globe and Mail* had said it wasn't necessary for me, as a Canadian correspondent, to depend too much on the British, so it was well over a month before I rang Stewart's secretary for an appointment.

When I entered his office he told me he was not at all happy about the story I had done on diplomats in Peking. This was a piece I had written reporting how fed up diplomats were in the Chinese capital, which had recently been published in newspapers in Toronto, New York, London and Melbourne. His was the kind of remark a reporter might expect from an editor, and a sharp reply was on my tongue. But since it was I who had requested the interview to pay my respects to Stewart, I merely asked, "Why?"

He said the British had opened their doors to me, had asked me to parties and club functions, and that he wasn't happy over my saying that British morale in Peking was low, maintaining that the morale in the British Embassy was very high. "I did not report that morale was low, didn't even mention the word morale," I said.

We argued the point a bit longer, and then Stewart said the club was open to me but hinted that I wasn't to use it as a reporter's listening post. In protest I stayed away from it for a couple of months.

Some weeks after this initial tiff, Stewart became most friendly, especially when my wife and family eventually arrived in Peking. He asked us to several dinner parties and went out of his way to arrange a luncheon, when Lord Montgomery was in Peking, for Farquhar of Reuter's, Richard Harris of the London *Times* and myself, to give us an opportunity for a quiet chat with Monty. Stewart, like me, and in fact like most newcomers to China, was at first impressed by all the Communist window-dressing, at which the Chinese are past masters. And, like all of us, he maintained his admiration for many aspects of the Chinese Communist régime, although he too got heartily sick of their unnatural behaviour and their fanatical hatred of the West.

In some ways the diplomats felt even more frustrated than we correspondents were. Since their contacts with the people who matter in China are almost non-existent, they have little chance of knowing what is really going on in China. They are starved of reliable statistics and facts. The Chinese authorities maintain an air of superficial courtesy toward them, but most times the diplomats are ignored. The Chinese don't mix with Westerners on a social level, and diplomats in Peking are treated like unwelcome guests: the less notice you take of them, the better.

The natural reaction of the Westerners to all this is to dream of the time when their Governments will release them from their China posting, after which they will put their stay in Peking down to experience—an unpleasant experience preferably not to be repeated too soon. I met diplomats from Britain, Ceylon, Norway,

Sweden, India, Pakistan, the Netherlands, Denmark, Switzerland, Yugoslavia and Finland who could not wait to leave Peking. Those from Eastern European Communist countries told me they longed for the end of their term. There was a total lack of contact, not only with the Communist masters of China, but with the Chinese themselves. In China, which is a world of its own, foreigners have always been looked down upon as uncouth barbarians, and today this is truer than ever.

The diplomats found Peking an inconvenient post. There is nowhere to go in the evening, no Western-style shops in which secretaries and wives can spend a pleasant hour. "We are the prisoners of Peking," a Pakistani diplomat said. "Many of us feel the best thing would be if they threw us out. We can't travel anywhere without a permit. They loathe us, and all we can do is to hate them back."

Occasionally the diplomatic prisoners were allowed out on carefully conducted tours of the country. Several times each year the Wai Chiao Pu played host to foreign diplomats and took them sight-seeing to various provinces. Usually three were invited from each diplomatic mission, and the party was shepherded around communes, factories, and canal and dam sites by large numbers of vigilant Chinese escorts.

In describing these visits, the diplomats spoke with a mixture of feelings about Chinese methods. They praised and criticised. Sometimes there was envy in their voices, and often abhorrence. The Indonesians, Indians and Pakistanis in particular hit out freely at the Chinese for the way they conducted communes. I talked to many of them after they had returned from a tour through Shantung province. In the City of Tsinan they saw an urban commune where the women were paid about thirty yuan (about four pounds) a month. Of this salary, ten yuan went to the community dining-room. Mothers paid eight yuan a month for each child attending the commune nursery, which meant that a mother with two children would have four yuan spending money at the end of the month.

"It was really depressing to see all those women working," an Indonesian told me. "They work from 7 a.m. until 6 p.m. and leave their children in the nursery for the week. The children spend Sundays with their parents." He said they were making clothes, ropes, toys and furniture and also costumes for Peking opera. One commune workshop consisted of 170 people who between them were paid 5,100 yuan a month. The diplomats estimated that the material (often consisting of soap and wastes) would not have cost the commune more than 20,000 yuan a month. "Yet we were told that the workshop's total earnings were about 60,000 yuan," my informant said. "This meant more than half the sum represented accumulated capital, yet the workers got only a bare living wage."

As is always the case in China, the journeying diplomats were impressed by the amount of work the régime got done, especially before the crisis years of 1960 and 1961. They saw water pumped up a mountain in five stages to an area that had suffered from water shortages ever since people settled on its slopes.

"They showed us how they turned a barren mountain into a peach orchard," a Western ambassador told me. For six weeks eight thousand workers were employed in digging crescent-shaped pits, and carting earth and trees along newly-built paths. In this way the entire hill had been transformed into an orchard. The local people said that last year the three million young peach trees planted had yielded one million catties of peaches (a catty weighs just a fraction over one pound), and that by 1963 they expected a harvest of fifty million catties of peaches per year.

I spoke with a Swiss Embassy official. "Both in the cities and in the countryside it was difficult to find an idle person. Everybody was working. Old men stood in smoke-filled rooms cooking tea for commune workers. Little courtyards had become outdoor factories."

"What is so flabbergasting," added a Dutchman who went on the trip, "is that this constant work is going on not only in Peking or near Peking, or in the few places we see—but right across China. One person's output may not be high, but multiply it by hundreds of millions and the results are fantastic."

On these trips the diplomats hardly had a moment to themselves. Their Chinese hosts were with them wherever they went, and Chinese-speaking envoys were given especially strong escorts. The Shantung Province trip lasted a little over a week, and the touring party, including Chinese, totalled about 150 people. As the days passed, the diplomats found their hosts becoming more relaxed and talkative. The usual official stiffness dropped away, and the Chinese, glad to be away from the routine, began to enjoy themselves. But the very day the travellers returned to the national capital the bamboo screen went up again,

At work on the Miyun Reservoir, north of Peking.

The author being pedalled past the ancient gate of Tien An Men in the centre of Peking.

One of the Peking cabbage mountains which sprang up overnight during a glut of vegetables.

and at the next diplomatic function the Chinese were back to form—straight-backed, silent, very correct, too polite and quite unnatural. There was intense jealousy and bitterness towards the Chinese among other Asians living in Peking. At lunch upstairs in the Hsin Chiao, Farquhar and I would often be joined by a Pakistani diplomat. He was an attaché called Malik, a small, slim man with a sense of humour and a deep dislike for Chinese Communism. Malik symbolised the anti-Chinese Asian. Among the intelligentsia in most Asian countries, the feeling is growing that the Chinese must not be allowed to pretend that theirs is the typical Asian viewpoint. I met Indians, Indonesians, Burmese and Pakistanis in Peking who were more anti-Chinese than most Westerners.

Malik told me that he often tried to discuss things with Chinese officials but found, as did we all, that they were not interested in your opinion of them, but wanted to enhance their own position as Party members.

Malik would never eat alone at the Hsin Chiao, but always brought a male companion. One day I asked him the reason. He said he didn't like the Chinese food in the downstairs restaurant and wasn't going to climb five stories to get to the European restaurant.

"Why can't you catch the lift?" I asked.

He rambled on with a long explanation that he felt in Peking no diplomat could afford to be left alone even briefly with a Chinese girl. "How do I know they don't want to get rid of me?" he asked. "It would be the easiest thing in the world for the Chinese to frame me if they could get some lift girl to explain that I had interfered with her on the ride to the top floor."

Malik once gave me a typical example of how inflexible Chinese regulations can be. He had rung a Foreign Ministry official dealing with diplomats to ask whether he could travel to Tientsin the next day. He was told to come down and fill in the application himself.

"But you know me," he said, "can't you do it for me? You fill in my name on the form." This couldn't be done. Anyway, they said, he knew very well that he would have to give forty-eight hours' notice to obtain a travel permit to Tientsin. This was on a Friday. He hung up the phone in annoyance and presented himself personally at this department the following Monday. "Here I am," he said, "now can I have a travel permit for tomorrow? You remember, we were talking about it last Friday."

"Yes, please fill in this form, but of course you can't go tomorrow. You will have to wait the usual forty-eight hours."

Malik stamped out in disgust and said he would send a Chinese staff member of the Pakistani Embassy to Tientsin instead.

None of the foreign diplomats understood why the Chinese went out of their way to be difficult, and several were going home convinced Peking was the worst possible diplomatic post.

"Many of these people here will get good jobs in the Foreign Service of their countries," an Asian told me, "and you can bet your boots whenever they deal with Chinese affairs they're going to be as unpleasant to the Chinese as the Chinese are being to us here."

In their social contacts, the Asian envoys prefer the company of Westerners to Chinese. They complain that the Chinese are not prepared to discuss matters logically.

"They don't have discussions at all," one of the Indonesians told me. "They merely talk for the record, following the party line. If anyone then challenges their opinions they can point to a report of the proceedings and say, 'Here are my views'."

4

TIEN AN MEN

The place I went to most often in Peking was Tien An Men Square. It was quite close to the hotel. I used to walk along the old Legation Street, now called Tung Chiao Min Street, past the fine embassies, some of which had now become Government offices. One by one, the foreign envoys were being pushed out of their spacious compounds, beautified with flowering trees, lawns and swimming pools, into the new diplomatic quarter. A few managed still to squat on Legation Street. They included the Indians, Burmese, Dutch, and several Eastern European embassies. The East Germans had a magnificent compound a few minutes' walk from the hotel. I was invited there once to hear the East German ambassador explain his country's views on the 1960 Summit collapse.

Tien An Men means Gate of Heavenly Peace. The square gets its name from a beautiful old building which was the South central gate of the Imperial City. The original gate, built by a Ming emperor in A.D. 1420, was burned down and rebuilt in 1651. Marble bridges spanning the moat were added later.

In ancient China Tien An Men was the spot from which the rulers of the land issued their Imperial Rescripts—edicts and proclamations for the people. It was the custom to wedge the scroll containing the Divine Decree of the Emperor in the bill of a carved phoenix. This was then thrown over the parapet to officials kneeling below, and it was their duty to relay the contents to the nation. China's new rulers have not forgotten the political significance of the Tien An Men. It was here that Mao Tse-tung hoisted the red five-starred flag of Communist China on October 1, 1949. Today, right in the middle of the square, facing the old gate, is a simple white monolith called the Monument to the People's Heroes.

The architects and builders of the new China have thrown up two other monuments on the Square—monuments to speed, to work, to power—two great structures flanking the Square which were built in ten months. They are testimonials to the extent the Communist régime has been able to sway the minds and the bodies of its followers. Whenever I walked across Tien An Men, I found the entire layout highly symbolic. The vastness of the square itself is the vastness of China. The refurbished gate suggests that the rulers of the new China do not and will not forget the land's unhappy past. In the monolith I saw the single-mindedness of Communist rule, China's gigantic struggle to stand up, to reach for the sky, and possibly China's sword. The two buildings, the new museum and the National People's Congress Hall, stand as witnesses—and as warnings—that the Communist Party in China has absolute sway over the people it feeds and clothes and houses.

Each time I went to the post office to airmail a parcel of film to Toronto, my walk would take me through Tien An Men since the general post office faced the square. There was always something doing near by, parties of tourists having their photographs taken either in front of the grand new Parliament, by the ancient gate, or at the foot of the monolith commemorating Communists and soldiers who had died fighting for the cause. Before a big holiday, like May Day or October 1, workers and children would practise marching in the Square. Then there were the rallies, of course, when the usually silent Tien An Men became harsh and noisy with the well-rehearsed cries of hundreds of thousands. To me, this represented one of the ugly aspects of the new, over-aggressive China. At the end of these rallies, the Square would empty, and fall silent, as if exhausted. Several teams of sweepers, tiny and lonely in the empty vastness of the Square, cleaned up the mess. Little boys scrounged through heaps of litter in search of ragged flags.

But Tien An Men under a mantle of snow was also quiet, and at the same time very lovely. One wintry day I followed with my camera a man passing through the square on a donkey cart. He sat in the white silence of Peking with his eyes closed, slumped on his seat as his donkey padded through the soft new snow. To me he was China, this man on the cart, time-worn and tired, yet indomitable; China moving ahead resolutely, despite a constant and bitter world winter. The man did not see how the ancient grey streets of Peking had been transformed by the pure whiteness of the snow. Even long, box-like apartment buildings and the piles of bricks at the side of the roads lost their ugliness. Peking in the snow is beautiful, and the flowery names the City's residents gave to their favourite buildings and palaces take on new meaning. There is Chien Ching Kung, the Palace of Heavenly Purity, Chiao Tai Tien, the Hall of Heavenly and Earthly Intercourse, and Kun Ning Kung, the Palace of Earthly Tranquility. The man and the donkey jogged through Tien An Men Square, now a wide, white plain. To the right, a blue-black river of people wound up the steps of the new National People's Congress Hall. They had queued in the freezing cold to see the huge and ornate hall where their Communist government meets, schoolchildren and peasants, teachers with thin delicate faces and workers whose features seemed hewn out of rock. A few of the waiting people sheltered under umbrellas but mostly these were used to protect the bags and food packages they had put on the ground. This building is the showpiece of the new Tien An Men. It is certainly an impressive affair, this "Great Hall of the People", and the Communist claim that designing began less than a year prior to the building's final completion is difficult to believe. Most foreign experts think the project had been planned quite some time ago, and that many of the components of the huge structure were finished well before two thousand men arrived on October 28, 1958, to begin digging the foundations. In a matter of a few months, thousands living in the typical single-storey houses of Peking were sent to live elsewhere, their homes were torn down, the square was levelled, and building began. But even the feat of actually putting up the immense Parliament in ten months is fantastic for a country where slow, laborious construction methods have gone on since time immemorial. The frontage alone is over a thousand feet long and the architects ensured that the total floor space of 171,800 sq. metres was greater than that of all the small palaces in the near-by Forbidden City combined. The Parliament Chamber is gaudy, plush, too self-conscious in its architecture, and contemporary architects in Scandinavia, Britain, the United States or Latin America would be horrified at the old-fashioned design of this and many other modern Chinese buildings. "Decadent" they would say, and point out that the heaviness of the Parliament and of the virtually identical museum opposite with their marble pillars belongs to the European school of half a century ago. And yet one could never fail to be staggered by the vastness of the halls during any of the Congress sessions, the conferences, theatre performances and banquets which the

Communists held there during the Tenth Anniversary celebrations and in the months that followed. Also impressive were the
hundreds of lamps, ceiling and flood lights which, when turned
on to full strength, bathed the main auditorium in such brilliance
that it was easy to take pictures on ordinary film without flash.
It really became as light as day. The whole building is designed
as a show place. It is a smart but rather too expensive piece of
propaganda.

In 1959, as the October celebrations neared, and the project
was not going ahead fast enough, tens of thousands of people
were whisked away from their normal employment to help
complete this building and nine other grand structures which
were to symbolise the "great leap forward". Professors and clerks
worked with coolies and pedicab men, and the labour force was
deployed as for a military campaign.

After watching the party-generated enthusiasm inside the
Congress Hall, the well-organised clapping, the Chinese smiles
switched on and off like the lights in the main hall, it was always
a great relief to come out again into the Square. Tien An Men
somehow had a soothing effect on me. If you shut your eyes to the
physical poverty and pain of China, and your mind to the spiritual
cruelty of Peking, the Chinese capital became, in some regards,
a dream city. It had an appeal all of its own, and whenever I felt
sympathetic towards the Chinese, I gravitated back to Tien An
Men. Probably the Square was most beautiful on the sunny
mornings, and on the nights of celebrations when the sky above
it was filled with the rainbows of exploding fireworks. It is so
large that to walk around its perimeter takes twenty minutes and
even the traffic on its edges does not destroy the peaceful void and
solitude of the Square on a quiet autumn day.

Although I prefer to remember the Square in its splendid
isolation, away from the bustling, tired, dull, workaday Peking,
its use by the Communists as the heart of Chinese political
activity is the measure of its real importance. The Government
takes the monster rallies it organises on Tien An Men frightfully
seriously. Preparations are made days ahead. Special mobile
toilets, built for this specific purpose, are among the first vehicles
to roll on to the Square, looking rather like long buses with
frosted windows. The armies of demonstrators walk through a
door marked "In" at the rear of this new-fangled bus, and emerge
in due course through the only other door, near the driver's seat,

looking distinctly relieved. Naturally, there aren't enough of
these motorised latrines, and on the eve of a huge rally workmen
erect temporary canvas lavatories. Paving stones along the footpaths are taken up, and each makeshift toilet is connected with
the main sewers. The entire organisation is tremendous. The
ugly structures, hidden during the rallies by red forests of flags
flying all around them, are whisked away again the moment the
rally finishes. The Foreign Ministry officials I knew never seemed
to appreciate just how amusing this entire spectacle was, not only
to the foreigner but to many of the simple peasants who were
duty-bound to take part in the rallies. I once saw a pretty girl
carrying the most grisly anti-American poster who was rocking
with laughter. Many of the marchers regarded the rallies as an
occasion for an outdoor picnic. A massive demonstration in the
Chinese national capital was showmanship at its most grandilo-
quent, propaganda on a fantastic scale. For example, three million
persons are officially said to have taken part in the demonstration
against the United States following the collapse of the 1960
Summit Conference in Paris.

I attended a number of these monster rallies on Tien An Men
as well as a few in the ancient Forbidden City of Peking, and
several indoor demonstrations. The recipe was always the
same—red flags, shouting, slogans, angry speeches. Each rally
demanded split-second timing, dazzling colour and masses of
demonstrators. In my last two months in Peking one demonstration after another was held, and the locals seemed delighted to
have so many unexpected free days in the sunshine of late spring.
Usually I watched the demonstrators assembling behind the hotel,
near the old gate of Chung Wen Men, where the city wall of
Peking still stands. They always grinned widely at my cameras,
despite the bitter anti-U.S. posters and slogans they carried.
Individually, the Chinese did not like talking about their mass
rallies. Many of them were rather ashamed of the great time loss
involved. During two rallies alone, staged to back rioters in
South Korea and Japan, 2,000,000 Peking citizens, from schoolchildren to old, ragged pedicab men lost at least two full days,
writing slogans, making hundreds of thousands of little paper
flags, preparing silken banners, painting posters, drawing cross
cartoons about Uncle Sam.

The imaginative citizens attend rallies armed with all kinds of
equipment to ensure a pleasant day's outing—packs of cards,

books, magazines and newspapers. Teenage Young Pioneers in white shirts and scarlet scarves play various children's games, and as speakers bellow into microphones about "vicious U.S. imperialism and Japanese militarism" only a small percentage of the vast crowd is listening.

Groups of men are huddled around cards, while their placards lean peacefully against the nearest tree and nobody attends to their screaming legends: "U.S. get out of Japan. U.S. get out of Korea. U.S. get out of Taiwan. U.S. get out of the Philippines. U.S. get out of Asia. U.S. get out of Latin America. U.S. get out of Africa. Oppose U.S. imperialism. Oppose Western colonialism. Oppose Japanese militarism. Long live the solidarity of the Asian and African peoples! Long live world peace! Long live the great unity of the people of the world!"

The fact that these colossal displays, the costliest propaganda stunts Peking can produce, have virtually no impact on the outside world must infuriate the men who arrange them. Even foreign Communists consider them not only antiquated and childish but a dreadful waste of time and money. Peking's leaders cannot understand why the other Communist nations seem to have put aside monster rallies as a means of political propaganda except on the most important of days. The Chinese will still organise a demonstration at the drop of a hat. Almost any riot anywhere in the world becomes the excuse for a hundred massive rallies in a hundred Chinese cities. All kinds of people turn up, including girl soldiers of the Chinese militia carrying rifles and ammunition belts, troops with tommy-guns, security police with pistols. But the bigger the rally, the more difficult it is to discipline people's faces. Take a small demonstration in a hall. Everyone can be watched closely. Each pair of eyes must be serious. One can't go to sleep without getting a jab in the ribs from the comrade in the next seat. The liveliest are the big rallies, which disrupt both traffic and work. Government offices close, shops put wooden shutters over their showcases to protect the glass from the milling crowds, and first-aid teams in white appear at strategic spots. Extra loudspeakers sprout on trees and telegraph posts, and in the communes and factories people outdo one another in slogan-writing and poster-painting. If the leaders themselves did not take the rallies so frightfully seriously they would be hilariously funny. People shout to order, run to order, raise fists when the squad leader raises his, march home again when they are told to do so. The rallies are about as spontaneous as a military parade.

But, of course, when you get more than a million people massed together simply to listen for hours to speeches they have already heard so often, there are bound to be a great number of bored demonstrators. Having seen thousands of laughing, sleeping, sunbathing, card-playing, reading Chinese demonstrators (hidden from the eyes of the leaders by protective walls of young Communist zealots) I feel that individualism will win through in the end. At present, Chinese individualism is hounded by conformity and by Communist regulations to such a degree that most times it must remain hidden in order to survive at all. But to me, the rallies were proof that total indoctrination of a population is a near-impossible task.

At one rally I was almost arrested. The rally invitations issued to correspondents (you had to have an invitation to any function in Peking before you could attend, and it didn't matter if it was held in the city's main square) gave us the right to watch rallies from the special stand just below the gate of Tien An Men. But often I preferred being down among the crowds. Up on the stand one saw only a packed mass of black-haired people in blue and lots of red flags. The spectacle was colourful but too impersonal. In the crowd it was possible to catch the real feeling of the huge assembly. Often the impressions we reporters got from our perch on high were quite false.

On the day of my brief detention about a million people had been mustered to gather in and around Tien An Men. The square and a couple of miles of the Changen Boulevard were jam-packed. Thousands preferred sitting in the sunshine to standing up and shouting. One of my aims in taking pictures was to show that the ordinary people in China still had the same normal reactions as people anywhere else in the world, that they got tired of all the propaganda poured into their ears and pumped into their heads day and night. On this occasion I was walking to the stands with Richard Harris, of the London *Times*, who understood and spoke Chinese fluently. After hearing the voice over the loudspeakers for a time, he shook his head and said, "I'm sure they aren't listening. They couldn't be. So much of it is just nonsense." Certainly, if people were listening to all the anti-Western ranting, they were hiding it very well. I took pictures of children playing their games, men betting on dice and cards, women knitting, people reading paper-backed novels and magazines. One character whose job it was to carry a huge placard showing a mighty Chinese fist splitting open the head of "Uncle Sam" had placed his gruesome piece of artwork against a tree. He sat on the road dozing, using the placard as a backrest, his head shielded from the sun by a handkerchief. I couldn't resist the picture. I focused, took the photograph and was walking away when a hand landed roughly on my left shoulder. A little man in black, with a red ribbon pinned to his chest, held on to my coat persistently and pointed to my camera. Richard Harris had disappeared in the dense crowd ahead of us. A policeman soon appeared, summoned by the little man in black. The people around us were gesticulating and chattering noisily. It was one of the many times I wished that I could understand Chinese. I had the distinct impression the youths and young girls around us were on my side because they seemed to be pointing to the little man, and telling the policeman I had done nothing but take pictures. The constable beckoned me to follow him, and we walked about two hundred yards to his senior officer. I presented my invitation and Press card which the second policeman examined carefully. Finally, after a whispered conference, they decided the whole thing was going to land them in too much bother. They gave me back my papers, pointed to the stand where all the other foreigners were, and let me go. They didn't even take my film.

I still don't know whether I had disturbed the sleeping demonstrator; in all the commotion I forgot to look. But I still have his picture!

5

STAGE OF DREAMS

One of my first relaxations in Peking had been seeing the Bolshoi Ballet which Russia had sent into China for the celebration of the Tenth Anniversary. The Company came first to the capital and took it by storm. The great Galina Ulanova, dancing *Giselle*, had the audience on their feet, clapping, cheering, waving, and three other ballerinas, Maya Plisstakaya, Olga Lepeshinskaya and Ekaterina Maximova were also extremely popular. The Chinese couldn't have enough of Lepeshinskaya soaring through the air in brief glimpses of Walpurgis-night, danced to Gounod's *Faust*. Even though it was an acrobatic feat rather than true ballet, the Peking audiences preferred this aerial stage-craft to many of the classical numbers for it reminded them of the acrobatics in their native Opera. The girl who made male Chinese hearts flutter was ballerina Maximova. She danced in *Les Sylphides*, and had a leading rôle in Prokofiev's last work, *The Stone Flower*. As a young girl in love with an idealistic sculptor who has been lured by a fairy into her underground palace, Maximova was a figure of forlorn loveliness. She was charming, beautiful, very young—at nineteen, the youngest ballerina in the troupe—and she danced with the best of them. She didn't have the leading rôle in *The Stone Flower*, but the Chinese balletomanes made her the star of the night. Time and again they called her back, and Ekaterina Maximova stood smiling, with glistening, starry eyes, as the audience ran down the aisles to the front of the stage for a closer look at her.

For me, the Bolshoi performances meant temporary escape from the harsh Communism of China. The music of Chopin, Saint-Saens, Glinka and Khachaturian swirled me briefly back into the world I knew and loved, where people were regarded as ordinary, and often weak, human beings—and not tools of toil. For a few hours the alien Peking hotel room was forgotten.

I marvelled not only at the Bolshoi but also at the excellence of the young Peking dancing school, when I saw it later in my stay. It seemed incredible that such performances were possible in a land like China where drabness and sameness were so encouraged among the people. In the West, the stage is a reflection of the real social life going on around. Often, of course, it is an exaggerated version, but the similarity is apparent. In China, the stage, and especially the ballet stage, is the very antithesis of real life. The surging music and rich costumes, the golden stage gifts and the gaiety, the colour and the brilliant lights, all these are lacking in the workaday life of China.

Evening theatre performances in Peking generally start about 7.30 p.m. You walk in off the almost black, dimly-lit street, and take your seat among the workers, most of them in blue, and plump with cotton padding in the winter. Many of the men wear their boiler-makers' caps throughout the performance. The lights dim, the music sweeps aside the endless talk about work and production and progress, and for a time everybody can relax and forget. Only when watching the ballet does one suddenly realise that girls in China can have slim and beautiful bodies, pretty faces, pursed lips, and loving eyes. As I gazed at their scant ballet costumes I found that beneath the faded, baggy boiler suits they wore in the daytime, Chinese girls had white willowy arms and long shapely legs. I had been reading so much about Chinese women being merely workers striving for higher production, I had almost forgotten that they were females, too. In the ballet performances, all the hidden yearnings which exist in China as anywhere else burst forth in flaming passion. Several times I saw the new Chinese ballet *Maid of the Sea*, a production by the five-year-old Peking Dancing School whose artists had been trained by teachers from Moscow's Bolshoi Theatre. It was a first-rate ballet, with novel, delightful music and most graceful dancing, featuring also some of the Chinese acrobatics which are included in almost all of the local operas. *Maid of the Sea* is adapted from an ancient Chinese fairy tale about the love between a sea maiden and a huntsman. A jealous mountain demon kidnaps the maiden, but with help of friendly gnomes the huntsman rescues his beloved and marries her. Many of the scenes were sensuous as anything I have ever seen. There were tender love scenes between the sea maiden and the huntsman: girls in glittering, body-hugging tights danced crazily as the sea maiden offered her lover her coral crown in the ocean depths. Toward the end of the ballet the wicked demon tries to tempt the huntsman away from the heroine by offering him any number of gorgeous females, dressed—or rather, partly-dressed—in exotic costumes. They weaved their hips and stretched their bodies at him; they danced half-naked behind veils, in the transparent clothes of harem girls; they teased him with bewitching, open arms and provocative smiles, paraded before him with bare midriffs and plunging necklines. In one erotic dance, a girl in scarlet tossed herself at the breathless huntsman, and literally wound herself around his feet before clutching at his thighs. The audience sat spellbound as the haunting music rose and the stage atmosphere became hot with desire and lust and seduction. In the end, of course, the huntsman overcomes all the temptations and finds his true love, but the men and women who invented the ballet, and who danced it with a wild frenzy, had obviously thrown all the frustrations of life in Communist China on to the stage.

After one performance, I gave an interpreter called Hsu a dig in the ribs. "Do you know," I said, "I even saw the girls' navels. Those little pants they had on were just like the bikinis we have in the West. I hadn't realised Chinese girls could look so cute." For a fleeting instant he grinned. Then, quickly, his Chinese mask reappeared. "The story has a moral," he said, a mild rebuke in his voice because I had been flippant about Chinese art. "In a Communist society good always triumphs over evil."

*　　*　　*

The Peking régime's own cultural contribution to the stage has so far been very insignificant. The revolutionary plays and operas, dealing with civil war, Communism and industrial production, make the Western theatregoer's hair stand on end. The difference between modern Chinese drama and the great artistry of the old operas is so vast the two simply cannot be compared. The rough, over-realistic stage plays of the present day will be forgotten in future times when Peking, Shanghai and other operas will still be hailed by enthusiastic audiences.

The traditional operas were born in the imperial courts of ancient China, and practically every dynasty had its impact on the drama of its day. Opera grew out of the songs and dances performed for the emperors. The Chinese rulers had acrobats, jesters and story-tellers to amuse them and all these eventually took their place on the operatic stage. The golden age of Chinese

45

classical opera occurred during the Yuan period, in the thirteenth and fourteenth centuries, although experts claim that opera in various forms goes back to the Chou dynasty of the tenth century. During hundreds of years of evolution the Chinese traditional drama branched into various forms. Some local operas achieved national fame while others remained popular only in certain localities. Foreigners must attend various operas repeatedly to recognise the various schools. For example, Peking and Shanghai opera have similar costumes, similar music, but Peking opera actors wear highly elaborate mask-like make-up, which takes hours to apply. Peking opera employs far more stage symbolism than Shanghai opera. I had to be told by my interpreters that in Peking opera men impersonated female characters, while in Shanghai opera the girls impersonate the boys. In their costumes, I could never tell men from women.

The symbolism of Peking opera, simple on some occasions, can become so intricate that only the regular theatregoers understand what is passing. When an oar represents a boat or a flag an army, the meanings are not very difficult to follow; the same is true for the actor who exchanges a fan for an umbrella, to tell the audience that it's raining. But then it gets harder: two yellow flags held horizontally, each blazoned with a wheel, represent a chariot. Sometimes a general stands on a chair to show that he has climbed a high mountain. The actor must be a mime as well, a female impersonator picking up his skirts to climb stairs, very deliberately lifting his foot to indicate that he is stepping over the threshold into a house. The costumes are a study in themselves. Some of the stage clothing resembles that of the Ming period (1368–1644), when court and government officials wore such extravagant clothing even their slippers had soles embroidered in the finest silks.

The old stories of Peking opera, now the most popular and widespread across China, dealt mainly with mythology and history. There are legends about "The Butterfly Lovers" and "The Tower of the Bright Sun", many military operas telling of brave generals and weak emperors and faithful courtiers. There are great historical dramas, tales of chivalry and ancient thrillers about spies and murderers. In the olden days masks were often used in the stage plays from which Peking opera developed. These were replaced with stage make-up, except when actors depict animals like tigers, wolves and bears, for which parts they

46

may still wear masks. Each painted face has a definite meaning. Red paint on the face indicates loyalty and courage; the villain has a white, twisted face; blue means cruelty; green obstinacy or impetuosity; a mixture of gold and silver on the face tells the audience that the character has supernatural qualities. The Peking opera fan will recognise certain well-known characters from the paint on their face the moment they come on stage just as an English audience would know Falstaff.

During my theatre excursions from the Hsin Chiao I never failed to enjoy the spectacle, the symbolism, the artistry and traditions of Peking opera; but when it came to the singing and the music, which to Chinese ears are both beautiful and tuneful, I wondered why excellent stage performances were being ruined by so much jarring noise. The singing seemed discordant with the voice pitched too high, the music harsh, clanking and childish. Many of the musical instruments were so simple I was surprised they produced any music at all. Singers were accompanied by a sharp and raucous two-stringed fiddle of northern barbarian origin; or three and four-stringed guitars and bamboo flutes rather like the recorders of schoolchildren. The most fearsome noises were made by clanging bells, brass cymbals, barrel-shaped drums, hand-gongs and a single-skin drum which, I was told, was the leading instrument in all operas. The cacophony and dissonance which assaults the ears during a more exciting scene left me half deaf. I had the misfortune to be almost on top of the orchestra on many occasions because these were considered the best seats. Out-of-doors, where green leaves and the high sky absorbed much clanging and scratchy fiddling, I found Peking opera far more enjoyable. It was quite an experience to attend theatrical shows in the parks and palaces where the emperors of China once lived in unbelievable splendour. Today these belong to the Chinese masses. Especially on feast days, open-air theatres were popular, and a hedge or a large tree became the actors' dressing-rooms. The audience usually sat on the ground. Young couples would stand in the shade of willows holding hands. People clapped the best of the actors, laughed with the clowns and for me life in China, for once, became pleasant and relaxed.

6

THE FAMINE

It was a typical Peking morning in late November, the air crisp and clean, the sky a clear blue. I went out of the Hsin Chiao and followed the usual procession of donkey carts, coolies, pedicabs and the trucks which always hooted unmercifully at the overloaded pedestrians. The traffic stream passed through the ancient city gate of Hatamen, which the Chinese Communists have now named Chung Wen Men. The new government is fast pulling down much of the massive wall that once encircled the whole of Peking. The section behind the hotel still stood, a vast stone and earth barrier the top of which was on the same level as my third-floor window. Often I watched soldiers drilling there or practising with revolvers. Little boys climbed through the barbed-wire entanglements put up to stop people from ascending to the top of the wall. They played hide and seek or had great fun throwing small stones at the people on the street below.

To me, Communist Peking divided naturally into two distinct parts, the grey old city with its countless drab houses, and the rebuilt areas with their numerous red-brick apartments and office buildings. That day, after crossing the rail line that leads to Tungchow, I walked south in the direction of the Temple of Heaven. But I did not get far. Here was a new, green Peking. The street had become a river confined between long banks of cabbages. Cabbages blocked footpaths and small lanes. Giggling and gurgling children played on top of the green cabbage mountains as if they were piles of slack.

I raced back to the Hsin Chiao for my second camera. I rarely left the hotel without one camera slung across my shoulder, but this remarkable sight was too good pictorially to take any chances. The cabbage glut had been caused by various factors. Flood rains earlier in the year washed out Peking's vegetable harvest several times over. Each time an increasing number of people were urged to plant more and more, and now one of

48

Manpower is no problem in Communist China. These men were digging canals in Tientsin.

Travellers who came down the Pearl River to Canton carry their belongings on their shoulders near the waterfront.

Peking. The author's wife Audrey with Tsang, the amah, Shane and the twins.

The author's children astride one of the stone horses lining the way to the Ming tombs outside Peking.

China's famous mass drives had gone askew. The Peking cabbage harvest was three times as great as in 1958 and totalled 500,000 tons. The government was begging people to buy and store the vegetable. Around the city thousands of troops, office staff, workers and students were helping the communes to gather in the crop. As trucks, pedicabs and whole trains arrived with fantastic loads of cabbages, the bewildered people of Peking watched green haystacks growing in the streets. And it was indeed a staggering sight, even along that one street outside the gate behind the hostel. For hundreds of yards there were continuous mountain ranges of cabbages, sometimes six and eight feet high, on both sides of the road. I shot several rolls of pictures, then went back to the Hsin Chiao. I asked Yen, the interpreter, to order a cab.

"Where do you wish to go?"

"Can we just go for a brief drive around Peking?" I suggested. "I believe you've had quite a good cabbage crop."

This was the understatement of the year, but had I appeared to suggest that something had gone wrong with the city's food planning, Yen would not have accompanied me quite so willingly. Wherever we drove that afternoon, there were cabbages. Since Peking did not have adequate storage facilities for the crop, citizens were doing their best to minimise wastage, burying their cabbages in their little courtyards, hanging them on clothes-lines and spreading them on roofs, to dry in the early winter sun. Despite all these efforts, much of the crop had to be fed to animals and a great deal was simply left to rot.

The greatest tragedy of China is its impoverished millions and its uncomplaining masses whose one concern it is to find enough food for today, and maybe for tomorrow. No Chinese government in living memory has been able to solve the food question successfully, and the Communists have also failed. Despite the cabbage glut in Peking that November, 1959 had generally been a bad agricultural year for China. 1960 proved even worse. By 1961 the Chinese Communists were so short of grain that they had to import vast quantities of wheat, maize and barley from Canada, Australia, France, Argentina, and West Germany. As the fear of famine loomed across China during the second half of 1960, the Communists did everything they could to avoid a major disaster in food production, but their past insistence on industrialisation was working against them. Repeatedly the

Chinese Communists had boasted that men were now the masters of nature, and now, nature gave China such a fearful pounding that Peking virtually admitted defeat.

Even the diluted English-language versions of the party's calls to people to help agriculture had an urgent note of warning in them. When the word "famine" was mentioned in the Chinese Communist Party's directives on vegetable production as early as autumn of 1960, office workers and Communist Party cadres rushed into the countryside in their millions to aid the peasants. Whole factory staffs moved in a body from cities back into rural areas to help grow food.

Across China people built underground vaults to store the autumn harvest. They used shelves and ovens to dehydrate vegetables. Citizens dug up footpaths so they could plant more food, and in Peking cabbages were growing at the foot of the decorative trees planted along Changan Boulevard and Wang Fu Ching, the favourite shopping street. "Neighbourhood gardening" became the vogue throughout the nation in 1960. When the Communists established urban communes in April and May of that year, the order went out that citizens must help peasants grow food. Not long before leaving China, I saw in Peking, Tientsin, Shanghai and Canton all kinds of vegetables growing in streets, window boxes, parks, and school playgrounds.

"All manpower that can be spared should be deployed on the vegetable production front," the Party's Central Committee ordered. "Time lost can never be regained." The warnings were dramatic and, for the Chinese, surprisingly blunt.

Peking said that an area of farmland as large as Britain, Austria, Denmark and Switzerland combined (600 million Chinese mou or 100 million acres) had been affected by natural calamities such as flood, drought and insect pests. Each day editorials and articles appeared in the Chinese Press urging people to produce more food, and trying to explain why there wasn't enough to eat. "The population of the cities and industrial and mining areas has risen by about twenty million in the past three years," said the *People's Daily*, official organ of the Chinese Communist Party, in one editorial. "People engaged in industry, construction and water conservancy work generally require more food grain than the peasants. The number of people on water conservancy work alone was more than seventy million from last winter to this spring. All this accounted for the greatly increased consumption of grain." In a full-page article the following day, the *People's Daily* said grain production had to be doubled to meet current demands and to allow fodder for the development of China's livestock breeding campaign.

This return to agriculture is an obvious sequel to the blundering manner in which the Peking régime raced into industrialisation. Since orthodox Communism insists that industrialisation is the key to political and military power, the Chinese Communists, with too little planning, had diverted labour armies of many millions from the growing of food to the rebuilding of cities, the construction of factories and dams. This in itself was not a bad thing. It was the mad, helter-skelter pace of the programme which brought sharp criticism from the more conservative factions within the Chinese Communist Party. But these critics were quickly silenced. Mao's beliefs (and commune organisation was one of them) are inviolable in China, and anyone who disagrees with them is automatically wrong. It is, of course, another matter if Mao changes his mind, and this is what has happened in regard to agriculture. Harsh facts have proved that China simply cannot maintain her rate of industrialisation without going hungry in the process.

It is often said outside China that the Communists of Peking do not care one jot whether or not their people suffer, but such talk is unfair. Since they are dogmatists, they must follow the dogmas laid down first by Marx, then by Lenin and lately by Mao. During my time in China I came to believe firmly that, despite all their shortcomings, the fundamental aim of the Peking Government was to give its staggering population a better life—sooner or later. Much would have to be sacrificed in the effort, they said. The stated eventual goal had its human ideals. And whereas before, during the great Chinese famines, millions died, now the hunger was at least shared by all except a very few Communists near the top. Party members found they, too, had to tighten their belts although there can be no doubt that many of them got extra food and clothing rations.

The Communists had hoped that their mass drives in irrigation, in construction of farm machinery and improved education of peasants would overcome food shortages without too much trouble. But they misjudged the effect which their population movements, with whole towns and villages being transplanted, would have on agricultural production. Grain and vegetable output did rise, but not sufficiently to meet growing demands. Given the chance, peasants ate a great deal more. Also, the nation was healthier, and people lived longer. The population was leaping ahead at the rate of 15 to 18 million a year.

The Chinese Communists, of course, could not admit either to their own people or to the outside world that their industrial drive had created havoc in food production. And yet Peking's drastic measures proved that natural disasters were only partly to blame. When the order came to aid agriculture and streams of city workers headed for the land, they often found the transition difficult. The younger generation in particular complained at the unfamiliar conditions of their new life.

"League organisations must first of all mobilise those young people, workers and young dependants of cadres who have blindly flocked into the cities," said the Canton newspaper *Kwangtung Ching-nien Pao* in late 1960, "And check young people from blindly heading for the cities. Those who have already left should be educated and mobilised to return to the countryside to engage in agricultural production."

The Communist Party found that this new policy was baffling many of the young people who had been so persuaded of Mao's wisdom that they simply could not comprehend how things could go wrong. Several times each week the *People's Daily* was stressing that "agriculture is the foundation of China's national economy with industry the leading factor". But this kind of jibber-jabber did not change the tragic food shortages, and even stringent rationing could not avert near-famine conditions in many areas, especially in South China. In some provinces, hit badly by mid-summer typhoons, people were getting much less to eat in 1960 and 1961 than they had for several previous years. In drought-stricken regions and in areas where grasshoppers and other pests had laid bare the farmland, food rations were reduced to a minimum. Coming at a time when world opinion, including popular thinking in Communist capitals, was mounting against China's leaders for their extreme views about crushing capitalism, even if it had to be done by nuclear war, the food shortages created deep misgivings in Peking. The tragedy was that it needed a famine to prove to Mao Tse-tung that nature, and especially human nature, could not be mastered only by materialistic creeds and political dogmas. Lack of food, and the continued rationing of grain and clothing, has been rocking the Communist boat for about two years, and the Chinese leaders have been searching desperately for a remedy. This famine has been Chinese Communism's severest test, and yet out of China's great food calamity have sprung several very real benefits. Glaring and fundamental weaknesses in commune administration came to the notice of the Communist leadership. The nation's two greatest administrative evils, an excess of bureaucracy and a lack of transport, were more apparent than ever. Certainly, China suffered dreadful natural calamities, but there were also insane miscalculations, gross mismanagement, and criminal labour demands made on overworked, underfed peasants. For many centuries China has been under the scourge of a bureaucracy which has gnawed into the nation and sapped much of its vitality. The man in uniform, the official with a title, the intellectual on a salary—these people ruled, and often misruled, the country on orders from above. Too frequently the orders were vague. Commands issued from the national capital, re-issued from the provincial capital and then repeated all the way down the long bureaucratic ladder were constantly being misinterpreted, sometimes unintentionally but very often knowingly. This was so under the great imperial dynasties many centuries ago, and the Communists in Peking were up against the identical problem. The cadres, almost invariably members of the Chinese Communist Party, were blamed by their superiors for poor leadership in the rural communes.

Peking admitted that it has had to sweep away many selfish, useless Communist bureaucrats who used their position in the Party to feather their own nests. Daily stories appeared in the Chinese newspapers during the famine about cadres who "misbehaved", factory managers and production brigade chiefs who did not show "a true Communist spirit". The provincial Press carried letters and complaints from disgruntled peasants saying they had been unfairly treated by cadres. It was almost a revolution within a revolution. The top Communist Party leadership told the masses to criticise openly middle-ranking party men who were not pulling their weight, the new propaganda line being, "We trust the masses to assume more responsibility themselves."

Peking put forward many leadership methods which went by different colourful names such as the "2-5 system" and the "4-togetherness practice". Some of the communes adopted the

"5 sameness movement". This new Chinese numbers game might at first have sounded comical to foreigners, but to the five hundred million peasants the shake-up in the medium-level party leadership was of vital interest. The *People's Daily* explained the various commune systems to its readers. The "2-5 system", for example, meant that Communist Party officials, even those holding high posts in a rural commune, must participate in agricultural production on five days of the week. For two days each week they could study and do their other work. There was no mention of any day off. The "4-togetherness" signified that party people should eat with the peasants, live together with them, labour together, and consult them on commune affairs. The *People's Daily* told how the cadres of Anting commune, in Pingkiang county, Hunan Province had launched their "5-sameness" movement. "Under such a system," said the newspaper, "the cadres eat the same kind of meals as ordinary commune members, they are engaged in the same kind of physical labour, their work points are assessed and recorded in the same manner as those of commune members in general, they receive the same wages as other commune members, and their dependants are accorded the same treatment as those of other commune members in general."

A switch came in the distribution of personnel when Peking realised that too many of its ablest people lived in the cities. Even in China, Communist intellectuals had managed to maintain, in varying degrees, an urban existence. The cities provided them with better opportunities to exchange ideas, and with more chances of quick advancement. Many did their terms of "going to the country" (and often felt much better after six months or a year away from their desks). But sooner or later they gyrated back to their metropolis, to the citizens they knew and liked, and away from the stolid peasants whom they found hard to understand and whose manner of life was so foreign. During another agonising re-education campaign, party officials at all levels were told, "You must go on the land to help the peasants until China gets on its feet again." Although many Communists found the reversal a harsh blow, Peking's planners insisted that, when necessary, the best men and women had to go to the countryside to clean up the mess.

Peking's directives led to a gradual yet radical transformation in the commune system. Commune discipline had to be modified to counter apathy among the lethargic peasants. For some years past the Chinese work armies had tramped across the land, toiling harder than most people in other nations. When, as a reward, they got not more, but less food, the tired, hungry, disillusioned peasant slowed up and lost faith in the measures which had been devised to increase agricultural output. The communes were supposed to simplify and centralise authority by lumping some five hundred million Chinese peasants into about twenty-six thousand administrative units varying greatly in size and administration. I visited several communes in different provinces, and about the only similarity I found in them was that most commune chiefs would repeat, parrot-like, the slogans which had been drummed into their heads. "Communism is paradise and the people's commune is the ladder to reach it," was one favourite phrase. I could never be sure whether they truly believed in an earthly paradise. They repeated themselves often enough anyhow.

With the arrival of the rural communes in 1958 came a first flush of enthusiasm in high places which caused the most monumental statistical error in recent history. Commune heads, brigade chiefs and production team leaders went out into the fields and estimated how much grain they thought they could deliver to their masters in Peking. Veteran peasants who shook their heads doubtfully were ignored. This was Communism. This year's harvest was for the party. It had to be good! The Chinese Communists announced their 1958 grain production at first as 375,000,000 tons, a claim which staggered the world. But soon unbelieving Western experts were proved correct. There had been some miscalculations, the Chinese admitted. They cut the figure back to 250,000,000 tons, though actual production turned out to be only around the 200,000,000-ton mark; just over half the original claim.

Commune administration was first tightened, then slackened again in 1960 and 1961 when the Chinese leaders realised that too much centralisation was harming production. The commune did have its great advantages, especially in major projects needing a vast labour corps. Communes could muster tens of thousands of people to build dams, dig irrigation canals, throw up solid buildings to house pigs, chickens, cattle and other farm animals. Peasants in their hundreds of thousands were told in 1958 and early 1959 not to worry too much about the land. The crops were doing well, was the official line. Instead they were asked to build commune workshops and factories, and to produce steel in miniature furnaces. But the steel-making campaign of 1958 proved a hopeless flop, and by 1960 peasants were being released for farm work again to grow more food.

It was already too late. Floods, droughts, typhoons, pest plagues and plant diseases, coming on top of an already dis-organised agricultural labour force, brought confusion and hunger. The Communist Party's plans for a greater China had their worst set-back ever. Britain's war-time food rations were nothing beside the dire shortages which China experienced, and the peasant reacted sharply. Constant reductions in grain rations led to all kinds of abuses both on the land and in the cities. People coming out of China say that despite strict policing peasants had been hiding part of the crops of rural communes to supplement their own meagre rations.

In the cities the rice rationing system was changed to thwart those trying to outsmart the State. Citizens who were allotted a monthly ration found that at the beginning of the month the poorest rice was sold. Stores were ordered to get rid of all the worst grain first. There were impurities in the early rice, but as stocks dwindled toward the end of the month, the quality improved. When retailers ran out of the poor rice they were forced to sell good rice until their stocks were replenished by the State in the first days of the next month. People began to ration themselves in the first fortnight, buying well below their allow-ance of rice. As the quality improved they bought more, and in the last week of the month, when good grain was available, they bought up to the very limit of their ration.

The Communists, late in 1960, suddenly declared all ration tickets null and void until the end of the month. When people picked up their new ration coupons they found the new ones had to be used by a certain date, after which they became valueless. Black marketeers who had sold ration tickets or held them to exchange rice for, say, a permit to buy a bicycle, were caught napping.

Most things are rationed in China—cigarettes, clothing, gaso-line, soap, edible oil, sugar, certain vegetables and, of course, grain and meat. People must hand in food coupons when they eat at restaurants. Early in 1962 the Chinese Government started a new coupon system covering scarce foods (like cooked meat and biscuits) as well as about fifty items of industrial consumer goods (including radios, crockery, watches etc.). It was designed not only to boost personal savings but also to lessen black marketeering and to prevent inflation. In Peking, Shanghai and Canton workers found with their pay packets a number of coupons equivalent to ten per cent of their wages. In other cities which had even less contact with the outside world the percentage was much lower, nearer five per cent. In most regions half the coupons were for foods other than grain, sugar, eggs and those edibles already rationed previously. The other half covered what the government called "industrial production". A Chinese teacher who escaped from Manchuria in February of 1962 told me in Hong Kong that with his salary of sixty yuan he got 2.5 coupons each month. 1.3 were food tickets and 1.2 for consumer goods. His example epitomized the tragic shortcomings of Chinese production. To buy a watch costing fifty yuan he would have to hand over the cash—as well as fifty industrial production coupons. It would have taken him well over three years to save up for his watch. His food coupons were sufficient to buy about a pound of biscuits each month. People often found that although the currency was now stable, constant shortages made it impossible to spend the money they earned in a useful way. But at least they had money, which was more than could be said in the olden days. It is to Peking's great credit that the government tries to make its inadequate supplies go round, to distribute food and goods fairly equally among its astronomical population. But so far it has proved an impossible task. In richer districts, peasants who have seen the larger portion of their good harvests disappear down the road in trucks and donkey carts have often gone on what might be called a go-slow strike. "If we don't get more out of this," they asked, "why should we work so hard?" In time, this negative mood, a form of work-to-rule campaign by the world's largest peasant population, spread throughout the nation causing famine and industrial havoc.

People who know China can appreciate the over-powering difficulties Peking must tackle, but nevertheless it was odious to learn of the hypocrisy practised by the Communists in their continuous efforts to control the thinking of the most populous nation on earth. During the famine, street committee officials went on austerity campaigns suggesting to people that they cut back their food rations "voluntarily". Having pushed citizens into a position where they must agree, the Communists produced a form. Then came the propaganda spiel. "You have shown fine Communist spirit in volunteering to give up some of your rations for the sake of the community. But, as you well know, the Communist Party has the health and welfare of its people at heart always. On this application form you may ask whether you can volunteer to donate a percentage of your food ration. We will then consider your request."

The country's economy was full of contradictions. China still sold food to buy machines, yet she hadn't enough to feed her own population. Peking, in its rôle as the puritanical defender of Marxist dogmas, felt China must eventually become the leader of the Communist camp, and kept giving economic aid and food to under-developed countries in Asia and Africa, even to Cuba. Though her own economy was in such a critical state, she was spending hundreds of millions of valuable U.S. dollars buying Western grain. What hurt the dogmatists of Peking still more was the party's virtual admission that there is nothing as productive as free trading. Mao's brand of Marxism (designed to take several short cuts to Communism which were so drastic even the Russians recoiled in horror) was finally forced to fall back on individual free enterprise. In a frantic effort to find more food for the exploding population and to halt spreading malnutrition, Peking encouraged the establishment of rural trade fairs where peasants were allowed to buy and sell and bargain with more individual freedom than they had been permitted for years. The Communist Party insisted on what it termed "fair bargaining between both parties", but found it increasingly difficult to stop speculators and black marketeers who took advantage of hunger and misery in the country areas.

Early in 1961 China's rulers conferred in Peking at the highest level about what should be done to ease the continuing food crisis. From January 14 to 18 the Eighth Central Committee of the Chinese Communist Party held its 9th plenary session. One of the main items discussed was the famine. The party reasserted a policy already stated the previous year in a blunt communiqué issued from Peking: "The 9th plenary session of the 8th Central Committee held that, in view of the serious natural calamities that affected agricultural production for two successive years, the whole nation in 1961 must concentrate on strengthening the agricultural front; must carry out the policy of taking agriculture as the foundation of the national economy and of developing agriculture

and grain production in a big way by the whole party and the whole
people; must step up support for agriculture by all sectors and
occupations and must exert the utmost effort to win a better
harvest in agricultural production. In the rural areas efforts must
be made to consolidate further the people's communes, carry out
the various policies concerning the people's commune and the
rural economy, adopt effective measures to take good care of the
livelihood of the people's commune members, help them tide
over the difficulties entailed by natural calamities and make good
preparations for increasing agricultural output this year. The
departments of light industry should strive to overcome the
difficulties of raw material shortages brought about by natural
calamities, open up new sources of materials, increase production
and insure the supply of the people's daily necessities as far as
possible." And knowing that a nation which cannot eat, will
never work hard, Peking ordered that during 1961 (the second-
last year of China's Second Five-Year Plan) the scope of capital
construction should be reduced. The Central Committee admitted
that in 1961 the tasks faced by the Chinese people would be
"extraordinarily great and arduous".

While I have been writing this book in Hongkong, the famine
in China has grown considerably worse. Hongkong's China
experts always tend to magnify the misfortunes of the people
across the border, but during 1961 in particular there was overwhelming evidence to support the general belief that the Chinese
people were very hungry. For example, some hundreds of ships
are being kept busy for several years shuttling back and forth with
foreign wheat and barley for the suffering Chinese population.
And there were the food queues in Hongkong—food queues with
a difference. Outside the colony's post offices, people stood for
hours with food parcels for their friends and relatives in China.
Special stores sprang up dealing purely in gift food for China. The
Communists, forced to abandon their pride in the face of the
famine, set up post offices in Canton and at the Shumchun border
whose sole task it was to handle food gifts. In 1961, people in
Hongkong spent well over £7,000,000 sending food to
friends and relations in China by parcel post alone. About
a million food parcels a month went through normal postal
channels apart from food carried bodily across the frontier by
couriers and a large number of parcels ordered at Communist-
backed grocery stores in Hongkong and delivered from stocks

held in Canton. Almost everyone coming out of China reported a climate of disenchantment with Communism. Businessmen and diplomats told stories of sampans on Canton's Pearl River selling black market cabbages at two yuan each (more than a hundred times the price paid for a Chinese cabbage in Hongkong) while policemen looked on quite unconcerned. They said the people of Canton no longer seemed to worry either about their work or about what happened to them. They were too weak and hungry to care. The same story reached Hongkong in letters from Chinese complaining openly to relatives about the lack of food. Many babies of one year could not sit up properly because the lack of calcium had softened their bones, and beriberi, as well as oedema, the swelling disease which comes with malnutrition, was also said to be common. Although letters written in English were often censored, overseas Chinese who had gone home in 1958 and 1959 not because of a love for Communism but from a sense of national duty, expressed deep regret over their move in correspondence. United Nations officials in Hongkong were aghast at the bony, desperately ill appearance of White Russians and other Europeans being repatriated from China. Vague stories circulated through the colony that even Communist cadres were beginning to filter across the border. But the comment made most often by foreigners coming out of China was that people were so fed up with the famine in China, the Communists could no longer keep all public resentment under cover. Ordinary people were openly telling the Communists to stop talking about ideology and the brighter future, and start worrying about today's troubles. They openly blamed food exports to Russia and other Communist countries for their misery.

In 1961 there was so much unhappiness in China the Communists couldn't possibly punish every individual who complained. But most of the talk I heard in Hongkong about a general ugly mood growing among the peasants was, I felt, either wishful thinking or imagination. There may well have been the occasional uprising in communes. And there have been strikes in the new China. A British skipper docking at the port of Hsinkiang, near Tientsin, one morning in 1961, found the Chinese stevedores squatting in the sun. When he asked a Communist official what was the matter he was told, "The wharf labourers are resting."

"But they've been resting all day," said the freighter's captain. "In the new China," the other said haughtily, "workers have the right to rest for as long as they feel inclined to rest," and stomped away. Similar reports came from Shanghai. The depth of China's dilemma about internal food shortages, and attacks from the direction of Moscow, was indicated most clearly by the 1962 National People's Congress in Peking which was held in unprecedented secrecy. No foreign diplomats or newsmen were allowed into the sessions which began late in March. Even the Russian and other Communist ambassadors to Peking were barred. On March 27, 1962, an official ceremony marked the opening of the National People's Congress, and was attended by Mao Tse-tung. But many important names were missing from the list of leaders published by the *People's Daily*, and it is believed that some of the top men in Peking may have been purged as a result of internal failures, and the increasingly obvious Sino-Soviet split. The entire congress, the first Chinese parliamentary meeting to be held since the one I attended in March and April of 1960, was blanketed by an impenetrable wall of silence. Evidently the crisis in the two years between the congresses had been of such magnitude that even censored versions of speeches made could not be released, and yet any predictions of a counter-revolution occurring in China are pure nonsense. For although the Chinese are disillusioned about Communist promises and are eating less, today there is little choice. No one in China is strong enough to replace the Communists. "What about a revolt by the Army, or the militia?" people in Hongkong suggested. Such a rising would have no chance of success because of the intricate system of Communist intelligence under which anyone in a commune, factory, office, or in any other organisation might be a Communist Party spy. At best, there might come an internal revolt within the party which would shift the power permanently from the doctrinaire Marxists to the moderates. The famine badly weakened the ultra-leftists within the party, and the planners were once again given more say in national planning, but even this move may be only temporary.

"But doesn't the government want gift food?" American friends asked me. "We could give them plenty of food, and the moment the Communist régime was overthrown, we'd pour the stuff in. Grain, technicians, cash. Why those guys in China wouldn't know what had hit them." I always made it my job to knock these dangerous daydreams on the head because it is foolish to under-rate your adversary. The Chinese Communists have had serious setbacks, but they are a very long way from being beaten. If the situation grew so critical that an internal collapse was possible, the Soviet Union and other Communist states would rush troops and aid into China to keep the nation within the Communist bloc. No Communist will now deny that food is, and will remain for years, the cruellest of the nation's countless problems, and that somehow the régime must solve this crisis before it can claim final success in national aims. At the same time, no Communist in China would admit that the revolution had failed or that the cause was lost. Strangely, there was not always bitterness in the comments of refugees escaping to Hongkong. A good many of them said the Communists attempted to distribute the little they had but this still caused hard feelings in China.

Considering the nation-wide crisis that followed during the succeeding years, the 1959 food situation, at any rate in Peking, did not seem too bad. Nevertheless it was obvious that for any shopper, food was the first consideration. Already many times I had noticed that Chinese often ate like animals, shovelling food into their mouths with a tense, almost anxious look in their eyes. At the Hsin Chiao it was not always easy to forget that outside the hotel walls was the largest nation on earth, most of whose people did not have enough to eat. The hotel food was first-class, both in the Chinese restaurant and the European dining-room upstairs. Prices were very high, especially if judged by Chinese standards. A single hotel dish might cost far more than a factory worker would pay for his dormitory bed for two months. Sometimes the Western cooking tended to taste dull but at least there was a great variety of dishes. The menus were in English, German, Russian and Chinese. The Chinese was mainly for the waitresses who spoke only a few foreign phrases. There were among the staff English, German and Russian "specialists" who would be hastily summoned to a table during an emergency, as when a guest complained at receiving a plateful of Wiener Schnitzel after ordering wine.

The best food was available in the ground floor dining-room, where only Chinese meals were served. Usually I went there to have lunch, and my favourite meal was chicken slice soup (which came at the end of the meal and not at the beginning), sweet and sour pork, fried rice with egg, and toffee apple which was made by dipping cooked apple slices into melted sugar. It arrived at the table piping hot and you ate it by dipping the pieces into cold water. The brown sugar went hard, but the apple inside was soft and hot. It was absolutely delicious. Though I'm not a big eater, the chicken soup and the toffee apple often cheered me up at the end of a lonely Chinese meal.

At night the trouble with the Chinese dining-room was its gloom. The hotel staff practised economy, and the whole place was plunged into murky semi-darkness. The ceiling was fairly high, the few lights were dim and the resulting graveyard atmosphere drove most foreigners upstairs to the brighter European restaurant. I rarely drank anything but beer with meals. Chinese wines I tried only once or twice, and this was quite enough. Without being unkind to China's wine-makers, let it suffice to say that even poor quality Australian wines, after their long and shaky journey across the Indian Ocean, the Red Sea and the Mediterranean, are better when they reach London than the local wines I tried in Peking. The hot yellow wine that came with Chinese food was pleasantly sweet, but in making table wines, the Communists still had a lot to learn.

The one meal I dreaded each day was breakfast. With the best will in the world, I couldn't face grilled sea slugs with onion, braised shark's fin or egg and fungus soup early in the morning. So I never ate a Chinese breakfast. Upstairs it really wasn't much better. The Hsin Chiao didn't stock breakfast foods in packets since they are not manufactured in China. I began each day with eggs—fried eggs, boiled eggs, ham and eggs, just eggs. Back at home in Australia the clap-trap on the large packets telling you how one serving of cereal is more wholesome and nutritious than a plate piled high with meat and vegetables used to infuriate me. Couldn't these wretched advertising men, at least leave you alone in the mornings? Instead they forced you to look into the muzzle of a huge plastic gun which you can buy your son for a few pennies, or at pictures of goodies and baddies fighting to the death in the Wild West. Why the hell aren't they a little more sensitive and subtle, I used to growl at Audrey, my wife.

In Peking I would have been quite prepared to learn off by heart these fearful advertising slogans, and even chant them fifty times before breakfast—so long as I could have had a plate of cereal with cold milk in the morning. A few times I tried the Hsin Chiao porridge. When my family arrived the waitresses always looked awed as they carried in the plates—huge soup plates filled to the brim with rough, poor quality porridge and lukewarm milk. Not only do most Chinese in the North dislike milk, it's also very expensive. Unfortunately the Hsin Chiao's chef just didn't know how to cook porridge, and one morning after I'd found weevils floating in the milk next to the usual yellow blobs of fat, I went back to my eggs. It was the poor processing and inadequate refrigeration of the milk which also made it distressing to drink the Hsin Chiao's insufferable coffee. Occasionally I tried it black, with spoonfuls of sugar to drown the taste, but didn't enjoy it in the least. Later I received tins of instant coffee by mail, but the Peking milk gave it an odd flavour, and the high customs duty I had to pay irked me. One day I described my dismal breakfasts to John Small, a Canadian Trade Commissioner in Hongkong who was visiting Peking. Not only did he leave behind a huge tin of instant coffee, he even presented me with some Canadian soluble milk powder which I hoarded for weeks. Since our first meeting in Peking, John Small and I have become good friends. Back in those days his gift of three fine cups of coffee daily for eighteen days seemed enough to make me indebted to him for life.

The post office people once handed me a huge but surprisingly light parcel. With raised eyebrows, the Chinese Customs men ordered me to unwrap it. From beneath the wrinkled brown paper appeared four large packets of breakfast cereal. I'd written to Stanley Marks, my closest friend in Melbourne, about the woeful hotel breakfasts. He had promptly told the Kellogg's company about this man in distress in China, and at the main Peking post office several months later arrived the first packets of cornflakes these gentlemen of the Chinese Customs had ever seen. They peered at the picture of the large plastic gun, at the blonde girl with the blue, blue eyes slurping her breakfast. They tasted the foreign-looking food gingerly. They took one packet away, and it did the rounds of the post office. What a queer and barbarian fellow this Canadian correspondent must be who eats thin, leaf-like flakes, and has them sent to China all the way from Australia! The Chinese were so flabbergasted they didn't even charge me nominal duty. "This food has no commercial value in China," the Customs man announced gravely. Didn't it just!

It cost the Hsin Chiao quite a number of dollars in eggless breakfasts; I remember the day after the cornflakes arrived. There came a batch of *Globe and Mails* with several published stories from Peking, a note from my father asking why I hadn't written a series on religion, a new tin of Nescafé airmailed by my mother and two long and loving letters from my wife. What a morning it was! I sat gleefully in my room in the sunshine, the newspapers and mail strewn around me on the floor, and munched dry corn flakes.

7

MAKING HISTORY

My first Chinese visa was good for only two months. There were no hard and fast rules about how the Chinese issue their visas, but generally they give correspondents at least a month. At the end of that period most of the visiting Western correspondents who went through Peking while I was living there, managed to get a further month's extension provided they applied for it. I knew that the *Globe and Mail* wanted me to stay in China for as long as possible since we hoped to conduct the first permanent Western newspaper bureau in Peking. My editors realised fairly soon that straight news out of China was a rare thing indeed. What is more, the official Chinese News Agency, which had a direct radio link with London, could get the official pronouncements of the Peking régime out to the world far more quickly than any reporter living in China. The Reuter and Agence France-Presse men faced the problem of the American news agencies, Associated Press and United Press International beating them on one of the rare news stories to come out of China by monitoring Radio Peking in Tokyo. I concentrated on news features and background, and managed to keep my editors interested enough to give most of my Peking articles good display.

When I was summoned by the Foreign Ministry to see Hsu Huang, Vice-Director of the Information Department, I decided to ask for a "permanent" visa, good for six months, after which time such visas were usually renewed on request. Once you had a six-month visa, you could safely rely on being allowed to stay in the country for a reasonable period. At the interview, Hsu Huang would not give me a direct answer.

"No matter, no matter," he told me with an energetic wave of the hand. "But it does matter to me," I said. "I have a wife and four children living in Australia and we don't want to be separated for very much longer. If I knew you would grant me a visa for six months I could make arrangements for my family to join me here." Through one of the interpreters, Hsu Huang's translation came back to me. "The Vice-Director wishes to say that the arrangement between him and Mr. Dalgleish (editor and publisher of the *Globe and Mail*) was that it should be of a permanent nature. It is immaterial whether the card is for two months or six months." I then replied that it would help my own planning if the visa were extended for a further six months, and added that I wished to apply formally for such a "permanent" visa.

Hsu Huang nodded pleasantly. "We will let you know," he said in English, and added as I walked out of the office, "I hope to meet your wife." He never did. He was transferred later during my stay to the Chinese Embassy in East Berlin. A few days later I learned that I had been granted my six-month visa. Even an official as high up as Hsu Huang evidently did not have the authority to tell me whether or not I would get it. His assurances that the arrangement was to be permanent were an indication that he knew there was every likelihood of a longer visa extension being granted, but he had to go higher for final approval. This unwillingness, or maybe it was an incapacity to make decisions, I noted time and again in China. People either would not or could not make decisions on their own. They always had to be made either collectively or by some higher authority.

When news got around that I had been given a permanent visa, the Communist correspondents especially were very surprised. There were about three dozen of them. I had become the first newspaper correspondent from the Western Hemisphere to be allowed to remain in China under the Communists longer than a few months. This was not, of course, my doing but was due to the *Globe and Mail's* policy of realism toward the Peking régime. Unlike many Western newspapers, we were not afraid to come out and say bluntly how ridiculous it was for Chiang Kai-shek's Government to be represented on the Security Council of the United Nations. The *Globe and Mail* attacked the U.S. policy of containment not only toward China, but in South-East Asia generally, on the ground that although Communism might present its immediate problems it was an empty doctrine which appealed to poor nations and which would not take root in the Western democracies. Despite the *Globe and Mail's* anti-Communist attitude, its honest picture of the new China had evidently persuaded the authorities in Peking to give one of the paper's correspondents a trial.

"Well, boy, you've made history," the veteran Communist writer Alan Winnington told me when we next met at an official banquet. Winnington, an Englishman, was on the Chinese side during the North Korean war and lived in Peking as an expatriate. He was a pleasant enough chap to meet personally, although I could never agree with his politics. He was the die-hard Communist who believed firmly in the way the Chinese were tackling their own special problems, and yet he seemed eager for the constant conflict between East and West to slacken. He was obviously pleased that I'd been allowed to stay on.

"It's never happened before, boy," he said, "so now it's up to you."

"Not at all," I said, "it's up to the Chinese." I said it was impossible to live here as a Westerner without criticising many aspects of the régime, and he agreed. "But it's the way you do it," he said. "Whether you stay beyond your eight months will depend on that."

All the reports I sent from China were received in Toronto without a single word altered. It didn't matter whether the stories were cabled or air-mailed—the Chinese Communists let them out uncensored. Often I wondered whether Peking's security officials had a look at them, but there was never any real evidence that my letters had been opened. I guessed that any security system would be forced to take an occasional peep at a foreign correspondent's mail but I had no definite proof. The fact that no censorship whatever existed, and the international play the stories got were the main causes for the eventual failure of the Peking venture. When the reporter must rely purely on himself for censorship the result is often worse than useless. I decided if I started censoring myself I would cease being a reporter. My problem was how to write objectively and, at the same time, stay in China. But events proved that these two factors were in bitter conflict. Either you were prepared to shut your eyes to any number of weaknesses in the Communist system or you were faced with expulsion. Unfortunately, although the Communists kept saying to me wherever I went, "We would appreciate your criticism," they really wanted only praise. They were too accustomed to getting their own way to be open to any criticism of their policies, especially by foreigners. No honest and objective

Western newspaper correspondent required to interpret as well as report will be able to stay in China for long until some form of censorship is introduced by the Peking régime.

The Chinese Foreign Ministry never seemed to understand that the Western newspaper reporter had to have something to write about. I believe they expected me to be like the news agency correspondents whose main duty it was to cable Peking's pronouncements—especially if they knew they could beat news agency correspondents in other centres such as Tokyo, Moscow or London—and then to give their own interpretation of the latest policy moves. This was not my job, but evidently it took the Chinese quite a number of months to realise it. There was no point in trying to compete on straight news with the agencies, and since I was not permitted much travel, I fell back on feature-type articles and attempted to explain the contemporary Chinese scene to the Western reader, trying to alternate my stories. One week I would send a series about irrigation and electricity schemes, then switch to interpretive articles on the parrot philosophy of Chinese Communism or explanations of why Peking's thought-control methods were frequently successful. This, of course, meant writing that the Western mind must consider many aspects of the new Chinese way of life quite abhorrent, but I tempered this by pointing out that it was not necessarily as unpleasant for the Chinese, for they had never known the civil liberties we take for granted. The Peking Information Department must have pointed out to those people who were against my presence (and there were certainly very many) that I was also writing about equal distribution of food supplies, the rapid advances in industrialisation, the attempts being made to educate the illiterate masses, and any number of other positive articles. It would have been false not to recognise their achievements in many fields. The cleanliness and honesty of the average Chinese, the purposeful manner in which the Government is organising its vast pool of labour, the admirable attempts at reafforestation, drought and flood control—all these deserved the richest praise. Against this had to be debited the cost in human terms, the toil and the tears of hundreds of millions who had been hoping that at last their life might become a little easier.

One of the people who helped me most in Peking was Richard Harris, correspondent of the London *Times*. Harris had been brought up and educated in China, where his father was a mis-

sionary. He spoke fluent Mandarin, and understood the Chinese
mentality better than most Europeans I met there. One of his
remarks I will always remember. Although he was never afraid to
criticise the Communist régime, he said, "The Chinese have at
last got a standard of living. In the olden days they had only a
standard of dying."

Richard and I spent many hours together, and he told me a
great deal about his life in China before Communism. We rode
together on Peking trolley buses, walked through the streets and
parks, sipped Shanghai beer in the Hsin Chiao and compared
notes on the few interviews we were granted. Like all visiting
correspondents, he had handed in a number of requests to the
Information Department. Most of the interesting ones were, as
usual, refused. Or rather, they were simply not granted, a quaint
distinction the Chinese Communists like to make. They don't
refuse interviews but you don't hear anything more about your
application. My talks with Richard Harris were of particular
value because he was one of the few people prepared to give an
unbiased view. Too many people I met were either all for the
Communists or dead against them. The ideological bitterness
between Communism and free-enterprise was enough to prevent people from talking and behaving objectively. But Harris
had the capacity to stand back and simply to observe, and then to
report honestly.

He told me how as a lad in Shantung Province he had watched
the woman who came to clean his parents' house collect the
fallen leaves in the yard to use them as fuel. One day, as a little
boy, he stole out of the compound around the house to visit this
woman's home, a hole dug into the ground, covered with a rough
roof. Apart from the tiny entrance there were no openings.
Young Richard walked down the mud steps into virtually total
darkness.

"I sat down on a mud shelf," he told me. "In this cramped space
lived the old woman, her daughter and a tiny baby which was
crying. The husband was away on some job." It was nothing
unusual in his town, on the bitterest winter nights, for about
half a dozen people to freeze to death in the streets, because they
had nowhere to go. They lay down in the street in the evening,
and by morning were frozen stiff.

After the war, when Harris worked for the British in Tientsin
and Shanghai, death was still visible in the street. "I used to be

able to walk around, look at a dying man in the gutter and estimate roughly how many hours he had to live," he said.

*   *   *

I found talking to people who knew China helpful, but after a couple of months of sitting in my Peking hotel I was longing for a change. I was afraid my stories would become stereotyped, and the six-month visa extension I'd been granted encouraged me to travel. I applied for a permit to visit Tientsin and to my surprise this was granted without a murmur. The train journey took only two hours. I had been charged in Peking for a telegram to the Tientsin Travel Service informing them of my train and even my seat number so that my Tientsin interpreter, named Chen Liang, had no difficulty at all in finding me on the station. Whenever a foreigner moved out of his usual location, Chinese security arrangements were first class.

European traders once used Tientsin as a port from which to export Chinese merchandise, and during the first half of the present century the big European powers, as well as Russia and Japan, filled the streets of Tientsin with large, imposing buildings. At different times nine countries have held foreign concessions in the city—Britain, France, Germany, Russia, Belgium, Austria, Japan, Italy and, for a brief period, the United States. Though they would dearly like to wipe out all traces of this former foreign domination, the Chinese Communists can't afford to do so—not yet, anyway. The Tientsin buildings erected by the foreign powers are old but solid. Most of them look far more permanent than many of the new high-speed buildings being thrown up in China today. These old buildings were now being put to good use for the first time, Chen Liang said.

He pointed out the former British Municipality headquarters, with its turrets and towers, which now houses the Communist Municipal People's Council. Behind the fine stone pillars erected by the Kailing Mining Administration, once a wealthy private company, are the Tientsin Communist Party offices.

We drove to my hotel past British and French banks, their windows still covered with heavy iron grilles, which had become libraries, post offices and art museums. In its architecture the Tientsin Hotel, too, was so true-blue British I thought that at any moment a pink and cheerful face would appear at the door, and ask in perky Cockney tones, "Did you ring, sir?"

The ancient red velvet curtains in the bedrooms reminded me of Blackpool. The bathroom taps carried the label "Twyfords of Hanley". The old lift, with its panels of polished wood and its seat with the floral cushion, was made in London, and the excellent parquet flooring was surely laid about half a century or more back by English craftsmen. The white crockery with its royal blue border displayed the old name, "Astor House Hotel". What had changed in the Tientsin Hotel were the guests, now men and women in blue, Communist functionaries and production brigade chiefs, the society leaders of the new China. They did not seem to use it as a hotel, but as an eating house and a meeting place.

On our way from the station I had asked Chen why the city streets were so jammed with human traffic, and he had explained that the port was an inlet for the machinery and goods needed to build up the industrial centres of Manchuria and Inner Mongolia. The result was an overwhelming traffic and transport problem.

"So we're now repairing our old canals, and digging new ones to relieve the congestion," he said. He took me to a canal site where one of the construction chiefs Cheng Tao Peng, boasted that on any one day eighty thousand people were toiling along many miles of old canals which had silted up through disuse. I watched young people working in cold slime using most primitive methods to move soil. Cheng, a small, confident man, said the labour force included soldiers, office workers, students, factory hands and peasants from local communes. Almost anywhere else in the world the civic authorities would have built new roads. But housing is at a premium in China, and the Communists can't afford to knock down old buildings to make way for better roads. They can build canals (needing only unskilled manpower) through waterlogged fields. Primitive wooden barges can be made more easily than huge lorries.

"In the past decade we have gone from nothing to something. Now we want to go from something to more," Cheng said. To do this means that thousands of girls must carry mud to deepen the canals, using nothing more than a stick, some rope and a piece of sacking. Only the force of a disciplined and indoctrinated society could tackle such major construction projects as Tientsin's canal network with the speed and vigour so evident here. If the mass psychology is sufficiently subtle, the people do not always ask why living standards are not improving more rapidly. The answer is spelled out in thousands of small stones pressed into the side of a completed canal section. "One thousand generations," say the white pebbles, "will benefit from one generation's labours." Peking's slogans at times were reminiscent of some used by Adolf Hitler about a quarter century before.

The following day, immediately after lunch, we drove to the new harbour of Hsinkiang. I was still rather green, and realised only when we had got half-way there that the cab was costing just about as much as my hotel room for several nights, my meals and the interpreter put together. The hiring of cars was, by far, the costliest aspect of life in China. We had been driving toward Hsinkiang for two hours, drawling past smoking factories and commune buildings and apartments, and the stream of slow traffic was so thick, the car often had to come to a halt.

"Are we still in Tientsin?" I asked the interpreter.

"Well, not really," he said, "but we do refer to this place as Tientsin's new harbour." Hsinkiang, on the Gulf of Chihli, where the eastern coast of China bulges inward as if it had been punched by a giant fist, now takes 10,000-ton cargo vessels, but anything above that must stay further out, at Taku Bar, discharging cargo into lighters which ferry it to Tientsin.

In the harbour office I met the director, Tsang Kuo Wei, who showed me a huge model of further plans for development, with everything from towering office buildings to small freighters and minute trucks carved from wood, exactly to scale.

"In time we want to accommodate eighty ships at Hsinkiang," Tsang said. "It will take many years to complete the project because it will be an entirely artificial harbour. We have to reclaim a lot of land, and deepen the sea bed in several places."

In conversation the Chinese constantly refer to the past and the future, but speak seldom of the present, which is still harsh and primitive. "The past," the Chinese would say, "was very bad. But we are working for a much better future." They tried to hide, perhaps also from themselves, the stark truth that living standards in China are still miserably poor.

"It used to happen in China that a suit of clothing was handed down from one generation to the next," Chen Liang told me on the drive back to Tientsin. "A man would hand down the trousers and jacket in which he was married to his son, who would wear it only at his marriage or on very festive occasions, and would keep it in turn for his son. Today you can see young people going around the streets well and warmly dressed. They are wearing their work clothes, and when they come home at night they change into better clothes. And some will even have a third set of clothing for best occasions. In the old China this was impossible for the working man."

Next day I visited a tractor factory where motor engineers were also experimenting with automobile construction. They had built several prototype models of a six-seater car which had been christened "Peace", and asked would I like to test it. For a Chinese-made car, Peace looked very sleek, with a gleaming grey-brown body whose lines were only a few years out of date by Western standards. When the driver took me for a brief spin I noticed a decided shudder, and realised that he never used the first gear.

"This car has three forward gears but only two are used. It's a technical innovation we have worked into the machine!" he explained. Like all Chinese drivers, he changed gear long before the car had gained sufficient speed. This was done to save petrol. Evidently it hadn't occurred to them that such short cuts ruined the engine. "If it were my car, I would use first gear," I said as I took over the driving seat, "but since you insist I will kick off in second." I drove for one block of the sprawling tractor factory at about ten m.p.h. and then my companion pointed out that I had forgotten to release the handbrake, though it really didn't make much difference. The footbrake was loose, the gears rattled, and though the steering was fair Peace was still a very sick car. Crawling along at a steady twenty m.p.h. I asked what the top speed was. "About 120 kilometres an hour," said the driver and he didn't even blink.

My final request before leaving Tientsin was to see a rural commune. In Peking the Foreign Ministry had conveniently forgotten my early pleas to be taken to a commune, but Chen said a brigade leader he knew in a commune near Tientsin would be only too glad to show me round. In China everything became so much easier and friendlier away from Peking.

That afternoon we drove about seven miles out of the city to a place called Shinli Village People's Commune. The weirdest misconceptions about communes have arisen both outside and inside China because of the vastness of the land. It is certain that even Communist Party cadres who found themselves far from Peking when the first rural communes were born in 1958 completely misinterpreted certain orders issued from the capital. In the Western world, especially in the United States, communes were said to be hurriedly-erected military barracks divided into three distinct sections—one for men, another for women and the third for children. Such segregation of families may have happened in some instances, but was not true in most cases. None of the communes I saw in China resembled in the vaguest sense my own mental picture of a people's commune. There were never long rows of dormitories, no barrack-like buildings. In fact, dormitories were far more common in the cities. In the Tientsin commune the same ancient mud and stone buildings which had obviously stood for several decades were now commune homes or offices or communal kitchens. Chen's friend, Pien Min Tao, a former Red Army officer and now one of the brigade leaders of the commune, met our car. He ushered us into his headquarters, a primitive low-slung house with a cardboard ceiling, dirt floor and buckling walls, and began:

"The Shinli village commune is roughly rectangular in shape. It is twenty miles long and fifteen miles wide. The population of the commune is 110,000. Some forty per cent of the commune population work." Here Pien looked at me closely as Chen translated. He was evidently waiting for a reaction. I took a gamble.

"That's high, even for China," I said, and this pleased him mightily.

"We produce mainly rice and vegetables," Pien continued, "but Shinli village also has its own fish ponds and small-sized industries. There is also some animal husbandry."

There may not have been barracks at Shinli but labour organisation was along army lines. The commune had ten administrative areas, each divided into production brigades and sub-brigades. "We have forty production brigades and 400 sub-brigades in our commune," Pien explained. "My production brigade comprises 3,000 people." Even in his old boiler suit he looked as if he could get a good deal out of his civilian troops. A pleasant, forceful man, he gave the impression of power, and was obviously wrapped up in the work. He spoke enthusiastically about the jump in rice and vegetable production, of the tomatoes, cucumbers, and hot peppers his brigade was growing in mud and glass hothouses. The commune had 40,000 pigs and 250,000 chickens, he said, but between them the 110,000 commune members had exactly seven trucks and thirty-four tractors to help them till the land. Most of the work was still done by hand, and transport was handled by 1,000 carts. To pull the ploughs and carts and stone rollers which thresh the grain the commune had 4,000 horses and donkeys.

The central organisation of the Shinli village commune was divided into seven main departments. Most of the labour was handled by the irrigation and industrial departments while the finance and trade office looked after cost and distribution. The cultural, welfare and education office was in charge of crèches, kindergartens, primary and secondary schools, old people's homes, maternity and health clinics, adult education, sports and entertainment. Finally, there were the general office, the subsidiary food office, and the military and legal office. "Military?" I asked. "Yes," said Pien, "the commune has its own militia." Later during my stay, while travelling through Manchuria, I saw China's militia training in the fields. Teenagers handled rifles well, and in Peking I watched even school children being drilled. They used toy guns made of wood, shooting at imaginary American invaders with fierce glee.

The highest organ within the commune, Pien went on, was the meeting of commune representatives—"our own commune People's Congress," he called it—which met twice yearly with one representative for every four hundred people. These meetings elected a working committee, a commune chief and deputy chief and the various executive officers. Of the commune's expenditure, about 50 per cent went into an accumulation fund, 7 per cent in taxes to the State, 2 per cent into a public interest fund, and most of the balance in wages.

Pien made no secret of the fact that the commune members were very poor. The average wage per head of population, he said, was 170 yuan a year, or just over fourteen yuan (rather less than two pounds) per month. Top monthly wage in the commune was $66\frac{1}{2}$ yuan, the lowest wage about $16\frac{1}{2}$ yuan. But food cost very little—some people paid only one yuan a month, Pien said.

We left his quaint office, with its painted cardboard ceiling, and watched men laying bricks—"for my new headquarters," Pien smiled. In his brigade area, there was still private ownership of houses, with people paying no rent provided they had a place of their own. Pien knew his commune's statistics by heart. It had 415 communal dining rooms, 110 small factories which made clothes, shoes, soya sauce and towels, 500 crèches and nurseries, 229 old people's homes and twenty-two maternity clinics. All the buildings I was shown were rather primitive, apart from the commune's new central brick offices which reminded me of a suburban shopping area in Melbourne. As our cab finished its tour, we passed some women and children and a few old men walking from their commune kitchen along the commune's narrow dirt roads carrying bowls of rice and mashed vegetables. "Some of the people eat in the commune dining-rooms, but others prefer to take their lunch home. They can please themselves," said Pien.

After a brief farewell with smiles and handshakes we drove back to Tientsin, and in the evening I returned by train to Peking.

8

LAND OF NO CHRISTMAS

On Christmas Eve I went out with Yen, my interpreter, to have a look at the city. Our first call was at the main department store in Wang Fu Ching which was no more crowded than usual. Men in sheep-skin coats were grouped around old-fashioned, pedal-type sewing machines, selling for the equivalent of £15, a sum a well-paid city worker might earn in two months. "These are quite new," the shop attendant was saying, "They have just arrived from the Peking Sewing Machine Factory." On the steps leading to the toy department sat a peasant woman breast-feeding her baby, a simple picture that had far more of a Christmas spirit about it than the shabby grey church we visited next. Men on ladders were putting golden Chinese characters above the door. "It says 'Celebration of Christmas'," Yen translated for me. Inside was a roughly-made crib surrounded by miniature-coloured lanterns and the sorrowing altar was decorated with pink and yellow paper roses. "Only nine years ago I knelt down and prayed three times a day when I was going to a church school," Yen laughed.

"And now?" I asked. "Never again! I only prayed then because my father wanted me to learn English and French." Obviously Yen's Christian education had paid off. He spoke English almost faultlessly. We asked a man at the door whether there would be a Christmas Mass at midnight. He said there would be, and that Archbishop Pi Shu-shih was the celebrant. I suggested to Yen that we should try to obtain an interview, and without much delay we were shown into a large room, the walls of which were covered with many photographs showing the Catholic clergy with Communist leaders such as Premier Chou En-lai and Chairman Chu Teh. Dominating the room was a large picture of Mao Tse-tung. Pi Shu-shih, a small, squat man, said he was the Chairman of the Chinese Patriotic Catholic Association, and Archbishop of Shenyang, in Manchuria.

He had been given his post when the Communists finally won their battle against the Christian churches in China, and forced Catholics to form their "Patriotic" organisation. He now lived in Peking. In the first "big leap forward" year of 1958, the Vatican broke with the Chinese Catholic Church after Pope John announced that a schism had developed. As I listened to what the archbishop had to say, it became obvious to me why Rome could not possibly continue to have dealings with the Chinese Catholic hierarchy. Pi Shu-shih, smiling too widely and too often, talked in the best Marxist traditions, and had all the favourite Chinese Communist Party phrases at his fingertips. I couldn't make up my mind whether his fixed smile was embarrassment or just smugness. Not once during our long talk did he look up at the tiny crucifix hanging on the wall above a big clock, though a few times he glanced at the picture of Mao, as if to make sure that he was listening too.

The great problem facing all Communist régimes which claim to give their people complete freedom of religion is how to attain peaceful co-existence between the atheistic state and those citizens who happen to believe in God. To the outsider the contradiction seems too great. I asked Archbishop Pi Shu-shih how Chinese Catholics could back the politics of the Peking régime. How could atheistic Communism and Christianity walk hand in hand? "Catholicism and atheistic Communism have one important common ground," he replied. "It is the task of this association to make the marriage of Chinese Catholicism and Chinese Communism into a happy and lasting union. Our common ground is the fact that we are all Chinese. We want to see happiness and prosperity in our country."

Three persons in the room were taking notes—a representative of Chairman Pi, my interpreter and I. The black-robed chairman looked pleased with his answer. "All Chinese Catholics—archbishop, bishops, priests and laity—are eager to help the Government in socialist construction," he went on. "We agree with the Government's policies, and wish to join in the fight against imperialism." How did priests and bishops help in socialist construction, I asked. "We now integrate our pastoral work with socialist construction," he said.

No matter how hard I tried, I could not think of Pi as an archbishop whose pastoral duty it was to preach Christianity— the gospel that teaches men to love one another, whatever their

79

race and beliefs, and not merely their fellow Communists. Despite the fact that Communism is atheistic, it has certain superficial but startling similarities with Christianity, but an essential difference is that the Christian creed calls for love among all men, while Communists are told to love only each other, and their friends, and to hate their enemies. Christian love and tolerance were lacking in Chairman Pi, despite the archbishop's ring that adorned his finger.

The archbishop told me that student priests spent only part of their time studying at seminaries, and also worked in communes and factories. Even bishops and archbishops had been called up to do physical labour for the Communist cause in China. "If the great leaders like Chairman Mao, Premier Chou En-lai and Chairman Liu Shao-chi can go and work on the dam at the Ming Tombs reservoir, why shouldn't bishops help in socialist construction?" he asked. We turned to education. There were now no Catholic schools in China, he said, since all education was handled by the Government. "What about the confusion that must arise in the minds of Christian school children?" I asked. "At school they are taught atheistic Communism, but in church they hear sermons about belief in God."

"We are allowed to preach to students and young citizens whatever we wish—provided it is done inside the church," said Pi. "We are following the policies of the state. In China the Catholic Church is not in conflict with the Communist state. There are no contradictions." According to the archbishop nobody interfered with the internal affairs of the Church provided its preaching was done inside a church. Naturally he did not mention all the churches that have been locked, and all the parishes which have been abandoned, nor all the priests and nuns who have been jailed as "traitorous reactionaries".

When the interview with Chairman Pi Shu-shih was over we walked away from the church. Like all educated Chinese Communists, Yen knew the average Westerner had grave doubts about the freedom and the future of the Christian religion in China, but now he thought the talk with Pi had reassured me. "Well," he said with a smug grin, "are you satisfied?"

"Yes, I'm satisfied," I said. I was, too—quite sure that Christianity, and especially Catholicism, was on the brink of extinction in China.

"What can I get you for Christmas?" I asked Yen later, as we walked past the shops of Wang Fu Ching.

"Give me as a gift your friendship," he said. It was nicely put, but he could not have meant it since he knew that true friendship between a dedicated Chinese Communist and a Westerner was virtually impossible. We walked on in silence. There were hardly any Christmas trees for sale, but since Mr. Hsu and several of the female interpreters at the Hsin Chiao had wished me a happy Christmas, I bought them a potted wild rose with tiny pink blossoms. The flower-shop girl assured me the miniature rose would stay in bloom all winter if kept near enough to central heating. Unlike Yen who had no family, Hsu had three children, and for his youngest son I bought a Chinese toy acrobat, and pushed it firmly into his hand when we reached the hotel. He began shaking his head. In China, all foreign gifts are taboo. "It isn't for you," I told him. "It's a Christmas present for your little boy, and he can't say no." "He cannot speak English yet," Hsu smiled, accepting the gift.

I had not anticipated a hilarious Christmas in Peking, but I didn't expect it to be quite so miserable. About eleven-thirty at night I walked to the Catholic church on Wang Fu Ching for midnight mass, one of the saddest church services I have ever attended. The pews were filled with close on a thousand grim-faced people, all the women sitting to the left of the aisle and all the men to the right. The atmosphere was heavy with sorrow and the hymns, though sung by children, were more like melancholy dirges. At one-thirty in the morning I sauntered back through the cold night in a mood of black depression.

Christmas Day was just another working day for Peking. I had arranged to have lunch with the Houghtons who were attached to the British Embassy, but at 10 a.m. there came a call from the Foreign Ministry.

"You have requested an interview with the Education Ministry," said a voice. It was always the same kind of voice. Precise, not exactly unfriendly.

"Yes, that's right. I'd like to talk to somebody about education in China." I had written my application for this interview many weeks earlier.

"We have arranged for you to see an official of the Education Ministry at two o'clock this afternoon," said the voice. "You may take your own interpreter."

There went my Christmas dinner. To be in time for the interview I would have to be on my way by about one-thirty and I couldn't very well ask the Houghtons to put their Christmas dinner forward by about an hour just because the Chinese Foreign Ministry were using one of their little niggling methods against foreigners. I had recently written a story about China being "The Land of no Christmas" and doubtlessly the Christmas Day interview was my reward. I was determined not to let the Chinese get the better of me.

I had a lone Chinese Christmas dinner of sweet and sour pork and fried rice, and presented myself at the Education Ministry offices at two o'clock. For three hours I was absolutely fascinated by the official explanations of educational trends in the new China. The Ministry spokesman tried to impress me with what was being achieved, adding that education for children and adults alike had to be mixed with physical labour to be worthwhile. In Western countries, he said, only the rich and the bourgeois middle classes could afford to give their children proper schooling. The average worker was handicapped by a system which favoured only the monied class.

I didn't interrupt. There was never any point in trying to tell the Chinese how wrong they were. Most of them had never been outside their own country and, moreover, they had been exposed to Communist propaganda for over a decade. My job as a reporter was to listen without comment to all these odd tales about life in the free world, and at least it helped me to understand that the Communist system in China is built on an abysmal ignorance by the population at large about what goes on in other lands.

By a quarter past five it was getting quite dark outside. "I think I have kept you long enough," I said. "But I've answered only two of the four questions you put at the beginning of the interview," the official replied.

He lectured me for another three quarters of an hour, after which I went home and wrote a disgusted letter to my wife telling her all about my Christmas Day interview which took four hours, eleven cups of tea, and a visit to the toilet at half time by each of the four people present. As usual, two interpreters had been taking notes of our conversation.

Christmas in Peking convinced me the Chinese were hoping that as the older Christians died, their religion would die with them. I tried several times to penetrate the barriers which the Communists put up between the foreigner and the true state of the Christian faith in China. In the cities I visited I stopped at different churches or asked questions about various religions.

The Chinese always gave the standard text-book reply laid down by the Communist Party: "There is complete freedom of religion in China, but of course, I'm not a believer myself and can't tell you much about religious activities." In Peking, Harbin, Dairen, Tientsin, Shanghai and Canton I saw churches that had become schools, Communist meeting halls, factories, warehouses and offices. Many Buddhist temples are now bazaars. One closed Catholic church near the Hsin Chiao was used as a bottle-yard and vegetable market.

Although Catholicism was the strongest of the Christian religions in China, many other missionaries worked for decades in China's cities and in the countryside spreading the gospel of Christ. Today the Catholics are said to number about three million and the remaining Protestants of various faith a good deal fewer. Nobody is sure of the exact figure, but it is believed to be less than a million.

One Sunday in Peking I attended a Protestant service. The main church was quite empty. There were red flags and a piano, but no pews. These had been removed to an adjoining smaller hall where several dozen worshippers were sitting listening to the sermon. I asked a man who was obviously the equivalent of a church warden which denomination this was. Were these Anglicans, Presbyterians, Methodists or Baptists?

"He says it's all the same these days," the interpreter said. "This is a combined Protestant service." The official term for this Protestant union in China is the Three-Self Patriotic Movement. Months later, during a brief stay in Shanghai, I visited Pastor Li Tzu-wen, of the Shanghai Community Church, who explained the "three-self movement" briefly but clearly. "It means that the Church in China must be self-governing, self-supporting and must have self-propagation of the gospel," Pastor Li said. He spoke fluent English, had travelled extensively in Europe and was obviously sorry that he had to talk with me in the presence of an interpreter. It was impossible in China to have a lone, long conversation between two people. A third party always turned up either to take down the talk for the records, or to act as an interpreter, or just to listen.

There had been a strong urge for Christian unity in China, according to Pastor Li. "The rank and file Christian had no real conviction about these different denominations. They might mean a lot to people overseas, but even before Communism they did not seem very vital in China. The Christian community was divided into denominations by the foreign missions. We have decided to have more co-operation between the protestant denominations now." Although he could not tell me how many Protestants there were in China, or even in Shanghai, he estimated that his total congregation at two Sunday services numbered about five hundred.

The Peking régime keeps up a façade of Christianity because of the small numbers involved. And while the Communists insist that "You Christians may preach your doctrine inside your churches and we'll do our talking on the outside" there is little danger of Christianity swamping Communism. In fact, the opposite could well be the case. In a land that has no Christian background and traditions to speak of, Communism could engulf the insecure Christian religion in a flood tide of ambitious materialism. And today the clergy are made to toil along with other Chinese because Peking must prove to them, and to all others in China, that the party's power over human beings is supreme. No man, be he intellectual, soldier, peasant or priest, may question or doubt the Communist Party's top-level directives. Anyone who does is classed as "an enemy of the Chinese people". Priests and ministers are worked as hard, often even harder than most to make them forget and forsake their faith, to help them exchange their Christian beliefs for Communism. Since it is utterly impossible to believe in Christianity and Communism at the same time, Chinese Christians, be they Protestant or Catholics, have deep doubts about their present way of life. This is admitted in Peking, though never in conversation with foreigners. I studied numerous statements by the so-called Christian leaders of China and realised the mental and spiritual battle many Christians are waging with themselves and with their political masters.

The intermediary between the Protestant Church and the Communist state is the national committee for the Church's self-administration whose chairman, Dr. Wu Yao-tsung, has said openly that Christians had misgivings as regards acceptance of Communist Party leadership. "With respect to the taking of the socialist road," Wu said in a speech about Protestants in China, "ideologically we still proceed rather from the viewpoint of personal interest than from the viewpoint of collective interest. Our eyes are fixed more on the past than on the future." He spoke of the conflicting sentiments and contradictions between the collective and the individual life, of inadequate Christian understanding about what the Communist Party means by its "mass line". Christians, he said, still faced many problems "in the work of self-reform". He criticised himself and his followers, presumably in order to please the party bosses, and said, "The bourgeois stand and viewpoints still stubbornly capture our brains. We have not only been deeply influenced by the selfish individualist thinking of the bourgeoisie, but have also been subjected, over a long time, to the influence of slave thinking, of worshipping the West and despising our own country, a thinking which was inculcated unto us by imperialism under the religious cloak."

Frequently in China I found the arrogance of the Communists mingled with feelings of inferiority toward the Western visitor. His education system, his language, his logic and his entire thought processes were obviously so much simpler and more direct than the circuitous Chinese way of doing things that the progressives of Peking secretly envied this. At the same time, a combination of Chinese traditionalism and Communist orthodoxy does not allow them to emulate Western ways openly. It must be done obliquely, by devious routes, to make it appear as if the Communist Party had invented everything that is good about the new life in China. Social welfare, like hospital and medical benefits, subsidised education, homes for the aged, as well as trade unions and elections were born in the West under the banners of democracy and Christianity. The Chinese Communist Party has snatched to itself all these Christian democratic ideals, has retained those aspects which suit Communism, but has thrown aside anything it did not like, particularly free will. Communists kept stressing the need for Christian self-reform. What is self-reform? What do the Communists mean by it, and what do they wish people to do? It is their way of breaking men's wills, of crushing all individualism within human beings until they become the docile, unquestioning, faithful servants of the State. This extreme form of Communism can be forced on a desperate people searching for leadership, but it is an impossibility in an educated society. Also in China it cannot last and this must already be obvious to those members of the Party who have any vision at all.

The hurdle which Chinese Christians face when they view the Communism preached by Peking is the fact that they received a liberal, democratic Christian education, aimed at furthering the individual, at elevating the human mind, and not geared to eulogy of the supreme state. No truly free mind can accept Chinese Communism, yet Peking likes to use the word freedom. The Chinese speak of the revolution as the "liberation" and are forever hailing the new-found freedom of women. But there is only one freedom the Chinese Communists understand fully— the freedom to serve the State—which is why they do grant people the right to join a religious group, as long as the religion is subservient to the Communist Party and the State. The freedom of either not agreeing with, or, worse still, opposing the Communist state is a concept utterly foreign to Peking. I had great admiration for the Chinese Communists in a number of respects. They wanted their vast land to be independent of foreign domination; they wanted their illiterate masses to be better educated, to have at least a vague understanding of the meaning of life; they wanted more food, more buildings, more wealth. But when they talked to me of freedom, a cold emptiness enveloped me. Silence, grim silence, was always the best reply, for it was futile to argue with them. They had not the faintest notion of the true meaning of freedom.

9

NORTH TO MANCHURIA

The day after Christmas I left for Manchuria. "Go by train," people in Peking urged me. "It's much faster than the plane." And when they saw my smile they assured me that many old China hands still insisted that travelling by train often meant reaching your destination sooner. For although China's Government-run airlines have an excellent safety record, the planes cannot be relied upon to take off on time. This lesson I learned for myself—the hard way.

The morning I was scheduled to leave for Harbin the sun was brilliant and the sky was that soft blue which gives the winter scene in China's north its mild and tranquil quality. I strode toward the squat two-engined plane when our departure time of eight-fifteen drew near, but was escorted gently back to the large and airy waiting hall by a young hostess. "There is some fog at Shenyang," she said. "Will you please wait here."

For one hour I waited, and for another hour, then at 11 a.m. an elderly English-speaking Chinese told me, "You had better have your lunch now. The plane will not leave before noon." "When will it leave?" I asked. "We have not yet decided," he said. It was after 1 p.m. when the plane finally took off.

From the air the North China Plain looks like a great yellow-brown sheet, the frozen canals glistening in the winter sun like strips of silver paper. Half an hour out of Peking we reached the hills, and now the ground below was like a relief map made of papier mâché. Not a single tree seemed to be growing on those hills, but in the valleys I saw villages, with houses and roofs the colour of baked earth.

Fly across Canada, Australia, the United States and even many parts of Europe—and often there is virgin land below, but not here. On the plains, among the hills, along rivers and little streams there were settlements, some large, some consisting of just a few houses surrounded by cultivated fields. The man-made terraces, wrung from the rugged hills after generations of toil, look from the air like staircases built for giants.

During my first flight across China, I realised why the Communists seem not to fear nuclear bombardment. Despite her populous cities, China remains fundamentally an agricultural country whose population is spread far and wide. As she industrialises, some of her leaders are becoming increasingly aware of the possible consequences of an atomic war, but there can be no doubt that China would survive nuclear bombardment more successfully than most other great nations. For thousands of years peasants have eked out a bare existence from the earth of China, which has been sometimes kind to them, and often cruel. If war came, the Chinese peasants would go back to tilling the land with the age-old methods handed down by their forefathers for countless generations.

In the hundreds of thousands of places where the Chinese live—from the sprawling population centres like Shanghai with almost ten million people to tiny mountain villages with a sprinkling of primitive huts—the Communist Party's call to peasants and workers to make China great is loud and constant.

Crossing the pale blue skies of China, I realised that below me was a proud, powerful nation which, by sheer weight of numbers, could some day conquer the world. As the people of the West grow more spoilt and pampered, China grows stronger, despite her present troubles. For two hours I had been musing like this, tapping away at the typewriter, when, peering down, I saw that the pilot was following a railway line into a city. We put down at Mukden—the official Communist name for the city now is Shenyang—and found the fog to be mainly smog from the scores of chimney stacks which had been visible from the plane. They belched black smoke, and the airsock showed there was virtually no wind to blow it away.

"Two hours to Shenyang, and another three hours to Harbin," the young man at Peking had told me as he escorted me to the two-engined Russian Ilyushin 14. I decided it wasn't worthwhile getting off the plane. I'd be in Mukden, anyway, later in the week. Everyone else got off. "Harbin?" I asked one of the passengers. He smiled. He knew a little English. "Tomorrow morning," he said. It was just after 3 p.m. and already the sun was low over the North China horizon. No more flying today! The Mukden terminal resembled a very old-fashioned railway station in a European village. Nine of us piled into a little bus, drove for five minutes to a row of brick houses, and got off again, evidently at the Mukden airport "hotel". My room had four iron bedsteads in it—the bedding was clean but the unbleached sheets looked uninviting. At Peking airport I had waited only four hours, but the Mukden stop-over lasted more than seventeen hours. Since China still has very few air travellers, her airlines are in no hurry, and a twenty-one-hour wait to cover an air distance of about seven hundred miles was nothing unusual. An English businessman staying at the Hsin Chiao waited four days to catch a plane to Shanghai. Daily the flight was cancelled owing to bad weather. He could have been there and back by train in that time.

Although in 1961 Peking began to buy British airliners, the Chinese still use mostly Russian-built aircraft on the 22,000 miles of air routes. Peking is linked by air with more than seventy cities within China and abroad. When it comes to international travel, the air traveller can fly only in a westerly direction if he wants to leave China by plane, as there are no direct air connections with India or Japan. Although both Canton and Hongkong have excellent airfields, there is no air travel between the two cities.

I was in no great hurry and I didn't mind the overnight stay at Mukden. Nobody spoke English, but the Chinese fed me well and gave me a lukewarm bottle of local beer. The delay helped me to catch up on several stories I had promised the *Globe and Mail*. I typed noisily until about 8 p.m., then realised that the six Chinese, who had all been put into one room next to mine, had put out their lights, and were trying to sleep. So I read and sipped some instant coffee my mother had sent from Sydney.

* * *

The following morning we all got up rather early, had breakfast (I was supplied with an egg and more beer) and began our wait at the airport building. When it looked as if we would have to wait until noon, I managed to find a cab and an English-speaking airline official, and we drove through Mukden, a drab, poor, dirty, intensely cold city. I bought a pair of padded boots and a fur cap I could fold under my chin, and also tried to get razor blades. Later, in other cities in Manchuria, which is supposed to be the industrial heart of China, I asked for razor blades but couldn't buy a single one. In every shop, attendants shook their heads, to the great embarrassment of my various interpreters. Chinese shops were invariably short of the consumer items people needed most like soap, towels, cigarettes, gauze face-masks for protection against the dust and the cold, and of course food and clothing. Though Chinese men do not have to shave as often as Europeans, razor blades come into this category.

My airport guide had rung up from the city about the time of departure, and was told the plane would not be leaving for quite a while. "We'd better drive back and see," I suggested. When we arrived, the plane was moving away from the terminal building. I raced out on the tarmac with my bag and my type-writer, clambered up a rope ladder they threw down, and we were off. Quite unpredictable, those Chinese planes!

We had left Peking only about a third full. Several passengers had got off at Mukden, and now there were only four passengers for the twenty-four seats. Airline officials had put lead weights under several seats to make the aircraft heavier, and had packed several of the seats with luggage and freight which blocked the windows. The cabin was quite dark, looking more like the interior of a mail and cargo carrier heading for outback Queensland than a regular daily airliner.

Below us there were now some timbered hills, quite a contrast from the totally denuded and rocky hills near Peking. The further north we flew, the lighter was the colour of the ground, frost covering the soil of North China with a transparent film of alabaster. Rivers of milk snaked across the fields and even large reservoirs were frozen solid. Soon we were over the sprawling city of Harbin, glittering in the winter sun of Man-churia. Harbin has beauty and grace and colour. After the utter drabness of Mukden, it looked from the air like one of those delightful and quite unrealistic models the Chinese often show visitors. Many of the apartments, factories and institutions were painted cream and yellow, light grey or some other pastel shade. The Chinese pilot banked his two-engined Soviet IL-14 sharply, and roared low above the housetops. It was lunchtime, and tiny figures were ice-skating. Miniature donkeys and carts were crossing the Sungari River—a mighty stream frozen solid by temperatures which drop to about twenty degrees below zero. Soon after we landed I went to the frozen river, which at its widest part is almost a mile across. Some daring lorry drivers were crunching across the ice with loaded trucks, but my cab driver was less brave. "It's safer to walk," he said. The white Sungari was paradise for the little boys who skidded down the white river bank on their simple sleds. They were so well padded, and their sleds so small, they seemed to be sliding on their stomachs. Older children and men pushed themselves along on larger sleds—using sticks as if they were gliding through a shallow canal. With a new interpreter, I drove along wide gracious avenues lined with trees, past beautiful Russian Orthodox churches, whose pear-shaped cupolas added splendour to the city's skyline. Although the Communists were not pulling down the churches, most of them were locked and abandoned because the White Russian community has dwindled to little more than a handful of people. The White Russians in Harbin, which is just over two hundred miles from the Soviet border, are an embarrassment both to Peking and to Moscow, and the Chinese are looking forward to the day when the last of them leaves, either to go north into the U.S.S.R. or south to Hongkong.

About forty years ago Harbin was a city of refuge for the White Russians who had escaped the October Revolution. They built fine new churches and schools, prayed before the ikons, reared children and thrived. At one time they numbered thirty thousand, but less than three thousand remain. I saw some of them in the Harbin streets—decrepit, sad-eyed people, clinging to life because of man's deep wish to live no matter what the circumstances. Many who are without jobs have had to sell all their belongings for food, and now wait either for release or death. They write desperate letters to Church and refugee organisations, to their relatives in Western nations, begging for help. But often the only reply is silence because most of the White Russians are old people whom nobody wants.

I was shown several sprawling industrial plants in Harbin and went through a typical factory dormitory. It was a large box-like building, only a few hundred yards away from the pounding looms of the Harbin Linen Factory. A grass patch had been fenced off, and to get in you first had to pass a small caretaker's hut by the fence. Each person leaving or arriving at the dormitory was seen by the gateman whose job was to stop anyone without a home from intruding. In China it is still a privilege to have a solid roof over your head and a dry cement floor under your feet.

With three factory executives and the interpreter I went into a room with five double-tiered bunks, two of which were piled high with luggage. Eight girls lived in the room, and each had the wall next to her bed plastered with pictures—family snaps, Chinese film stars, newspaper cuttings of Mao. At the head of each bed were books and magazines, and one girl had a radio.

There were only two women in the room, one in her thirties, an obvious activist, who began lecturing me. The interpreter repeated all the dull propaganda in English. She was nattering on about production targets until I became heartily sick of it. For a time I listened then turned to the other girl who was sitting quietly on her bunk. A young, beautiful creature even in her simple clothes, she wore slacks and a printed cotton blouse.

"May I know your name?" I asked her. It was Yu Ching-po— in English "Clean Wave", said the interpreter.

"What do you consider more important," I asked, "romance or machines?"

"Machines—of course," she said. The "machines" was the standard answer. The "of course" showed some originality.

"But why of course?"

"You cannot separate love affairs from your work," the girl said. "You meet your sweetheart at your work, and you have common interests."

Ching-po said she had no boy friend. But didn't she want a husband and children one day? I asked. Most girls in the West hoped to marry and raise a family. The pink of Ching-po's cheeks turned crimson. This was not the kind of question a foreign visitor should put to an emancipated woman worker employed in the fine-yarn workshop of the Harbin Linen Factory. She said that in the old China girls also thought first of romance, of finding a good husband who would keep her, and be kind. But this was important only because women depended on husbands for their livelihood. Today this wasn't so in China. Women worked on an equal basis with men. Her glowing face, framed by curly black hair, looked very sweet. A shy smile was on her lips, and I would have given much to read what was behind those large black eyes. For a time we talked of other things. She said her next shift was from 3.30 a.m. to noon. No, she didn't have an alarm clock, nor did she need one. Somebody came around to wake the early morning shift workers.

"What do you do with your free time?"

"There are films, or I read here in my room."

Each bunk had a thin curtain to give a little privacy.

"It is quieter with the curtain drawn," Ching-po assured me. Like other single girls, she ate in one of the factory canteens, saw films in the factory club and claimed that her first and foremost interest was in factory production. She took daily showers in the factory, but once a week, on Saturdays, the plant's boilers sent hot water to the dormitories for the workers' laundry. Ching-po, one of five-thousand workers, was now twenty-four and had been employed by the factory since the age of sixteen. We chatted mainly about her work, and I purposely kept off international affairs. She was so feminine that had she brought up the time-worn Chinese line about "U.S. imperialist aggressors" it would have ruined the whole atmosphere of the interview. As we were about to leave the room, Ching-po stopped me at the door.

"To answer your earlier question, I do wish to marry and have children. That is only normal." My day was made by this small incident, because despite the factory delegation accompanying me the girl was admitting that she loved men and children's laughter better than the noisy machines in the fine-yarn workshop.

On New Year's Eve I caught a train south to Changchun, a little under two hundred miles from Harbin; my main purpose in stopping there at all was to visit the Changchun motor works which I found disappointing. Virtually all the workshops in the huge plant had been shut down because of the New Year holiday. I tramped for an hour through the No. 1 Automobile Plant, China's biggest motor works, after a hopelessly futile interview which had proved what a trap it is for a nation to exaggerate its statistics. An article I had read in the February 1959 issue of the monthly journal *China Reconstructs*, had carried the flaring head-line "Altogether for 150,000 cars a year!" It was a poorly trans-lated, misleading title for the article, which consisted mainly of Communist propaganda prose. The most interesting aspect of the story was the claim by the management that the 1958 output of 30,000 cars and lorries would be pushed gradually to 150,000 vehicles a year. But things had not changed in the slightest when I visited the factory a year after publication of the *China Reconstructs* article. I asked how many cars were now coming off the assembly line. Tso Ying, one of the plant's executives, told me quietly, "We are producing 30,000 vehicles a year. We plan to produce 150,000."

"But you are talking about lorries," I insisted. "What about private cars?"

"The plant's main product is trucks," said Tso Ying. "So far we have made only small batches of cars."

"Can you give me any idea how many private cars the plant will turn out in a year?" was my next question. "Most Western people have cars and are interested in cars."

"We are turning out only high-quality sedans, not poor-quality vehicles," said Tso. "Our plan of production is still very rudimentary." One of the engineers, Liu Ping-nan, came to his rescue. He said technological improvements were still being made to the new Chinese car, the Red Flag, but for the time being automobile production would be less than ten per cent of the Changchun plant's total annual production.

"At that rate it will be many years before a Chinese worker can buy his own car," I said.

"But this isn't China's only automobile factory," Tso replied aggressively. "There are many." Asked where they were, he mentioned two cities, Wuhan and Nanking. This constant tendency to exaggerate everything is one of the Chinese Communists' gravest faults. The Soviet Union in 1953 sent hundreds of advisers to Changchun to help them build a plant with a capacity of 30,000 trucks a year, but the Chinese had pulled it apart again to suit political ends. By using the mass line they could improve on Soviet techniques, they said. The plant's modernity, reported *China Reconstructs*, had its drawbacks. "Because the plant had been equipped with the most advanced techniques, it was pervaded with a kind of technological superstition," the journal reported. "Standard designs and processes were untouchable. Everyone in the plant belonged to one of two categories. In the 'front' were the workers and technicians engaged directly in production. In the 'rear' were the designing office personnel, who shut their doors and immersed themselves in 'international standards'." But Peking insists on Chinese standards, where the workers are the bosses and the intellectuals the ones who must obey, so the orthodox Soviet system could not last. Before long, the plant director was putting on a boiler suit to work as an apprentice in the steering-gear shop. *China Reconstructs* said designers saw that their "aloofness from reality" had harmed the plant; administrators admitted that their "bureaucratic ways" had done the same. "Administrators and engineers taking part in shop work are one aspect," said the article. "The other is workers taking part in administration. Formerly, each production team had a foreman. Since last March the responsibility has been divided among several elected secretaries—for tools, labour discipline, economics, technical innovations, labour protection, etc. Each keeps a record book of problems arising and action taken which is hung on the wall for public inspection."

When the Changchun motor plant wanted to find out how it should carry out the Communist Party's general line most effectively, it asked its workers and personnel to put up 400,000 tatzepao (Chinese wall newspapers) used for self-criticism, criticism of others and for suggestions. With more than 20,000 employees in the plant, this meant twenty wall newspapers each. The countless hours wasted by the Chinese in drawing wall posters of leaping horses, of rocketing production charts, and paintings of how China is catching up to Britain (usually painted as a paunchy, sickly-looking little man in a bowler hat) was absolutely unbelievable. The time workers at all levels spent at meetings and conferences in criticising themselves and others must, over the years, have added up to a staggering number of lost man-hours. Toward the end of 1960 and in 1961 there came many modifications in the Chinese Communist mode of living and one was, to the delight of hundreds of millions, fewer political meetings and shorter hours of study after the day's work was done.

10

MUKDEN, ANSHAN, DAIREN

From Changchun I caught a train down to Mukden, where a tall, serious man of about thirty plucked me out of the journeying crowds. It was quite baffling how rapidly most interpreters found me amid the teeming crowds which poured in and out of the Manchurian stations in their tens of thousands. During most of my train and plane journeys I was the only Westerner travelling. Occasionally I saw a Russian, or the wife of a foreign expert heading for home, but the Chinese have cut themselves off from the rest of the world so thoroughly one can travel for days and see only Chinese faces. Although Peking obviously does not like the idea of foreigners, Communist or otherwise, breezing through the country, these suspicions are rarely evident among individual Chinese I met.

Everywhere he goes the European visitor gets red-carpet treatment from the mild-mannered officers of the China International Travel Service, and the further away from Peking you are, the nicer people become. When officials politely refused to accept invitations to join me in a meal, I would ask to have my food sent to my room in protest. "I'm not used to eating alone in an empty dining-room meant for fifty persons," I explained to several of them, with rapid results. My next invitation was accepted and the compliment was returned with a first-class meal. The huge dishes of pork, chicken, beef, fish, shrimps and vegetables, the fruit and the wines served embarrassed me considerably. How could I enjoy a vast meal a few hours after visiting a commune where the headman assured me that in two years or so his peasants might get meat once a month? Today it was an impossibility to give them meat each Sunday, but they did have meat on certain national holidays.

The Manchurian hotels were old-fashioned but comfortable, and the staff scrupulously, almost frighteningly honest. If I was due to get one cent change, waiters walked down three flights of

Soochow Creek, Shanghai.

Street artist with admiring onlookers.

Young modellers of Shanghai. They are Young Pioneers playing at the Children's Palace, a youth club housed in a former millionaire's mansion.

stairs to fetch it. When I was in China you could leave cash, valuable cameras, clothes and suitcases standing in the middle of the street, and nobody would touch anything. But as the famine got worse, honesty also declined. Room boys were generally most attentive, and though at times their interest in my comfort was a little overdone, in Manchuria I appreciated it.

Rail travel, after a few days, became extremely tiring. Trains were always slow, often ran behind schedule which meant long waits in dreary railway rooms, and carriages had no temperature control. At times it was so hot in my sleeping compartment I stripped down to a pair of shorts, although outside the temperature was about minus twenty degrees centigrade. On some trains piping hot steam was passed through the carriages for a time; then it would be turned off for an hour. As the temperature dropped, I put all the pullovers I had peeled off back on again. Then the steam would come hissing back. How the Chinese could sit in the trains still wrapped in their cocoon-like padded clothing was to me an absolute mystery, but probably their meagre diet had far less calorific content than was needed to heat the human body properly.

Mukden, where on September 18, 1931, the Manchurian warlord Chang Tso-lin was assassinated in a bomb plot, signalling the Japanese seizure and occupation of Manchuria, is typical of the mushrooming north-eastern cities which are absorbing some of the excess population from the fertile south and centre of China. As a result urban populations in Manchuria have rocketed to new heights. In the five main industrial centres I visited, Harbin, Changchun, Mukden, Anshan and Dairen, there live almost as many people as in the whole of Canada. Mukden is the largest with more than 6,000,000 people in the city and suburbs. Then come Harbin and Dairen with over 3,000,000 each. Anshan and Changchun each have city and suburban populations of at least 2½ millions. Since these 17,000,000 do not include the growing populations of the many smaller cities, towns and villages between the five main centres, there must be at least twenty-five million people living along the railway line between Harbin in the north and Dairen near the tip of the Liaotung Peninsula, a straight stretch of only about five hundred miles.

The large-scale movement of Chinese from south to north also has its strategic aspects. Manchuria has long been the springboard from which aggressors have staged their invasions of China. The Japanese came into China through Manchuria, and three hundred years before them the Manchus subdued first Inner Mongolia, then headed southward taking Peking and the ancient capital of Sian.

Today the Chinese realise they must have a strong Manchuria. They do not want to be invaded via Manchuria again, and are keen to bring Outer Mongolia, whose Communist Government at Ulan Bator has for years faithfully followed the Kremlin's dictates, within their sphere of influence. The Chinese know that nothing is more capricious than history. By moving people into Manchuria and Inner Mongolia, Peking is merely ensuring that should history throw Mongolia into China's lap, there will be people around to catch it. The Communists have realised that containment of China is the main aim of U.S. foreign policy in the Far East, yet the population pressure along their eastern coastline, and in the valleys of the great rivers must be eased somehow. One method is the massive movement to the north-west, to the far-western regions of Sinkiang and Tibet, and to Manchuria. A bird's eye view of the north-eastern industrial cities, beautifully camouflaged from the air by constant smoke-screens of the filth being belched from tens of thousands of chimneys, proves that the Communists are strengthening this region with a vengeance. Other schemes are to make Heilung-kiang Province which borders on south-eastern Siberia, into an important wheat and timber-producing region; to raise cattle on the great plains of Inner Mongolia; to squeeze oil from beneath the deserts of Sinkiang. To the north and to the west of China lies the Soviet Union, the world's largest single nation. It is very significant that China, the country with the largest population, is telling so many of her young people, "Go north! Go west!"

I spent two days trudging through Mukden's factories, and listening to Communist complaints about "the fearful Japanese occupation with its cruel Japanese militarists who had forced Chinese to work like slaves in the Manchurian mines." The hatred for the Japanese was stated intense, and it surprised me since the Peking Press had lately been putting out feelers toward Tokio.

After Mukden, south again, to Anshan, which the Chinese call the nation's steel capital. But it is more than that. It symbolises the new China, for it is a city of toil, an industrial colossus, rebuilt from the ruins the Japanese left behind them because of Peking's determination to industrialise China at top speed. Anshan's sprawling Iron and Steel Company is the largest integrated iron and steel works in the country, employing 170,000 workers. Like Shenyang, Anshan was drab and dirty, its atmosphere laden with coal-dust and smoke. Although the steel city people looked weary, Anshan was tremendously impressive. I arrived at night, and the glow from the city's blast furnaces had turned the night sky an eerie red. The place never slept. The shrill whistles of trains, the trundling of trucks and trams, the pounding steam hammers and the screaming metal saws created a nightmare of noise that penetrated into the large, comfortable hotel room I was given, and kept me awake a long time. Anshan was making iron and steel with that baffling enthusiasm which startled all visitors to China up to the summer of 1960. The lethargy and disenchantment which was to come later that year and in 1961 was not yet apparent.

Even hard-headed industrialists from Europe who had visited Anshan had come back to Peking wide-eyed. The city seemed to be nothing but one huge factory after another. Anshan produces more than one third of the nation's steel and has been developed solely as an industrial centre. Apart from the massive iron and steel complex, there are scores of other large enterprises and smaller blast furnaces with hundreds of chimney stacks breaking the skyline, sending black filth into the atmosphere day and night. I spent a whole day driving past countless plant installations, inspecting steel-rolling and tube-making factories, walking through shaking buildings where ore was dressed, visiting sintering, iron-smelting and refractory material plants and factories that made nothing but rails for China's growing railway system. I saw Anshan's blast furnaces, higher than thirteen storey buildings, which needed entire trains to take great cauldrons of molten iron from one part of the plant to another. Cranes lifted the containers, and then the metal was poured, a glowing orange waterfall cascading through the sub-zero temperatures of Manchuria. Men toiled so close to the open-hearth furnaces the heat tanned their skins. The workers wore excellent and comparatively new protective clothing. They were obviously experts and handled red-hot steel tubes or rails as if they were giant candy bars.

From the city we drove to the open-cast mines outside Anshan, along a bumpy dirt road past endless lines of workers walking between the plants and their homes, through outlying suburbs of mud huts with straw roofs to where metal teeth were biting into the mountains. It had been snowing, and the brown ore was hidden under a layer of white. Hulking machines transferred the iron ore into trains which were kept busy shuttling back and forth between the ore dressing plants and the mines. The same night I caught the late train to Dairen, snatching five hours' sleep during the journey. After the grime and noise of Anshan, the port of Dairen was a gracious, almost quiet city, as beautiful as Anshan was ugly. Fresh air blew in from the sea, and the people in the streets did not have the ashen, weary, coal-dust faces of the industrial workers further north. Down by the seashore were fine old villas, converted into sanatoriums and rest homes. Along wide streets were large department stores crowded with singularly relaxed shoppers. Each of China's great cities has its own rhythm, its own particular mood, and Dairen was smiling, obviously in good spirits.

A quarter-hour's drive out of the main shopping area, and you are by the sea. To the east is Korea Bay, to the south the Yellow Sea. Dairen had also had some of the snow which was falling in Anshan, but now, at noon, the sun was out again. Half the beach and some upturned boats were still a few inches under snow. After all the pounding machines of the North-east, the wet, white beach with its crystal rowing boats and the sun gliding across the water was most soothing. The mode of life in Dairen was more normal than in the big factory cities I had visited earlier. Many people lived in pleasant suburban cottages which had their own gardens. There were quiet, narrow streets which could have been lanes somewhere in Scotland. Unfortunately, the Chinese Communists were disfiguring many of the streets with their large and unsightly red-brick apartments. Next to the old-fashioned but charming cottages, most of them still in excellent repair, the newer buildings looked like high, square barns.

By the time I had reached Dairen I was having nightmares about factory inspection. "No more factories," I insisted. But I was keen to see the Dairen shipyard. China is today building her own 10,000-ton cargo ships, and executives of the Dairen shipyard told me proudly of plans for 20,000-ton ships which were well under way. The 10,000-ton freighter I saw under construction had a fierce-eyed red dragon painted on the bow. The shipyard, employing 13,500 people, was built originally by Czarist Russia, then the Japanese used it, and in 1945 Soviet Russia occupied Dairen. Between 1952 and 1954 the Russians helped the Chinese to rebuild it, I was told, and by 1955 China took over the enterprise completely.

I wandered around below the tall, spidery cranes of the ship-yard with the manager, Chi Wei-hsin, who said China was spending millions on establishing her own shipping fleet, not only in Dairen but in shipyards at Shanghai and Wuhan. He said Dairen was not as big a ship-building centre as Shanghai, but that it was growing. "We don't just make ships," he assured me. "Out in the suburbs we have our own pig and chicken farms as well as sheep and oxen, also farmlands and orchards where we grow apples and pears and cherries for our workers."

Chi said about twenty ships were then being repaired in Dairen. I saw welders and painters at work on a large Russian freighter, propped up in one of two dry docks. The hulls of two large tugs and another 10,000-ton merchant vessel were well under way. Although, for the most part, China is still concentrating on such small ships as trawlers, coastal freighters, river and canal boats, barges and tugs, she has begun building her own fleet of submarines and other warships. Early in 1962, British naval experts put the combined strength of the Sino-Soviet underwater fleet at about 429 nuclear and con-ventional submarines. China, of course, will not have an atomic-powered submarine for many years to come. But there was no point in discussing naval defence with Mr. Chi, who wouldn't have told me a thing. Nor did I broach the subject with Li Yu-tang, my interpreter in Dairen, whom I liked far too well to pump him on a matter which could have landed him in trouble.

Li Yu-tang was a man after my own heart. How he knew I will never guess, but he seemed to sense how tired I was of industrial interviews. He did not assail me with a string of statistics, with Communist Party chatter, with propaganda and proposals for factory visits, with talk of production and emulation and forward leaps and backward capitalists. Li Yu-tang was first a human being, and only after that a Chinese believer in Communism. He was another China International Travel Service man, and if China wants more tourists it will have to look for interpreters like young Li Yu-tang who talked to me about his children, about the smell of the sea on a summer evening, about fishing and shopping.

"On my day off," he said, "I go fishing and nothing else seems to matter. I forget even my family. All I want to see is what's at the end of that line." We discussed Australian and Chinese beaches, and when he saw the photographs of my four children on the hotel desk he insisted I put a picture of my wife next to them. "It is impossible to have four children without a mother," he announced firmly, and smiled happily when I put Audrey's picture on the desk.

Li Yu-tang's very ordinary small talk and normal reactions were not only a great relief but a most pleasant surprise. China today is geared for work and for work alone, and discovering an amiable individual who did not constantly try to rub Communism into you was like discovering a pearl among the pebbles on a beach.

Mr. Li was very happy with Communism. This was quite obvious, and I did not even have to ask him. He, his parents, his wife and children were much better off now than before. The Japanese had been in occupation, and Li told me they had not been kind masters to the Chinese. Only those Chinese children whose parents worked for the Japanese could go to school.

For once, a Chinese also showed a little interest in the land I had come from, and the places I had visited.

The Communists were not only generally polite to me, but often far too polite. They were courteous even when I knew they disliked me for the things I had written. But there was never the slightest attempt to make me feel at home, and never did anyone show the vaguest interest in what was going on outside the Middle Kingdom. Canada and Australia, they used to say, were countries which had very small populations. In the United States, people had lots of cars. "This is why we must work so hard to catch up." But no more. Never once was I asked were people really oppressed by monopoly capitalism as the Chinese Press made out? Nobody seemed interested in what foreigners in the West thought about China. Yen, the tall interpreter at the Hsin Chiao hotel in Peking, had read books about Australia, knew that Sydney had one of the longest single-span bridges in the world and even that Collins-street was Melbourne's main shopping street. He had learned that London and Paris had underground railway systems "like Moscow". He had travelled a little in Czechoslovakia with a youth delegation. But he wore the usual Communist blinkers and our chats, which began fairly informally, became very stiff as the months passed. Yen was probably warned that I was criticising certain aspects of China, and was told to keep his mouth shut.

Li Yu-tang had none of these inhibitions. He spoke about the schooling he had had with the Maryknoll Catholic missionaries in Dairen, after the Japanese surrender, without bitterness. The admission that he had been educated by Catholic teachers was unusual enough, but it should have been accompanied by propaganda talk about how the foreign missionaries had duped and deceived the Chinese people. Instead Li said the Catholics had taught him English. We yarned about the most innocuous matters. Down on the beach he posed for photographs, and said how much his children loved swimming. Touching the freezing water, I told him that in the same ocean, way down south in the Australian summer, my children were probably playing in the surf along a Sydney beach where they were holidaying. He smiled, and said, "I hope they will come to China, and then to Dairen for holidays. You should bring your family here. Dairen is such a lovely city." He was justly proud of his home town.

Li had been an interpreter with the Chinese Travel Service for only six months. For five years before that he had been teaching English at a local school. After vainly trying to stifle his yawns, he explained that since he had had to meet me soon after 4 a.m. that morning he hadn't slept a wink. He thought he might over-sleep and miss meeting my train. Before lunch it was my turn to utilise the Chinese method of propaganda and persuasion. "Please join me in a meal," I said. "No, no. It is not necessary." This was the standard Chinese answer whenever I invited any of the interpreters. With some, who were obviously polite only as a matter of form, and whom I disliked as much as they distrusted me, that was often the end of it. With Li, I insisted.

"I know it may not be necessary, but at the same time it is vital for you to come to lunch. I don't want to sit at a table all alone, and you would be failing in your duties as an interpreter if you allowed me to eat by myself." So he agreed, and we had some wine to celebrate the occasion. After half a glass he became a little funny, and much more tired, and immediately stopped drinking. He said he didn't smoke, and never drank. Would I excuse him? He didn't think he should have any liquor. "The wine isn't strong, I know, but I really didn't sleep. If I'd slept more I could have a little more wine, too." Instead he drank burning hot coffee which he said didn't hurt him "because I have a throat of iron."

Straight away after lunch he excused himself and had a brief rest in his room. We spent the afternoon wandering through the streets, looking at the shops, and watching children at play. Li was as pleased as I to escape another round of factories. When he saw me off in the evening, we parted good friends. He was the only Chinese official I met in Manchuria who was filled not only with pride for the new China but also had some warmth and understanding for a stranger alone and far from home.

I was really glad to be heading back to Peking. I had emptied two drawers and had told the room boys to put mail and any papers into my desk as it arrived. I had already decided on a form of rationing, in order to stretch out the news from Audrey's letters. No more than two or three letters a day, even though eight or ten might be waiting for me.

Again I had a compartment to myself but couldn't enjoy it. The radio was going full blast—Chinese opera, Chinese marches, Chinese chatter—always this ear-shattering din on the trains. When the attendant came into the compartment, I pointed in desperation at the radio. He grinned broadly, went to a knob I'd been twirling vainly for hours, gently manipulated it, and there was peace. At the stations it wasn't as easy. Just before we reached Peking, the train stopped at a small township. It was already eleven-thirty at night but the station radio made sure everyone stayed awake. The smaller the station, the worse the records. The alleged musical entertainment here was a worn-out gramophone disc being assailed by an ancient needle. The total result was bedlam. I got off the train, and, as an experiment, stood beneath the lamp-post to which one loudspeaker was attached. Several people were lounging about quite unconcerned. The wailing, howling record made such an unbelievable din I couldn't bear it for more than a minute and walked a good fifty yards away to watch the station scene from there. Most of the Chinese didn't seem to realise the inferno of sound even existed. Time had immuned their ears. But one young man heard. To the sepulchral yet piercing strains of what had once been a dance tune he performed a weird waltz. His steps were rhythmic, stiff, puppet-like. But his face was glowing in the lamplight, and obviously the music pleased him. The scratchy, screeching record had fulfilled its purpose. Evidently it had made one man happy.

COMMUNIST PARROTS

"And now we will give you a brief introduction." Not only in Peking and Manchuria—but everywhere I went in China the sentence haunted me. Invariably it was the beginning of any inspection tour in China. Kindergarten teachers, factory managers, commune brigade chiefs, bosses at dam sites and canal projects, guides in museums—they all insisted on their "brief introduction" first. I always settled back in resignation to listen to a lecture on the wonders of Communism, generally lasting from one to three hours. In an industrial plant the brief introduction covered every aspect of factory life, from production figures to social welfare, and the textual similarities were frightening, everyone parroting faithfully the same well-worn Communist phrases. The visitor is told that the workers are wonderful, that the workers are the masters of the plant, that the workers have speeded up production, have invented new methods and are improving the administration of the factory, that each worker is, in fact, a miraculous gift from heaven. If only one factory manager in Communist China had told me his workers were a lazy lot of good-for-nothings who needed shaking up he would have become my lifelong friend. Each official talk with a Chinese was not only an interview but a ritual one had to go through to learn anything at all. The uniformity of this ceremony at all institutions (be they communes or factories) is startling and disturbing.

Invariably you arrive by car. Somebody has been watching for it from a window, and the moment the car pulls up, a door opens, and several officials are there on the threshold to welcome the guest. They are always charming and smiling. The visitor is never shown into an office, but into a large room where the furniture consists mainly of armchairs, sofas and low tables that stand about two feet off the ground. Hats and overcoats come off, and tea is poured. The next few lines the interpreter need hardly translate.

"Please sit down," comes first. Then, "We welcome you to this factory," and "We are always pleased to see foreign friends." The Chinese never talk about "foreigners" or "visitors" since everybody allowed into China automatically becomes a "foreign friend."

Then follows the dreaded "brief introduction" during which you learn over and over again that the factory is functioning solely because it is under the leadership of the Communist Party and Chairman Mao Tse-tung. Before, things were dreadful, now they're wonderful. After reciting statistics often going back as far as 1949, the Communist executives tell you that the factory has established canteens, kindergartens and nurseries, dormitories, clubs and spare-time schools where workers can learn anything from English and mathematics to music and painting.

After visiting a dozen factories in a row I felt I could have recited interviews (apart from detailed production figures) off by heart before they began. Questions are possible, of course. But you have to be quick. Some of my Chinese lecturers have openly resented being interrupted during their "brief accounts". But I found that by asking questions it was at least possible to reduce the length of the interview. The monotonous Communist propaganda, the drear repetition of production slogans, the similarity of the phrases used to explain the national plans of the Peking régime left me suspicious and disheartened. I felt that through their political education, the Communists were turning the Chinese people into a race of human parrots, where everyone had to talk and think alike. Near the very top, of course, are the real planners who can use their brains as well as Western executives. But behind them in an endless stream strut the parrots who repeat the leaders' phrases with such utter accuracy one imagines they need only press the red badge on their lapel, and the record inside their brain begins to turn. Only rarely did I talk to Chinese who had been over-seas, who knew that there are other ways of life and could think for themselves. But they are a dying breed. Flooding out of the nation's schools and universities today are the up-and-coming executives of China who see the whole world only from one position, who are told that Communism, and especially the Chinese brand, is the only worth-while form of government.

What is so hard to understand is that the great revolutionary leaders of China like Mao Tse-tung and Chou En-lai, who with a handful of followers had to pull this huge land out of chaos, cannot see the immense dangers in the parrot society they are creating. China's newspapers are forever hailing the infinite creativeness of the masses, telling how the people themselves make roads and reservoirs, build new cities and factories; but in fact, all construction work, every mass move begins and ends with the Communist Party. The party leads in all fields and the people must follow. With the present emphasis on breeding only the parrot brand of party members, the Chinese Communists could soon find themselves in a position where they have no real leaders left. For today, unless you are prepared to be a mimic, you are an outcast, and that is why people I met never seemed ashamed that the Communist Party had remoulded them into walking tape recorders. In the not-too-distant future China alone will have a population of a thousand million. The great Communist dream is that these thousand million people will work and behave and think as the party sees fit. I saw the effect of Communist education best in my own interpreters, most of whom were young Communist mocking birds; but some were definitely more likeable than others. Take Mr. Hsu, whose duty it was to look after the foreigners at the Hsin Chiao, a pleasant little fellow of about thirty-two, who could at least relax when he got away from his hotel watch-room. He spoke reasonable English and some Russian. Hsu sat in a small, cold office not far from the one and only entrance to the hotel, and his dark eyes would dart to the lift door and the stairs to see which of the hotel's residents were leaving the building. Hsu smiled more readily than most other Chinese officials, but he, too, followed Communist dictates to the letter. He was trying to improve his English, and often when I came into his office he would be reading the English publications most easily available such as *Peking Review*, *China Reconstructs*, *China Pictorial* and other Communist propaganda published in English.

Only rarely would Hsu and the other interpreters who shared the office be reading a book published in England or America, although these could be bought at the second-hand bookshop in the closed market off Wang Fu Ching. There was every conceivable work to be had from Shakespeare and Dickens down to books by scores of Chinese travellers like Peter Fleming and Edgar Snow.

There were books in all languages, but especially in English,

French and German, while another section of the bookshop sold only Russian books. I spent hours browsing through the shelves; one day I bought a battered copy of *Twilight in the Forbidden City*, by Reginald F. Johnson, the English tutor to the Emperor Pu Yi. On another occasion I found a vast volume of 625 pages, printed in 1935, called *The Theory and Practice of Ice-cream Making*, by Hugo H. Sommer, Professor of Dairy Industry at the University of Wisconsin. I wondered whether any Chinese hotel manager would dare to buy it. I almost bought it for Hsu to present to the Hsin Chiao manager but decided he mightn't take kindly to the jest.

Hsu was the only interpreter in Peking who told me something of himself. He had a brother, who was a Chinese businessman in the Philippines. Hsu in his earlier years had lived in Hongkong where he had received some of his education. But he was not interested in business and had preferred to return to China. He had three children, two of whom were living with their grandparents at Amoy, in Fukien Province, just across from the off-shore island of Quemoy. His youngest child, a boy of two, spent his week at a Peking kindergarten. Often on a Sunday the little chap, roly-poly in his padded jacket, would race around the lobby of the Hsin Chiao, or play quietly in his father's office. But Hsu never talked about his wife. In the evenings, after accompanying me to some theatre or ballet performance, I would drive him home in a cab. Not once did he invite me into his rooms. None of the Communists I knew asked me to their homes. I felt sorry for them because their abode, more often than not, consisted of one or maybe two rooms, and I guessed they had neither food nor drink to offer me. But I believe most foreigners would prefer a steaming cup of weak tea shared with a Chinese they like in his own quarters, however mean or humble, to the artificially sumptuous meals served up to most visiting foreigners by party or government officials.

I got to like Hsu, mainly because we both enjoyed music. He would be the first to tell me if a visiting ballet troupe was appearing in Peking, and would be doubly delighted when I asked him to buy two tickets, one for him and one for me. I always assured him that an interpreter during these theatre shows was a must and he gladly agreed with me. Hsu, who loved Western music sat whistling symphonies and concertos to himself at his desk for hours as he absorbed Communist propaganda. Once, during my first visit to the Summer Palace on which he accompanied me he really let his hair down. We tramped along the usually silent paths singing loudly several of the solemn themes of Tchaikowsky's *Pathetique* symphony. Yet neither he nor any of the other interpreters ever let the side down. They might criticise themselves at times (self-remoulding was considered a great asset in a good Communist) but everything the party did was perfect, at least officially.

The interpreter I used most regularly was a young man named Yen, who spoke excellent English, but as time passed our relationship became increasingly strained. Instead of giving straight answers to my questions, Yen tried to be a little too clever, the Chinese equivalent of a smart Alec. He virtually admitted it, and one day told me his wife had put up in their dormitory a public notice (or Tatzepao) criticising him for being too arrogant.

Yen, tall, good-looking, confident, cared far more for his clothes than most interpreters. He liked browns, often wore a brown woollen jacket and brown corduroy trousers, and had several pairs of smart grey flannel slacks. A few times, when I saw him wearing a suit, white shirt and tie, he looked quite a man of fashion.

It was during my first two months in Peking that Yen and I had our most valuable conversations. He would accept my invitation to lunch, or join me in a cup of coffee on the sixth floor. He had obviously been given the nod that I was, as yet, harmless. After several meals at my expense he insisted on paying for his own lunch. One of our coffee talks became a debate about individualism and individual tastes. Why was China against individualists, I asked. Just what were the advantages of collective living?

Collective living was selfless, he said. It was important to be interested in your neighbour's welfare. He explained how children were taught about the collective ideal already in kindergarten. "Suppose there are thirty children in a nursery," he said. "Each of them gets a white handkerchief. But one of them says, 'No, I want a green handkerchief.' You will admit that if the child were living at home it would nag its mother until it got a green handkerchief. But at the crèche it must take what all the other children get."

Surely, I argued, if out of thirty children one wants something different it must prove in some way this child should be singled out from the others. There must be a reason for it wanting a green handkerchief. Maybe the child is smarter than the others, or perhaps it is merely stubborn. "But by forcing the child to take the white handkerchief you may be killing some imaginative spark which in later years could invent new machines for China," I said.

"We believe that what is good for the community is good for every member in that community," said Yen. "If it is a good thing for twenty-nine children to have white handkerchiefs, it must be good for the thirtieth child also."

To Yen and Hsu and the many other interpreters I used must go some of the credit for the stories that were sent home to Toronto. Without interpreters, I would have been lost. At first there was so much to write about I didn't even have time to think about taking Mandarin lessons. And later, when the bureau folded up, there was again no time. You could make yourself fairly well understood by signs, though there were, of course, certain fundamental traps.

The best story I heard about sign language in China concerned a German businessman who arrived in Canton tired and thirsty. He was a teetotaller, and wanted a cold bottle of orange juice. The room attendant was a young, plump girl in trousers. He tried to tell her in reasonable English what he wanted. She understood not a word. So he motioned that he wanted to drink. She brought him a glass of water. He smiled, shook his head and drew a bottle in the air with his finger. The girl smiled back, and brought him a bottle of beer. Again the German shook his head. He searched around the room for something which would tell the girl that he wanted an orange liquid. As any good Communist should, the room girl was wearing a reddish badge near her heart.

"Ah," said the German, when he spotted it, and gave the girl a beaming smile. He walked up to her and, making quite sure that he was not touching her, pointed to the badge on her ample bosom.

The Chinese lass nodded her comprehension and came back with a bottle of milk!

12

BEHIND THE INVISIBLE WALL

When I was in Peking I spent the greater part of each day working in my room. There was so much to be learned about China, both old and new, that I could have put in ten hours a day reading. My first Hsin Chiao room was bright, and reasonably large, that is before I began spreading myself. Soon newspaper files, books, Chinese papers and magazines and the bulky New China News Agency reports were piling up in every corner. I called for an extra table, even though it considerably reduced the amount of uncluttered floor space. In the first few weeks I kept both of the beds which were in the room when I moved in, using one as a depository for papers, maps, suitcases and odd bits of clothing. While it lasted, the second bed was rather handy. When the room became too untidy I shoved a whole heap of rubbishy papers and dirty shirts beneath this ideal hiding place, and would retrieve them only when the mood took me. Later, when I was more organised, I had one of the beds removed.

It was a cosy room, but suffered seriously from schizophrenia. One half, nearest the door and the bathroom, was a bedroom. The few square feet next to the large window had all the trappings of a newspaper office. The walls were plastered with maps, and after a time, from the initial incredible mess, emerged a weird and wonderful filing system which functioned bravely over the months, without a filing cabinet which was unobtainable in Peking. The built-in wardrobe became a storage space for old newspaper files. I filled my entire shoe drawer with scores of rolls of film, both black and white and colour, and chucked my shoes under the bed.

The décor of my third floor bedroom was, to put it kindly, very plain. The room, like all others in the hotel, had a terrazzo floor, a small carpet, a second-rate Chinese scroll, thin brown curtains and armless upholstered chairs with cream-coloured loose covers. White lace cloths over the backs of the chairs were supposed to stop the covers from becoming stained with hair oil. My bed was of metal, with a comfortable mattress. The room was roughly twelve feet square, but after I invested in a fine Chinese rosewood desk, and knew that Audrey would soon be using the *Globe and Mail*'s Peking Bureau as her boudoir, I moved into a room which though only a little more expensive was about three times as large.

The best and possibly the most surprising feature of all the Hsin Chiao rooms was their attached bathroom and the almost constant flow of piping hot water. Quite expensive hotel rooms in North America and Europe today offer guests only a wash basin and shower recess when the architect feels that a bath for each room is not necessary. The Hsin Chiao was justly proud of its large white porcelain baths. One night a baby bat that had found its way up an air vent into the bathroom disturbed my ablutions. But apart from this single adventure my baths were taken in peaceful solitude.

Though several diplomats and foreign businessmen visiting me swore that rooms occupied by foreigners were wired for sound, I never had the feeling that my room had been tapped or searched. I'm sure that the hotel boys, in the process of cleaning, had a good look at most of my belongings, but there was no evidence that an official search of my belongings had been ordered by the Communists. The Chinese did, of course, have plenty of opportunities to go through my room while I was out of Peking, or even while I was travelling around the city in a cab. But there was no need for them to go to all this trouble. Their censors could see all the material that came and went in the mails, and since the *Globe and Mail*'s was the first North American news bureau established in the Chinese capital, the man sent to staff it would hardly have been a spy.

The greatest difficulty working in Peking was the sense of isolation and the loneliness of being among people so alien in outlook and ideals. I wrote to Dic Doyle, the *Globe and Mail*'s Managing Editor: "I never knew that a hotel could be, in many ways, so much like a prison. It's a most comfortable one, of course, and naturally a prison by choice. But all the same, the inability to go where you want to go, when you feel like it, has its psychological effects."

A few foreigners, visiting correspondents as well as business-men—who might spend up to six or eight weeks at a stretch in

The author's twin daughters, Nicole and Michelle, near the Marco Polo bridge, just outside Peking.

Young Pioneers.

Miniature Chinese jeeps are being made in Shanghai to replace pedicabs.

Men and women work together in factories as virtual equals.

Peking—told me they talked to themselves to relieve the silence. But although I was often desperately lonely, I found no relief in that. Instead I bombarded the *Globe and Mail* with stories, and my letters to Audrey and the detailed reports about the frustrations of the Peking operation which I sent to my Executive Editor, Tommy Munns, got longer and longer.

The weeks passed, and the arrival of the mail grew into a vital daily event. Letters from Audrey, as well as newspapers and mail from Toronto, became as important as food and drink to me. The isolation of Peking was so intense it was now a matter of great urgency to maintain contact with the West. The mail always arrived at the hotel at about 9 a.m., and on the days when there were no letters at all I felt terribly depressed for about half an hour. I'd go upstairs for a bitter cup of Peking coffee and possibly a brief talk with one of the other Hsin Chiao inmates to cheer myself up before starting work again.

I was always grateful when Chinese hotel managers provided me with a short-wave radio that could pick up the B.B.C. or the Voice of America. Once, in Harbin, I found that I was suddenly deeply thrilled to hear Radio Australia playing "Waltzing Matilda". Another time, in Anshan, I heard all about a baseball match being played in Minneapolis. I'm no baseball fan but I listened to this game for about an hour.

As the winter wore on it seemed as if there was an invisible wall around the hotel. I began to know how prisoners must feel when they receive news from the world outside. My main sources were the newspapers which came to me both by air and surface mail. It used to take up to three weeks, sometimes even a month, before I saw my own stories in print. Each time a well-played story turned up, it cheered me immensely. But most important of all were Audrey's letters. They brought normalcy into this odd, prison-like existence. She chatted away about the children, the garden, painting the house in case we would have to let it. And she said she missed me. So did the children. She sent me clippings of some of my stories which appeared in the Melbourne papers, and encouraged me to keep writing in the same vein. "Keep up the pictures," she wrote. She had found that people were almost more interested in seeing pictures of the Chinese at work than reading about them.

At least there was never any lack of reading material. Apart from the *Globe and Mail*, I got the weekly edition of the *New York*

Times, and the air mail edition of the London *Daily Telegraph*. Both papers occasionally printed my material. The editors of *Die Welt* in Hamburg began sending me some of the articles translated by them into German, and the Vancouver *Sun* and the Chicago *Sun Times* kept me supplied with a regular clipping service of the pieces they used. Seeing the results of the work made a great difference. The published stories, both negative and positive, seemed to make up for the many hours spent at my typewriter. Often I would get a bit of a jolt at seeing headlines like "Mao's Chinese Parrots", "Chinese Eat at the Price of Their Liberty", "Chill Wind Still Blows in Peking, Cold War Ice Not Even Cracking", "Hostile Eyes Glare at China", "West's Envoys Are 'Prisoners of Peking' ", "Chinese cannot have real Yule where Mao dominates Crucifix", and "Parrot Philosophy stifling individual enterprise", and wondered how long I would be staying in Peking. Several newspaper men passing through asked to see the type of material I sent out. I generally picked out a dozen negative stories which they read with raised eyebrows. But then I would give them a dozen pieces portraying Chinese industrial development, forestry programmes, irrigation projects and other pieces which I had written in trying to balance the anti-Communist stories.

As a Westerner who was not a member of the Diplomatic Corps (although the Chinese and some of the Communist diplomats often treated correspondents as though they were) I had no set circle in which I moved. The constant round of Peking's social life, luncheon parties, cocktail parties, dinner parties, supper parties, bridge parties, mahjong parties, not only bored but worried me. This was diplomacy at its worst. Had I wanted to, it would have been easy to skip from one party to another without doing any reporting and writing at all. I refused a good number of invitations, and certain people didn't understand. Ronnie Farquhar of Reuters and I got a bad name for being late at parties. Often we came and went together, and would take it in turns to dream up excuses. He undertook to make apologies for getting to a place late, and I would explain why it was essential that we both leave early.

Among the few good friends I made in China were a young Norwegian couple who were married the day before they left for Peking. Kaare and Liv Holum were both blonde and blue-eyed and still very much in love. Kaare was Secretary-Archivist to the Norwegian Embassy in Peking and she was a former nurse who found the very social life which most of the diplomats' wives led somewhat trying. Both of them felt rather as I did. One week of parties night after night, with some daytime functions thrown in for good measure, left them too tired to enjoy their new life in Peking. Sometimes I lunched with them, or had an evening meal, and on each occasion the warmth of their little home enveloped me in a soothing mantle of friendship. I think the charm of the Holum house was that they were truly happy, which in China was a rare thing. Most foreigners were unhappy because they felt complete social outcasts, and this hurt and annoyed them. The Chinese officials, partly because of their extreme arrogance, and partly because of the comparative poverty of their own residences, did not see why they should mix with these representatives of the hated imperialist class. The ordinary Chinese people, though very much more pleasant than their Communist masters, could not mix with foreigners for fear of retribution by the State.

Had there been a free and easy atmosphere on the streets, such as may be found even in the most overcrowded, filthy parts of Hongkong, this quality of happiness would not have been as unusual. But there was none of this. People may have been reasonably relaxed on the occasional free Sunday, but they worked too hard during the week to be glad about living. There is a rigidity and a tension about the Communist way of life that has no time for human joy.

At the Holum's house I realised how much I was missing music, not just classical music but any kind of Western music. Chinese music jars most Western ears, and only very few Europeans learn to appreciate its tuneful qualities. People say that once you get to understand Chinese music, it is really very beautiful. I'm afraid I never did, and several times each week had to beg the waitresses in the hotel dining-room to turn down the din. It was wonderfully comforting to walk into Kaare's home or some other European residence in Peking, sink into a soft armchair, drink ice-cold beer with your hosts and listen to *Swan Lake*, or South American tangos—any music, in fact, that wasn't Chinese. It never failed to refresh me, and I would return to my hotel room determined not to let my icy Chinese hosts get me down.

All of Peking's diplomats, but especially the Westerners, lived an isolated existence. Many of them found solace in their round of parties. They dressed up for each other, and it always amused me to see the severely-dressed Chinese officials, either in navy blue or grey Communist uniforms, buttoned to the neck, standing just a little way from the others. The Chinese guests were never part of the milling crowd at a foreign diplomatic gathering, but looked on silently and spoke only when spoken to.

Most of the diplomats lived in what we knew as the "diplomatic ghetto of Peking", a series of rectangular box-like brick buildings, thrown up by the Chinese a couple of miles from the centre of the city. There was one main apartment building and behind it, built around a huge courtyard, half a dozen other apartment blocks and a shopping centre. Near the "ghetto" the Communist embassies built several streets of fine new offices and apartments. Communist envoys from Poland and Czechoslovakia and other Eastern European countries, on moving into their new accommodation, told me how pleased they were to be getting away from "that red-brick dormitory around the corner".

Though most Westerners resented being pushed around by the Communists, there were constant debates within the diplomatic community as to whether it was preferable to live in the flats or in one of the quaint Chinese houses in a Peking lane or "hutung".

These narrow streets often hide the most charming residences. The Chinese formerly built all their houses with windows facing into courtyards. From the outside, to the stranger, the Chinese house is just a brick wall with a door in it. But through that door is often a lovely home with one or more courtyards. In the past its size depended on the family's needs. Wealthy Chinese had huge establishments with many courtyards. The entire family unit would live there—parents, uncles, aunts, grandparents and children. This custom is now dying fast because the Peking régime insists that communal living is a good thing only when the individual looks upon the State as the community, and the entire Chinese nation as his "family". Yet the top Communist officials prefer to live in the comparative privacy of a Chinese house to having to share the vast dormitories being erected.

Among the Westerners living still in the old style were the Holums; their quaint Chinese house was situated in a "hutung" not far from the sterile-looking offices of the *People's Daily*. But the Peking housing authorities want the old-styled Chinese houses for the new élite of China, which is why Europeans are being transferred to the "ghetto".

For entertainment, foreigners had to fall back on their own devices. There are no night clubs in Peking, no night life of any kind in the European sense. Occasionally, the diplomats might attend Chinese theatre performances, or on special occasions go to see visiting artists from Russia and Eastern European countries. But after the show, you head straight for home. There are no bars, no public restaurants that serve meals late at night. Hotels will feed their permanent guests until about 10 or 11 p.m. The only clubs I went to were the British Club, and occasionally the International Club, where many Communist diplomats gathered on Saturday nights, and danced to a brass band playing impossibly old-fashioned music. The British had an unwritten rule that their staff could not go to the International Club and, in fact, the British Club often attracted a bigger crowd to its competitive Saturday night dance.

In Peking, wherever a group of foreigners gathered, the talk always drifted back to the communes, the shapeless girls in their boiler suits, the food situation and China's disputed seat in the United Nations. In these arguments it was fairly easy to put people into separate, watertight compartments. Those I liked least were the men with closed minds who could see either only good or only evil in China. Some had shut their eyes to the fact that China had progressed, because their hate for Communism was too deep, too intense. It blinded their judgment to a fantastic degree.

Newcomers were usually the most enthusiastic, and the monastic hotel prisoners the most critical, during any China argument. But by far the worst offenders in any debates were the Communists from the West who gave more allegiance to the Chinese in Peking than to their own country. There was Gavin Greenleas, for example, under normal circumstances a likeable man in his middle years. He was a fair dinkum Australian and a good bloke—provided he kept off politics. But once the subject was Communism, he became a fanatic. To Gavin everything in China shone with hope and brightness, while in Australia the workers and unionists were struggling under the capitalist yoke. Perhaps his enthusiasm was understandable. In Australia Gavin Greenleas had been a journalist on a Communist newspaper, but in Peking he was an important English-language adviser employed by the New China News Agency. He had a car and a chauffeur at his disposal, lived in an apartment, and was not subject to the stringent food and clothes rationing imposed on his Chinese colleagues.

Just as biased as Greenleas, at the other end of the scale, were the cynics who admitted China's need for rapid development, but who spent their time poking fun at the régime's attempts to give its people a higher living standard. When they saw a large new apartment block, they would walk into it, find the first spot on the ceiling and say, "Sure, they're putting up big buildings fast, but look at the workmanship! Look at the ceiling! One good shower of rain and we'll be afloat."

The most numerous and for me the most valuable of the transient visitors were the foreign business men. They stayed longer than most. They talked more honestly than the diplomats, who were afraid of compromising their governments. I would find the foreign traders, mournful and lonely, in the funereal top-floor bar of the hotel waiting for their interviews with the Chinese trading corporations. Many came to Peking regularly each year, and some every four or six months, knowing that each trip would entail a lengthy period of just sitting and waiting. Fuming about all the unnecessary, infuriating delays, they told me why they came back time and again for more. Often, they said, the results were really worth while. In the long, low, grey headquarters of the Ministry of Foreign Trade on Changan Avenue, less than ten minutes' walk from the Hsin Chiao, they might talk to Chinese officials in hundreds of thousands or even millions of yuan. They were trading with a nation of seven hundred million people, and felt that although China was poor, its vast population created a tremendous potential consumer market. A good few of them had in mind not a quick profit but visited Peking with an eye to the future.

There were the merchants who could be very good-natured and philosophical about having to spend two trying months in China to clinch a deal which anywhere else took only a fortnight, and there were others who simply couldn't stomach the wearisome weeks of negotiation. One of the angriest men I met was a member of a Finnish trade delegation. He couldn't stand the Chinese. After each interview with them he would stomp into my room, slam the door, order fearful locally-made brandy and pour out his heart about the cruelty of having to do business with Peking's

Communists. He was a table-pounding type, which created an impossible situation. If there is one thing the Chinese won't take from a foreigner, it's table-pounding. At one interview he became so annoyed he got up, went to get his overcoat and threatened to leave the conference. The Chinese persuaded him to sit down again. A few moments later, when a point of conflict arose, the Chinese spokesman also got up. But since he didn't have a coat in the corner he merely walked around the room twice before sitting down again; this was the official's gesture to "save face".

A far more merry merchant was Otto Schilling, a short, bald, twinkling man who had a big metal import and export business in Hamburg. He was middle-aged but had tremendous energy. He returned to the Hsin Chiao from a visit to Anshan, the Manchurian steel centre, one evening, unshaven and bleary-eyed, but took the trouble to come to my room. "Grossartig", he said. "Grossartig!" Then he switched to English. "I've never seen a steel works as big as that anywhere in the world. It's really fantastic."

He walked across to the window and gazed out over the roofs of Peking, even greyer than usual in the dusk. "Communism seems to have done more for these people in ten short years than feudalism and capitalism achieved in centuries. No wonder the Chinese still back the Peking Government even though they don't eat enough and must work so hard."

The businessmen I spoke with had no illusions about the advantage the Chinese enjoyed in any trade negotiations. They told me that often it was obvious from discussions with various export and import corporations that their cables had been scrutinized by the Chinese authorities. This applied both to outgoing and incoming cables.

The Chinese would watch the kind of advice businessmen got from their head offices, and would then negotiate a trade deal accordingly. Some of the Western traders even accused their Communist counterparts of plain dishonesty, although they could never prove it. They said that a "mistake" would occur in some cable giving world commodity prices, and this would always happen on the day they were due to confer with the Chinese trading corporations. A day later they might get word from the Chinese telegraph office that an unfortunate mistake had occurred in transmission. The price was really such and such. By then it was too late, the contract would already be signed. The mistake, they noticed, invariably favoured the Chinese side.

Naturally, to me the most refreshing transients were other Western correspondents. I became so starved of newspaper talk that each time a newsman checked into the Hsin Chiao it called for a celebration. Swiss and Scandinavian correspondents in particular were given Chinese visas from time to time, and occasionally we sighted a Fleet Street man, grimacing up in the bar about the taste of Peking whisky. I got the shock of my life when, of all papers, the London *Daily Express* got visas, not just once, but twice. First their Moscow man came for the tenth anniversary celebrations and later Norman Smart, of the foreign desk, flew in from Hongkong. Smart was on a world trip looking up *Daily Express* foreign correspondents, and was most surprised when the Chinese gave him a visa. The *Express* has been trying to get a permanent man into Peking for years, and Smart made this the main purpose of his visit. After an interview with the Foreign Ministry he told me he doubted whether they had much of a chance even though the *Express* has repeatedly condemned the dangerous absurdity of excluding China from world conferences.

When Norman plonked himself in my room, it was like a little bit of Fleet Street invading the sombre atmosphere of Peking. There was just a touch of London in his voice. His gossip about English journalists and journalism (the cut-throat practices along Fleet Street hadn't changed, he assured me) were a reminder that there was another world apart from China. One tended to forget this in Peking.

Like most newsmen passing through, Norman didn't write much from Peking. The visiting Western correspondents knew that the Chinese didn't impose any censorship, but often they preferred to keep stories in their notebooks until they got beyond the borders of the People's Republic. They wanted to get back in again some time in the future, and felt psychologically it would be wiser not to write critical material which might be seen by officials while in China.

Among the most interesting visitors to come to the Hsin Chiao during my eight months there was a well-known novelist. One morning a striking woman wearing smart tweed slacks and a voluminous woollen sweater came into the breakfast room. Han Suyin, writer of tingling love stories, was no longer the young girl of her books, yet she carried herself with grace. She had a magnificent presence, and when she entered a room—not only

at the dowdy Hsin Chiao but in a colourful place like Hongkong
—people took notice. She had that dynamism which lifts her
novels well above the average, especially her famous *A Many
Splendored Thing*, a confession of her dead, lost love, which touched
me deeply when I read it in Peking. Han Suyin was the first
person born and bred in China who talked to me frankly about
her country's problems. She was no Communist, I felt sure. I
think she might have liked to be one years ago, but now it was
too late. She was a wealthy woman with houses and gold shares,
and the outside world offered freedoms she would have missed in
China. She had a deep desire to write in China, about China,
but was afraid of the restrictions that might eventually be imposed
on her. I liked Han Suyin. I didn't find her as physically attrac-
tive as many men do, but I thought she was a fascinating woman.
She was vibrant, forceful, and at the same time highly emotional
and quite womanly.

I'm certain she did not use the same terms about Communism
to me as to, say, Premier Chou En-lai, whom she knows, or even
to the head of the Foreign Ministry Information Department,
Madame Kung Peng, an old friend from her schooldays in
Szechwan province. But it was very valuable to speak at length
to somebody who could see the new China both with the eyes
of a Westerner and the mind of a Chinese. Once Han Suyin and
I spent an amusing half-hour chatting about Chinese slogans.
The Communists lead the nation with slogans, and each month
some new slogan is added to the party list. The favourite one
while I was there was "Go all out, aim high and achieve greater,
faster, better and more economical results to build Socialism".
This jibber-jabber translated into English sounds clumsy and
childish, but when Han Suyin spoke the slogan in Chinese it had
power and beauty. I would have considered it impossible that
the slogan "Let us hold even higher the revolutionary banner of
victorious Marxism-Leninism and march forward to new and
greater victories for peace and Socialism" could have sounded
poetic. In English this is no slogan. It's an essay. The effect of
the slogan is lost completely. But translated into Chinese, this
rigmarole is considerably condensed. Often a few sounds in
Chinese express a word picture or idea which in any European
tongue needs an entire sentence to give it meaning. Han Suyin
agreed that the translations of some of the slogans were very
quaint to Western ears and said they were translated too literally,

on a word-for-word basis. "I keep begging them to stop speaking and writing in Chinglish," she said.

Han Suyin was wildly glad that Chinese intellectuals were being made to work with their hands.

"Do you know," she said, "that some of these men have never held a hammer or a spade in their hands because they thought anything to do with physical work was dirty. Now they're coming back from the land admitting that the fresh air and the labour has done them a world of good."

When I told Han Suyin that I believed forcing a man to do physical labour against his will was to ignore one of the fundamental freedoms, she waved my objection aside.

"You have to realise what these people were like before the Communists came in order to understand," she said. "They were convinced that to toil with your hands was filthy." The conclusion which followed was that all manual workers were therefore also filthy.

The other objection to manual work put forward not only by foreigners but by many Chinese themselves was the fearful wastage of mental man hours. Why on earth employ a physicist who has spent eight years of his life training for his job at various colleges and universities on a canal project as a labourer? Why lower the standard of education in China by making teachers harvest rice? If there is one thing China does not lack it is manual workers. Surely it was insane for Peking to squander its insufficient brain power so foolishly? With the famine and the general economic disasters which befell China in 1960 and 1961, there came also a change of thought on this matter. People were not "sent to the country" in punishment quite as often. While it was still Communist policy that to "get dirt under your fingernails" was fundamentally a good and honourable pastime for intellectuals, the issue was not hammered by the party as consistently as during my stay. Many brain workers were forced into the countryside more as a result of natural disasters and reorganisation of the communes than through the party's desires to "correct their thinking".

The enjoyment of debating these issues with Han Suyin was her ability to listen and to understand—a thing which Chinese Communists didn't even pretend to do. They did not wish to hear honest and objective Western opinions of their system because this might weaken their own faith.

13

THIS HUMAN TIDE

I was ambling towards Wang Fu Ching with Norman Smart when we came across the citizens of Peking taking their Sunday stroll. All of them were in their boiler suits, tens of thousands of blue-clad people surging past in a constant stream which seemed to engulf us.

"How very terrifying," Smart said. It was the normal Western reaction to China's millions. "You know," he went on, "they're all quite well-dressed. They seem warm in their padded coats, they look fairly well-fed and reasonably happy. But isn't it frightening to see everyone in blue?"

There are so many Chinese and they are multiplying at such a rate that within some decades they may be able to impose their society on other peoples by sheer weight of numbers.

Trying to explain to Chinese Communists just what the European finds frightening about their present society is a problem, because people have been so conditioned by a decade of Communist propaganda and indoctrination they cannot comprehend our attitude.

"The West doesn't want a strong and healthy China," a Communist once told me, "and that is why it upsets your people when we do well, and pleases Western governments when we go hungry. You're all afraid because the party has succeeded in unifying China."

"Europeans are frightened for quite another reason," I answered. "We see in China—and especially in China, not so much in Russia or other Communist nations—a serious threat to our own free way of life." I was also frightened by the knowledge of how little the outside world knows about China. What you could not define for any Chinese Communist was the revulsion most of us foreigners felt at the complete submissiveness of the population. Yet this feeling was mingled with a certain fascination because the servitude of the many millions had given

China its own powerful, somewhat elusive rhythm. It was nothing you could see or touch, but foreigners sensed it and I wondered whether the Chinese themselves did too.

Each great city and land has its own rhythm. In a metropolis like New York or London there is a rapid higgledy-piggledy rhythm with each man seemingly chasing after his own affairs. Peking's rhythm was slower but far more surging. It was the pulse of a nation in harness, the constant beat of a people gaining a new identity as cogs in a massive machine. On one occasion I tried to explain this feeling of mine to Han Suyin.

"I think I know what you mean," she said. "I have a different way of expressing it. I feel myself carried along in China by the general wave of enthusiasm."

Enthusiasm for Communism fell sharply among the Chinese in 1960 and 1961, although the rhythm did not immediately falter. There was a willingness among the greater part of the Chinese population during most of the preceding decade to help the Communists rebuild a land ravaged by civil war and corrupt government. But a little over half a year after I arrived the danger signals were already flashing, and by the end of 1960 Peking was vainly imploring people to maintain their previous zest. In 1961 embarrassed Communist leaders were assuring cadres who had grown cynical over the many failures that private trading, stiff individualist bargaining and the healthy profits made by peasants at commune trade fairs were indeed one aspect of creating a Communist society. These rural trade fairs, established in 1960 to boost failing agricultural production, were a tremendous blow to Chinese Communist ideology and to Mao's prestige. Another humiliation lay behind the fact that the Chinese imported almost six million tons of grain in 1961 alone, with millions of tons to follow later. This must have hurt the Communists' pride very deeply. To be forced into buying food with hard-earned foreign currency was the last thing the régime had anticipated, and to make it worse, the cash was going to half a dozen capitalist countries. The Communists were pushed into buying capitalist grain by accusations within their own ranks that the party had committed a breach of contract. Chinese Communist propaganda since 1949 was nothing less than the highest promissory note ever written—an assurance by the Chinese Communist Party to repay to the people of China, in housing, consumer goods and food, the years spent in labouring for next to no reward. Instead, in the years beginning 1959 things grew progressively worse. Just before this book went to press in mid-1962, diplomats coming from China are saying that the morale among the working population has never been lower. They predict that rations could become even tighter—already grain rations are well below one pound a day for the average person—and that Peking's foreign community is now importing absolutely everything including, as one top British diplomat puts it, "buttons for my shirts and the thread with which to sew them on."

Despite grumbling and dissatisfaction among the peasantry and town dwellers, China's economic crisis has not changed the general obedience of the masses, for by their endless propaganda and indoctrination campaigns the Communists have managed to mould the Chinese population into the largest and most unified work force on earth. Few Chinese would now dare to question the commands of their superiors. In China you do what you are told; you do it not for yourself, or for the person who tells you, but for the State. You obey because you have no choice.

The entire nation is supposed to work purely for the State, even down to the men and women in China's prisons. In fact, in the same way as in Russia, certain aspects of China's policies towards prisoners are remarkably progressive and enlightened compared with Western attitudes.

The Communists use their methods of indoctrination to prepare their convicts for life in a Communist society. They are made to work long hours, they are lectured, they are taught to read and to write; they are told that in a Communist society there is no need for social outcasts. In this way, the Chinese Communists are building a nation where people do not question their leaders. They must try to show the same agreement, enthusiasm and delight as any party member when Communist decisions are announced. As a result, there is neither freedom of speech in China, nor freedom of silence. For silence could be taken as unspoken disapproval of Communism and of China's policies. Silence is suspect, and hardly existed in the China I saw. Despite these grim conditions Communism in China will struggle on, for the Communist bloc cannot afford a complete collapse of the present Peking régime. Even if the 1960's see big changes in Chinese public administration, the Communist régime will remain entrenched there for years to come. A hungry man may become disgruntled, weak, tired, ill, perhaps angry, but he does not forget the lessons he has been taught in ten years of solid propaganda. In the end, he is a resigned and obedient servant of the State. It is this blind compliance to commands throughout the length and breadth of the land which gave China her swirling years of success before the advent of the famine, for this rigid discipline was the main factor in China's progress.

The frightening power of the party was demonstrated most clearly in a single sentence of a brief story I read in the journal *Peking Review*. "Despite the cold weather in most places," said the weekly journal, "more than seventy million people are turning out every day to work on water conservancy projects in all parts of the country." That was early 1960. Visualise what this means—four times the total population of Canada, seven times the population of the Australian continent, just tackling one single task the Chinese Communists wanted done.

In the past, during the hard northern winters, the peasants resigned themselves to nature. They retired to their little mud hovels, found what nourishment they could, and waited for the spring to soften the frozen earth. This is no longer allowed. All Chinese manpower is put to work the year round, even in the regions where the climate is harshest. In the early dusk of Manchuria I have watched hundreds of peasants lining up for their bowl of rice and vegetables, served to them from a field kitchen. From the train I saw dam builders hard at work, attacking the earth with picks, then levering it up, great slabs of dirt as solid as rock. In Tientsin, canal diggers worked through the bitter night, reclaiming silted-up canals and digging new ones, and the blocks of ice they lifted into lorries to be carted away glistened under the searchlights flooding the work sites.

But the ability of China's Communists to keep their civilian labour corps straining must dwindle in time unless there are continuing incentives, and Peking knows this. When he is pushed beyond his capacity, the worker simply slows up. This is what happened between 1960 and 1962. It can be likened to a massive, nation-wide regulation strike. The Communist government reacted by introducing modifications, and is now waiting for the time it can reimpose restraints. Moderation is not a popular word in Mao's vocabulary, and his followers must avoid it if possible. Poor work is the peasant's only way of resisting the pressures of the State. The Communist zealots in China are still so engrossed in their revolution they tend to forget that most human beings are not revolutionaries by nature, and that the average man likes the quiet, not the tense life. Peking's solution is the attempt to mass-produce revolutionaries in the nation's schools, to persuade children and young people that by following the State's dictates blindly they can prove themselves to be true and worthy sons of China. The most successful remedy employed by Communists against sceptics is a gentle poison which the West knows as thought control. Advertisers in most Western countries use it themselves with remarkable success.

In the Chinese method no brute force is used to persuade the population that the party knows best, but these practices are at the same time abhorrent and frightening and evil. The Chinese people who are still casting off feudal customs and beliefs, have naïve and open minds, especially China's five hundred million peasants, and are easily taught to believe almost anything since previously nobody had bothered to teach them at all.

In my hotel, across the corridor from my room, the Communists practised thought control. Behind closed doors they held meeting after meeting, some of which lasted till three and four o'clock in the morning with much shouting and jabbering. For a nation which boasted so much about rapid production, China held a remarkable number of meetings. There were always production meetings, rectification campaigns, political rallies.

The time wasted was colossal. But the Communists felt that if they talked hard enough for long enough, the eventual results would be better than without this political education. They were proved wrong by the food shortages, and modified their meeting schedules. Since late 1960 there are fewer meetings. But the Communists have not changed their minds one iota about thought control, a factor which truly worries many educated Chinese who see untold danger in the parrot society. The Communists practise thought reforming all the same because it suits their massive work and production programmes. When you can control people's thoughts, you can also control their actions; capture a man's mind, and you can use his muscles to your advantage.

In the West, once a man becomes an adult he may choose his own road, but in China, when a child reaches adulthood, the need to conform grows not less but greater. A man's or a woman's— even a child's—central and single pursuit in the new Chinese society is work. The nation's entire mode of life revolves around grinding toil. The factories are the new temples of China, the machines the altars. In the cities people are being encouraged not only to work, but to eat and sleep, study, and play within the confines of their factory or office. Until they are old enough to go to school, millions of babies live at factories. While the old buildings still stand in China's ancient cities, not everyone can be housed in factory or office apartment blocks, but as the old is torn down and the new built up, the Communists are gradually rehousing increasing numbers of city dwellers. Each day countless thousands leave the former life with its tumble-down but essentially private houses, and march into the communal world, into more modern but very clubby, sociable community apartments. The Communists found it was not only convenient to have workers on tap and close at hand constantly. They considered privacy a breeding ground for individualists whose beliefs were often inconsistent with the policies of the State, and so they built communal dormitories for single men and women and small apartments for families.

During a tour of the Tientsin Textile Machinery Plant I saw how factory babies lived and played and cried in their nursery not far from the hissing machines. When I inspected the nursery, mothers in boiler suits who were feeding their babies quickly pulled their blue denim shirts down to cover their breasts, and proudly showed me their infants. The mothers, mostly in their twenties and early thirties, smiled and chatted gaily—as if it were the most normal thing in the world to leave your spindle for half an hour to breast-feed your child. The crèche was open twenty four hours a day. Women on night shift left their children with nurses when they went on duty, and picked them up again the following morning on their way back to their apartment block.

The Tientsin factory was typical. In the past couple of years accommodation for families had multiplied twentyfold, the plant's director, Ni Chun-teh, said as he showed me around. "Today the factory provides accommodation for more than a thousand families and has dormitories for 3,000 single men and women workers. Altogether there are 4,500 workers and staff in the plant." The factory had three dining-rooms which served meals around the clock. On the average each meal cost something like one and sixpence. The average worker including apprentices, earned about sixty yuan (£8) a month. "We have our own film projection team and five theatrical troupes," Ni went on. "Workers can see one film a week, and get tickets to attend the factory theatre once or twice a week. Theatre and film tickets in the factory are far cheaper than those outside the plant boundaries." This is one of the many methods the Communists are using to keep workers within easy reach at all times. People are urged to seek entertainment, medical advice, political eduation and sporting activities, even love and marriage within their own collective. The textile workers had formed eleven sports groups which included football, table tennis, volley ball, basketball and baseball teams. During our inspection tour, Ni made constant apologies for the mess outside some of the workshops, explaining that a big expansion programme was in progress which was why things were so disorganised. On our way back to his office we passed the nursery. Another batch of mothers was arriving to nurse their factory babies.

"Do they feed their babies in their lunch hour or during a tea break?" I asked the director.

"No, they get time off specially to do this!" Ni said proudly. "It's part of our social welfare here."

New generations forget the old ways readily enough, and after a decade under the Peking régime most Chinese saw nothing strange in their abnormal way of life. It merely made them tired, so very tired—especially when food ran short. And you could see it. Particularly at night, in the half light of Peking's dim street lamps, the strain of the nation's great toil began to tell. In the trundling buses, workers sat silent and exhausted as they made for home. The Communist Party has public behaviour splendidly organised. It can turn anything off and on virtually at will—anything from floodlights to people's laughter. At high-speed building projects, if the organisers are really competent and the slogans and the music bright enough, sweating men and women who should be weeping seem to jest instead. But when night comes, and protects the people's faces with a welcome veil, China relaxes just a fraction. Eyes that were laughing only an hour ago are now weary, showing the burden of the day.

One question visitors to Peking asked me repeatedly was, "How long can the people stand this pace?" It was impossible to answer. The Communist planners doubtlessly want to know themselves, and their zig-zagging internal policies proved they had not found any solution. All they could do was to press on regardless of consequences. Even among the government were those critics who warned that the Chinese Communists were risking their own fortunes and their country's welfare on a policy of power by population. China is already the home of almost one quarter of mankind, yet the most populous land on earth is doing nothing about birth control.

The Communists tried birth control campaigns in the mid-1950's but found the beliefs of Marx and Malthus did not mix well. China's Malthusians warned that the country would never grow strong unless its numbers were limited; they were defeated by orthodox Communists who said the nation's greatest asset was its people. It would be interesting to know how many Chinese officials are allowed to keep track of the population figures that must come pouring regularly into Peking's buzzing State Statistical Bureau. There are probably only a few, since population is the most explosive issue the Communists will eventually face. Professor Ma Yin-chu, a lone critic, now almost eighty years old, repeatedly attacked the régime's population theories until in 1960 he lost his job as president of Peking University. Ma insisted that in a Communist State, as in any other, quality was far more important than quantity, and like many other Chinese intellectuals, questioned the desirability of a population greater than a thousand million.

Not one Chinese official talked to me of the need to limit the nation's numbers; they repeated what was said in the Press —that China was short of manpower and needed more people. On November 1, 1954, the State Statistical Bureau of the Ministry of Internal Affairs announced that China's first complete scientific census had found the nation's population to be 601,938,035 at midnight of June 30, 1953, which by the Chinese traditional lunar calendar was the 20th day of the 5th moon. The figure included Formosa and overseas Chinese. The total living in China was more than 582,000,000. The present Chinese population is anybody's guess. Most demographers put it at well over 700,000,000, with estimates of China's annual increase varying from 12,000,000 to 20,000,000 people. The Communists admit to an annual increase of about $2\frac{1}{2}$ per cent. It is safe to estimate that within the next twenty years the number of Chinese will reach a thousand million, and unless the rate of growth is slowed drastically, by the turn of the century China's population will be nearing 1,500,000,000.

Far more impressive than written statistics are the crowds in every city, the lanes loud with children, the jam-packed streets. I had the impression that there was a tragic aimlessness about Peking's population programme, and that China's birth control schemes were abandoned not because they contravened Marxist principles, but simply because the Communists had found it impossible to carry them through successfully. Whenever I watched a human tide of men and women slaving to control the flood-tides of China's rivers, I was awed by the indescribable problems the nation still faced.

By the river Hsiang, west of Changsha, in Hunan Province, a man years ago asked himself another question. This is how he put it:

> Alone I stand in the autumn cold
> And watch the river northward flowing
> Past the Orange Island shore,
> And I see a myriad hills all tinged with red,
> Tier upon tier of crimsoned woods.
> On the broad stream, intensely blue,
> A hundred jostling barges float;
> Eagles strike at the lofty air,
> Fish hover among the shallows;
> A million creatures under this freezing sky are striving for freedom.
> In this immensity, deeply pondering,
> I ask the great earth and the boundless blue
> Who are the masters of all nature?

The dreamer who wrote this poem* was Mao Tse-tung.

* Courtesy Foreign Languages Press, Peking.

14

MAO TSE-TUNG

Mao Tse-tung. The world's modern statesmen speak the name with a touch of surprise in their voices. How has it been possible for this one man to climb slowly, laboriously up that long and terrible ladder which leads to absolute power in Peking, and having reached the summit to stay there? Mao has been perched on the very top of China's political peak for more than a dozen years now, and nothing can budge him. Not even three years of famine have unseated him. And long before he reached Peking, back in the late 1920's and early 1930's Mao was already a force to be considered within China.

Though I once stood just a few feet away from him at the Peking airport, when he was bidding Nikita Khrushchev farewell after the tenth anniversary celebrations, I found Mao the greatest mystery of all during my time in China. Peking's Communists had built him into a twentieth-century god. The personality cult of Russia, criticised so harshly after Stalin's death, was child's play in comparison to China's elevation of Mao Tse-tung. I was nauseated by the unbelievable number of photographs, paintings, busts and statues of Mao peering down from everywhere. Most of them were horrible. Once, in the Manchurian city of Changchun, I couldn't contain myself. Enormous paintings of Mao hung from almost every building. "Why must there be so many of these pictures?" I asked my guide. "Chairman Mao Tse-tung is the beloved leader of the Chinese people," he told me. The stiff answer illustrated a simple truth: Mao is indeed the most popular man in China, where a quarter of mankind revere him, despite his faults, despite his obvious errors in national planning. The most remarkable aspect of Mao is his staying power, his capacity in the past to sway the Chinese peasantry to quite an astounding degree, and now to keep their loyalty throughout years of hunger and hardship. He is the living legend of China's revolution, the peasant boy who became Peking's Communist emperor, after

132

a lifetime of struggle. Mao is almost certain to stay in power until his death. Though born in 1893, he still enjoys reasonably good health, and the question everybody in Peking asked was not when he would die, but who would succeed him. Liu Shao-chi, who as president is China's Head of State, seemed the most likely man. Liu, a Soviet-trained Communist, was obviously far less popular than Mao. He has a sharply-etched face and quick, cunning eyes. I imagine the Chinese propaganda machine could try to build him into a national hero, as it has done with Mao, but his thin face could never replace the plump father-image of Mao.

One day Liu Shao-chi came to the Hsin Chiao hotel for a diplomatic reception, and from a door I watched him as he peered into the hot television lights. Mao's face has a touch of kindness about it, sometimes an almost womanly softness. Not so Liu Shao-chi's. His was the face of a tough and ruthless politician. Whenever I saw the big four in line on the walls of so many rooms I entered—first Mao, next to him Liu, then the soldierly Chu Teh and finally the handsome Chou En-lai—Liu Shao-chi's pointed face always seemed somehow out of place. Liu Shao-chi was probably the main power behind the 1958 "Great Leap" plans which later flopped, and this is not likely to endear him to many of the elements who will play a leading part in choosing Mao's successor. But when he picked Liu as Head of State in April 1959, Mao indicated him as the natural successor. The two had been together as early as 1922 (Liu at that time was only about twenty-four) when they led strikes in Hunan Province, at Changsha, the Anyuan colliery and at the Shuikoushan lead mine. Mao was then chairman of the Hunan Branch of the Chinese Communist Party which had been formed in Shanghai in 1921, and Liu was already, four decades ago, one of his closest associates. With a wealth of experience in party operations, Liu's standing within the Central Committee and the Politburo is second only to that of Mao Tse-tung who retains the chairmanship of both these policy-making bodies. Liu Shao-chi certainly has a far better chance of gaining the top job than the personable Premier of China, Chou En-lai—unless there comes a major upheaval within the Chinese Communist Party.

Of all the leaders I found Chou En-lai the most pleasant by far. Several times I shook his hand, either at diplomatic receptions or airport farewells and welcomes, and I sensed that here was a man who could handle foreigners. Chou En-lai exuded the air of a man of the world, a rather un-Chinese diplomat, good-looking, with burning eyes that revealed an inner fire. I envied people like Han Suyin and Lord Montgomery who had spent hours talking with Chou En-lai, but this jealousy was lessened somewhat by the knowledge that the Chinese Premier would never have talked to a Western reporter except along the straight and narrow party line. For example, Chou was terribly disappointing in a television interview with English broadcaster Felix Greene. There was not a single new thought in the entire script—which had been vetted by the Chinese. It was the same with Chen Yi, the Foreign Minister. Visiting journalists from many countries would meet Chen, and he granted to several Scandinavians what Henning Nystad, a correspondent of the *Politiken* in Copenhagen, called "a *People's Daily* interview". Nystad came back to the Hsin Chiao rather deflated. "I'd read it all long before I came to Peking," he grinned at me through his russet Viking beard. This was at least one little comfort to the resident correspondent in Peking who found that all the top men in China were utterly inaccessible to him.

The Communist newsmen were no better off. When Chou En-lai gave Press conferences in Delhi, Rangoon, Katmandu and Phnom Penh in April and May of 1960, several Communist correspondents from Russia and East European countries complained to me that their colleagues in India had had more chances to speak with Chou during his flying South East Asian tour than they'd had in several years of covering Peking for their papers.

Mao, the enigmatic genius, was the least accessible of all. Even when you saw him from close up it was impossible to read anything into his face. With a different background, Mao Tsetung might have been a mystic. Looking at the man one can imagine him as a zealous Jesuit, a withdrawn hermit, a devout Buddhist monk, and, of course, as a fanatic Communist. I saw Mao only half a dozen times. After observing him in person, and studying the constant flow of photographs of him, I had the impression that Mao's mind was invariably far away. His eyes have the quality dreams are made of, rather vague, yet filled with great depth and hidden meaning. But taken as a whole, Mao has an unusually dull face, a moon face that cannot compete against the shrewd cunning of Nikita Khrushchev or the deeply pensive face of Jawaharlal Nehru. It hides remarkably well the severity and unrelenting hardness a leader such as he must have developed to scale the icy heights of Communist political power. It is the face of the son of a peasant who lived in the village of Shao Shan in Hunan Province. The peasant was a nonentity. The son has become a mighty dictator. As a boy Mao rebelled against a hard father who had called him lazy and futile, and grew to lead a revolution in the most populous land on earth. If power can be counted in terms of persons, Mao must today be classed as the most powerful man in the world. He dominates the political scene of China and his leadership of the Chinese Communist Party remains unchallenged. To the people of China, to the uncomplaining toilers who have never known the good life and who ask no questions, Mao Tse-tung is pictured as an almost super-human leader, a man who can do no wrong.

As Mao Tse-tung grows older, he sees his chances of joining the counsels of the global powers dwindling, and his bitterness increases accordingly. To compensate for the isolation imposed on him by the West, and particularly the United States, Mao wishes to prove that he and the Chinese millions who look to him for leadership can stand alone.

China's solitude has disturbed not only Asian giants like Japan, Indonesia and India, but has also caused grave misgivings in Moscow. Almost for its own protection, Russia must see that China takes a larger part in world affairs. Despite occasional back-slappings by Chinese and Russian leaders, and frequent stress on Sino-Soviet solidarity in the Press of Moscow and Peking, contacts between the two leading Communist nations are not nearly as strong as they once were.

The Summit collapse of 1960 helped to consolidate the alliance only temporarily, for Russia was even then not really keen to continue the cold war indefinitely. A far more dramatic crisis in the Moscow-Peking relationship occurred in October of 1961 when the Chinese Premier, Chou En-lai, suddenly stomped out in the middle of the 22nd Congress of the Soviet Communist Party, and flew back to Peking. The entire Chinese delegation followed some days later. China's anger was precipitated partly by Khrushchev's attempt to belittle the name of Stalin in every possible way. Late that October Stalin's body was removed from the famous tomb in Red Square, and Chou had shown his disdain for the revisionist Soviet Premier by placing a wreath on Stalin's tomb several days before. But the principal and fundamental reason was Khrushchev's oblique criticism of Chinese policy. The dispute was not merely over Stalinism, but about the entire future of the global Communist movement.

Although it was obvious to the rest of the world what was happening, both Moscow and Peking used Albania, a tiny and impoverished nation, as a scapegoat through which they could channel their differences. When Khrushchev was attacking certain Albanian policies, he was really whipping out at the Chinese Communists, and when the Albanian dictator, Enver Hoxha, the First Secretary of the Albanian Communist Party, abused the Kremlin and Nikita Khrushchev personally in November 1961, he was using a text which had the approval of Mao Tse-tung. The breach over Albania came as near to an open quarrel between China and Russia over their diverging internal and external policies as any political affair since the Peking régime came to power. But the wishful thinkers who said this fight was the beginning of the end of global Marxism and who claimed that the two Communist giants could now no longer be friends are hopelessly wrong.

In the same way as there is no absolute unity within the West— even in time of war—Sino-Soviet unity is a myth. The Communist alliance, on the other hand, is a reality. Political, military and economic co-operation of sorts between Moscow and Peking is about as indisputable a fact as Anglo-American friendship. The Sino-Soviet alliance will stand the test of the coming years, no matter what change of Communist command might come in Peking and Moscow. For it is an alliance in the truest sense of the term, a marriage (uneasy though it might be) of two powerful states with a common object—the overthrow of Western capitalist society and the creation of a Communist globe dominated by the dictatorship of the central State. This is why it would be sheer insanity for Western strategists and policy-makers to under-estimate the strength of the many bonds that still tie Peking and Moscow. And yet there are so many causes for friction they cannot be hidden.

First and foremost, China's Communism is far more orthodox and dogmatic than that now practised in the Soviet Union, and Russians in Peking have told me that Moscow is just as much interested as the West is in the eventual outcome of China's ill-fated experiments with communes. The fact that Premier

Khrushchev is known to have expressed his disapproval of the rigid regimentation involved in their establishment does not seem to worry Mao. From a standpoint of international Communism the Kremlin must, of course, side with China officially, yet Russia felt compelled both in 1960 and 1961, in view of China's verbal brinkmanship over nuclear war, and her defence of Stalinism, to criticise Mao and his followers for trying to shatter all hopes of peaceful co-existence. The official Soviet Communist Party newspaper *Pravda*, and other Soviet journals conducted campaigns strongly defending the Khrushchev policies of co-existence, and denounced unnamed "left sectarians". It was clear that these attacks were aimed at Mao. Newspapers urged tactical compromise with the West, and said that the extreme leftists who opposed such policies were dangerously mistaken.

The Moscow press conducted a "hate Albania" campaign in the winter of 1961 which intensified until both Russia and Albania recalled their ambassadors. The Chinese newspapers, while refraining from editorial comment aimed directly against the Kremlin, printed Albanian attacks on Khrushchev and his followers in full, and left their readers in no doubt that the Chinese Government could not agree more. While the Kremlin was recalling its ambassador from Tirana, there was zealous and friendly diplomatic activity between Albania and China, with both countries exchanging friendship delegations at the drop of a hat, from cultural societies to women's groups.

The Albanian affair was further proof that Mao has rejected Russia's ideological leadership, and has decided, once and for all, that China will go her own way. He is a fanatic believer in his own theories, and sees a breathtaking vision of a new world ruled by Communist principles, which will change human destiny, eliminate all evil, and bring lasting peace. But to reach the golden tomorrow, Mao has warned, Communists will have to overthrow all classes and systems opposing them.

The menace of Mao and his followers lies not only in their dominion over 700,000,000 human beings but also in their self-righteousness and their devotion to orthodox Communism. Many of them are well-meaning people who want to help the world and its people, and who will not believe that most of the world does not want Communist-type help. This is what makes them dangerous to the West, to other Asian nations, and even to Russia and Eastern Europe.

Some time during this decade, at a triumphal rally in Tien An Men Square, the Chinese rulers will tell their masses that they are saved—that they, the proletarian sages of the new China, have built and successfully exploded a nuclear bomb that will stop imperialist aggressors. China will certainly have joined the nuclear club by 1970, probably some years before that.

Mao does not seem to think that nuclear war will annihilate mankind. On the contrary, he has said he is certain Communism would benefit from a world war. This refusal to believe that mankind has the power to destroy itself is a tenet of Mao's religion of constant struggle against other social systems.

As dangerous as any Chinese atom-bomb is her isolation. The realists of the West who are prepared to look beyond tomorrow, to the day when China will become the political and economic giant of Asia, are already suggesting a two-pronged policy for peaceful co-existence with China. The immediate aim is to come to terms with the Soviet Union, which is also beginning to fear Chinese domination. The second and equally important goal should be to tear down the artificial barriers separating a quarter of mankind from the rest of the world. It is obvious that Peking's dominance over Asia is coming ever closer, and today the Chinese Communists are appealing not to the West, or even to Russia, but to all the have-not people of the world, to Africans, South Americans, to the poor of Turkey, Egypt, Algeria and many other nations. Peking first hopes to settle its differences with India, Indonesia and Japan. This done, the Chinese leaders believe, the Communist doctrine could be spread among hundreds of millions of impoverished Asians who still view the wealthy West with a mixture of envy and hate. China is trying to head this crusade of the poor against the rich. The only sure way to halt China's leadership of the poor is to help her—and indeed all the world's poor nations—grow rich more rapidly. More recognition of Peking, perhaps even aid for China are not popular views in many circles, but the peril for the West will be far greater if Mao and his men are allowed—or encouraged—to preach their extreme and extravagant doctrines indefinitely in the locked Communist temple that is China.

Khrushchev has been trying for the past several years to persuade Mao to adopt a softer line toward the West, and visited Peking in 1958 and 1959 for personal talks with Mao, who has refused to go to Moscow ever since 1957. The Chinese leader snubbed the Russians when he did not attend the Moscow Conference of Communist Parties in December 1960. Instead, he sent Liu Shao-chi, who must have had a difficult time debating China's case and explaining his party's aggressively militant beliefs about Communist world expansion in the face of Western nuclear weapons.

At Moscow in 1960 the Sino-Soviet rift widened. The Chinese asked why the Russians had made it so obvious by their sudden withdrawal of experts, a most startling and open evidence of the split, which occurred in the autumn of 1960, not many months after I had left Peking. In a matter of days, thousands of Russians, Hungarians and Czechs living in China pulled up stakes and went home for good. Foreign diplomats who have been checking reports ever since insist that this wholesale exodus of technicians was one of the most remarkable operations ever carried out.

In Canton, Shanghai, Peking, Changchun and Harbin, in big cities and at dam sites, the experts from so-called "fraternal nations" packed up in a matter of three days. Trains bound for Moscow rolled out of Peking jammed with Russians. Curious Western diplomats who had gone to the main station in Peking to learn what was happening were barred from the platforms. A Dutch diplomat saw a Russian family leaving by air, though the wife had to be carried aboard on a stretcher. The experts had orders to leave fast, pregnant women included. A White Russian from Harbin reported the rapid emigration also occurred in Manchuria, and claims from Moscow that the return of the technicians had been planned months ago as well as official statements in Peking that they had finished their tour of duty were disproved by the fact that no replacements, on the same large scale, have since gone into China.

The split became apparent to me after I had been in Peking only a few days. At Khrushchev's airport farewell (he hasn't been back to China since that October day in 1959), I saw what may seem a superficial aspect of the quarrel. But I felt it was one of its most important causes—the great difference in thinking and behaviour between the Chinese and Russian leaders.

Khrushchev, confident, jaunty, twirling his hat in his hand, wore bright check socks that peeped out from his trousers. Near him were Gromyko, his Foreign Minister, and other advisers—all looking obviously relieved to be heading back for home. They could have been U.S. business executives returning from a not very successful conference. The Chinese had gone out of their way to emphasise the contrast. The four top leaders, Mao Tse-tung, Liu Shao-chi, Chu Teh and Chou En-lai, stood rigidly in line as Khrushchev disappeared into the Soviet jet. Each of the four wore an identical Communist uniform, mid-grey soldierly suits buttoned to the neck. It seemed to me a rather forced way of telling Khrushchev they disagreed with his individualist approach to Marxism. The Chinese leaders remain to this day diehard, first generation revolutionaries, Communist crusaders still battling for their cause, but the Russian revolution has almost completed a full circle and Russian citizens are fast forgetting all the revolutionary notions the Chinese still try to keep alive.

In my reports I kept off the subject of the rift for a couple of months because I felt articles on Sino-Soviet differences would upset the Chinese even more than stories about their work armies, the national regimentation and Peking's controversial thought control. But in February of 1960 I did a piece which pointed out that Mr. Khrushchev must seem a very tame Communist to the Chinese who still cherish the memory of Stalin. The gap between the policies of Peking and Moscow was widening, I wrote, and a few days after this first piece appeared, the *Globe and Mail* ran a second story from its Peking correspondent headed, "Can the Sino-Soviet Alliance last?"

All the high-sounding talk about the everlasting Sino-Soviet friendship, and the love between the Chinese and Russian brothers (which will last, according to the *People's Daily*! "as long as there is water in the Yangtse"), could not hide the deep river of fear and suspicion between the two régimes.

A great deal is being written about the reasons for the crack in the Communist alliance, but the main one, I feel, is that the Chinese and Russians must view their relationship on a historical basis. Two countries like the U.S. and Canada, both highly civilised, highly industrialised, with predominantly educated societies, with one language and common habits, can afford to live in such peace and friendship that they need not defend the border separating them. But this is not possible, in the long run, for the Chinese and the Russians. The Chinese, as a race, are suspicious of any foreigner, the Russians, in turn, cannot trust a nation of over 700,000,000 where there is not even a semblance of a birth-control programme. The main cause of their quarrel hinges around the vital theoretical goal of a Communised world. Chinese Communists are fundamentalists who have become fanatically convinced that world Communism can be achieved only through global violence, whereas the leaders of the Kremlin, on the other hand, are realists. Khrushchev has said that "only fools and madmen can call for a new world war today". Both Communist leaders hope for a Communist world, but they are not agreed as to how this is to be achieved.

In 1960 there were any number of clues as to the progress of the rift, such as the very obvious policy differences at the Communist meetings of Bucharest and Moscow, and Branko Bogunovic, Peking correspondent of the Yugoslav news agency Tanjug, cabled to Belgrade that Chinese industrial production was menaced by the continuing exodus of Soviet technicians and engineers. Bugonovic had close association with the Russian and Eastern European Communists. He felt the rift had most vital implications, and asked me to explain to him why the U.S. seemed so indifferent in its attitude towards Khrushchev when he was one of the Kremlin chiefs mainly responsible for the uneasiness between Peking and Moscow. Certainly one major reason for the rift is an utter lack of understanding between Mao and Khrushchev. Though their basic and theoretical aims may be similar, as individuals the two disagree. For one thing, the Soviet Premier was never a diehard revolutionary like Mao and his men, but grew up with the Communist State. Khrushchev is a sophisticate by Chinese standards. He is a globe-trotter, a showman, a politician, a clever agitator and opportunist. And, in Peking's view, Khrushchev is moving dangerously near the road taken by Tito whom the Chinese have branded as traitor to the Marxist cause.

The present Kremlin leadership, according to Mao, has its priorities all mixed up. Moscow wants peace at all costs, believing that a historic fusion of capitalism and Communism will come in time, and that since the two systems are slowly but surely drawing nearer there is no need to go to war. Communism, says Khrushchev, will win in the future also by peaceful means. The top men in China are appalled by Moscow's new interpretation of Communism, and Mao in particular has expressed his dislike for Khrushchev with such vigour the word has gone out to cadres across China that the Soviet Union's top man is nothing less than an opportunist and a chauvinist willing to sell Communism down the river for the sake of national security. Mao also wants a peaceful world—but only after Communism has triumphed. He is prepared to make those nuclear sacrifices which Khrushchev wishes to avoid, and therefore he simply cannot understand the Soviet Premier's policies.

Mao Tse-tung is neither sophisticated, nor well-travelled. He is a strategist rather than a politician, a long-term planner rather than a realist. He is not a showman, but a man of immense stature. His military victories, his national planning (despite the famine and other recent failures), put him head and shoulders above Khrushchev as a Marxist revolutionary. Khrushchev, as Lord Attlee once put it, "is comparatively small beer" when stood up against Mao. Khrushchev wanted to besmirch Mao's efforts in China, and made it more difficult for the Chinese to receive Soviet aid. Of course, the young men in the Russian Communist Party must feel that Sino-Soviet differences will eventually be resolved after Mao's death, much in the same way as Russian Communism altered and moderated when Stalin departed the political arena. But perhaps the cult of Mao has been too deeply instilled into the young Communist intellectuals of China, who as yet have shown few signs of exerting much influence on Peking's decisions.

Where Mao, however, has failed is in his inability to appreciate, from his isolation within China, that the nuclear age has accelerated not only aircraft and rockets—but also political theory and global strategy. Khrushchev knows this very well. In his internal and international planning, Mao Tse-tung still looks to the Marxist principles which are outdated now. He studies Lenin to give him the answers to the innumerable problems China faces. And, most dangerous of all, because his interpretation of Marxism has partly succeeded in China (where the circumstances were, to say the least, very special), Mao believes what is good for China can be as well applied to the rest of the world.

Khrushchev does not. Although he may not have learned his lessons in Communist theory as well as Mao, Khrushchev is more of a realist who has been to Western countries and has toured lands where a mixture of democratic socialism and free enterprise brings the ordinary people very high living standards.

The Russians are beginning to believe that the present Western trend away from the former free-wheeling capitalism to a fairer free enterprise system—where State taxes are high and profits are shared out with greater justice than ever before—is proof that their side is winning. Moscow's planners say that by using correct tactics, peaceful transition to Socialism and finally to global Communism is possible. This is the thinking which Mao Tse-tung is prepared to attack with all the considerable might he has at his disposal. He believes that to win, the Communist side may have to fight. And despite their rocket rattling the last thing the Russians want is all-out nuclear war. The leaders in the Kremlin live today in a climate of fear, as do men the world over, because they have realised that history can now move at the speed of a Polaris missile. Russians, Poles, Czechs, Hungarians, Rumanians, and virtually all the other satellites have tried to persuade China that in the nuclear age even small conflicts present staggering dangers to the world. One slight mistake—and a local revolution could spark a global war with hydrogen bombs and atomic rockets.

When Soviet Premier Nikita Khrushchev was stomping through Austria in July of 1960, explaining his stand over the U.2 incident and the Summit failure, he said: "We don't want to push solving the question of Capitalism versus Communism through a war because all would be lost. What would war mean at the present time, now that we have atomic bombs and rockets? Everything would be destroyed. The few people who would survive would vanish because of horrible radiation."

Being men who deal in fundamentals, the present Communist leadership in Peking cannot and will never agree with the Russians that nuclear war in the age of the atom is unthinkable, and it is here that the possibility of an eventual complete break between Russia and China lies. Certainly, over the next few decades Moscow and Peking, the two great centres of global Communism, must pull together to prevent the total collapse of the movement. But in the next century, and perhaps even in twenty or thirty years, the slow movement to the left in Western countries, and the gradual liberalisation of Russian Communism will have brought Washington, London and Moscow much closer together. By then, China's population pressures could well cause a Sino-Soviet clash. But since the world's political future is utterly unpredictable, the present rift must not be unduly exaggerated during the next few years. The bonds that join Russia and China together are still stronger than the factors pulling them apart. This did not prevent the Russians from telling their truculent allies in China to stop talking light-heartedly about nuclear war when they did not even have an atomic bomb. In 1960 Peking's propaganda had stressed that the Chinese people must not fear nuclear war. China's Defence Minister, Marshal Lin Piao, once told a Chinese Army Conference: "We handle both weapons and men but attach greater impor-tance to man's rôle. The atom bomb of spirit, that is man's ideological consciousness and courage, is much more powerful and more useful than the material atom bomb." And General Fu Chung, deputy-director of the Political Department of the People's Liberation Army, urged the Chinese not to fear nuclear war because "atom bombs cannot occupy countries". He said, "This is finally done by men. Victory or defeat in future war will not depend on rockets or atom bombs but on men." When-ever Chinese leaders spoke like this it brought home the absurdity of excluding from all current disarmament conferences the Peking régime, which has under its complete control the largest land army in the world.

During my term in Peking there was a marked contrast between warlike pronouncements appearing in print, and what Chinese Foreign Ministry officials told me to my face. Hsu Huang, the Deputy Director of the Information Department, sounded like a most peace-loving man during our various talks, and only showed his teeth once. It was during an interview on February 12, which was to be my last formal talk with him, though I didn't get a hint of this at the time.

Hsu Huang began the talk by stressing that everything pointed to China's peaceful policy. On the Sino-Indian border, in Indonesia and Burma, China was following a policy of peace, he said, whereas the U.S. was preparing for war and extending nuclear bases. Though China was having serious troubles with both India and Indonesia I was not going to let myself in for a political debate. I merely said it looked as if China didn't want an early war with India. Then he launched into his one attack on my reporting. "You have distorted Chinese foreign policy and have written slanders about Chinese internal affairs," he said, talk-ing in a very matter-of-fact way and without venom in his voice.

"I'm a Westerner and naturally cannot view your country through the eyes of a Chinese," I said. "If you could give me detailed instances of where these distortions and slanders occurred it would help me greatly."

"Go back and look at your files. You will see what we mean," he said. "If you wish to express personal opinions of Chinese foreign policy you may do so, certainly, but possibly elsewhere. We already have enough people outside China slandering us. There is no need for you to do it as well." I repeated my request that he be more specific about his complaints instead of generalising, but this time he ignored the question altogether. Despite the sharp nature of the exchange both of us maintained an air of very reasonable men voicing their opinions. For some reason the Chinese often gave me the impression they regarded me as a semi-official representative of the Canadian Government. Probably the fact that their own writers and correspondents may operate only with State sanction caused this unnatural attitude.

Several times I tried to explain that the Western reporter who came only to praise and who shut his eyes to certain factors which were alien to him, would defeat his own purpose in trying to explain China to the people of the West. He would be considered a Communist, I told Hsu Huang, and would therefore not even get into print.

My main aim, and the *Globe and Mail*'s main aim, was to promote a more realistic Western policy toward China. Any criticisms were surely worth while in order to achieve this end. Hsu Huang mumbled something to Miss Chen who was interpreting. She translated: "The Deputy Director wishes to assure you that we never considered you as a Communist correspondent."

Hsu Huang turned to the matter of my reports appearing in other newspapers. They had been published in New York, London, Chicago and Hamburg as well as across Canada and Australia, he complained. Since I was representing only the *Globe and Mail*, he said, he could not understand this.

I said the cost of maintaining a news bureau in Peking was considerable. My paper sold these stories to selected newspapers to help pay for the operation. Surely the more people in the West read about China, the better the chances of improving relations, I said, but then asked whether he wanted the reports in the other newspapers to cease. "If you do, I suggest you might write to my publisher, though I would advise him as well. The fact that my reports go to other newspapers has nothing to do with me personally. As you are probably aware I cable and mail all my material only to Toronto." Hsu Huang gave me no direct answer, but added that he thought what had happened was not entirely consistent with what had been said during his talks with my publisher, though he admitted that no definite agreement had been reached.

"Perhaps the Foreign Ministry will discuss this matter by mail with Mr Dalgleish or perhaps Mr. Dalgleish might like to come to China," he added, then dropped the subject, switching to the Spring Festival. Had I seen how happy the people were? I replied I had written a story about the very relaxed, easy atmosphere in Peking during the Festival period.

"Before liberation only the rich could enjoy the Spring Festival," he said, "but now we are producing more food, and more goods and still we are not happy with the living standards of the people. We are not satisfied. We want to go farther. China is no paradise, and we know it. We do not pretend to be perfect. We are still very far behind the Western nations which had their industrialisation long ago. That is why we work so hard. We don't want to wait such a long time to catch up."

15

ASIA'S GLAMOUR MIGRANTS

"The twenty-second of February is a very close date to our hearts as it reflects and materializes an old and dear aspiration which dwelt for many generations in the consciousness of all Arabs," Cairo's Ambassador was saying. "That is the unity of two Arab countries and the birth of the United Arab Republic." This was still 1960 but the following year the unity being eulogised here disintegrated when Syria broke with Egypt.

Just before Ambassador Dr. Salah El Dine Tarazi began his speech at the United Arab Republic National Day ceremony, I had found myself standing next to a vice-director of the Chinese Foreign Ministry's Information Department, Kang Mao-chao, a moon-faced, serious man whom I had first met during the trip to the Miyun Reservoir. I had beamed at him brightly, and had asked "Have you any news for me about my travel permit to Shanghai?" But then the Ambassador had begun to speak. Kang Mao-chao had pointed to him and had put his finger to his lips.

"Both Egypt and Syria fought bravely and incessantly against imperialism and resisted all sorts of aggressions, conspiracies and manœuvres launched against them," Dr. Tarazi was saying, peering every now and again at a large painting of Liu Shao-chi which had been hurriedly put up in the Embassy's main reception hall.

I was sorry the other vice-director, Hsu Huang, wasn't there. He might have known something about my Shanghai application. Despite his recent lecture about my slandering China and giving a distorted account of her foreign policy, I thought Hsu Huang felt reasonably friendly toward me, and had the impression during our various meetings that he understood my problems as a Western reporter. Hsu had a teddy-bear look about him, and perhaps because of this several other correspondents, Communists included, called him a buffoon, but I think he had been given the job of vice-director because he was one of the few Chinese Communists who knew how to handle Europeans, and could talk their language. One step down the ladder in his department was Miss Chen, a typical Communist zealot. She was small and rather dainty, had bright, intelligent eyes that smiled only rarely, was the devoted, unswerving, unbending servant of the Communist State, and I couldn't help feeling that she thought of me as one of the enemy. I had seen Miss Chen at the reception, but thought Kang Mao-chao was a better bet when it came to pushing my Shanghai trip.

The United Arab Republic's representative in Peking was still talking, but the speech was obviously almost at an end. I turned to have another crack at Kang Mao-chao who had been standing right behind me. He had vanished. How he had managed to get through the dense crowd gathered in the reception room I will never know. Obviously he was not going to answer my question because I didn't sight him during the rest of the evening. Miss Chen it had to be. I had approached her on previous occasions on the question of Shanghai, so I just bowled up to her and asked whether my travel permit would be granted.

"I think," she said, speaking rather curtly, "that you may travel directly to Canton, and then you can finish your story about the fact that there is no freedom of movement in China."

I must say I was startled—not by the refusal of the permit but rather by the unusual course she had taken in telling me why I could not go to Shanghai. The Chinese hate to say "No" just like that, and will go to extremes to avoid the blunt Western way of refusing a request. Instead they will say "Your case is being considered" or "Yes, we are looking into that" or "Will you please ring in a few days when we may have an answer". But it is never "No". Being faced, for once, with plain Chinese honesty, I thought I would give a few blows straight from the shoulder too. "Well, let's face it Miss Chen, there is no freedom of movement for us in China. If you impose restrictions on foreigners, why do you expect us to keep quiet about it?" She made no answer.

Later, when I cooled down, I realised Miss Chen had hinted that at least I would be granted an exit and re-entry visa to meet my family in Hongkong. I had been making arrangements for some time for Audrey and the children to join me but had not been sure until now whether I would be given a re-entry permit. If the Chinese had issued only an exit visa, Audrey would have had to bring the mob up from Hongkong herself. When I began discussing the family's journey to Peking, I hadn't been too optimistic about Audrey's reaction, since I had painted a fairly grim picture of life in my letters. It was not going to be comfortable for a family, and a vast change from our house-and-garden existence at Eaglemont, one of Melbourne's more agreeable suburbs. I argued it would be interesting not only for her but for the children, who were reaching an age when they would remember at least something of China later on. The main thing was, I had said, that the family would be together again. I had received a cable from her in answer to a letter telling her the Chinese would allow her and the children in, and that we should get moving on final travel dates. "Wonderful. Really thrilled. Getting busy and longing to see you," she had cabled. For the rest of that day I had walked on air.

When I reached my room after the Arab reception, I brushed aside the mass of paper on my desk. There was Audrey's cable preserved beneath the glass top of the desk, next to photographs of five smiling faces. I grinned to myself. Who the hell cared about Shanghai anyhow? Audrey and the children would be here soon, right here at the Hsin Chiao! We'd show those wretched Commies with their niggling hate tactics a thing or two!

The next days flew by in a whirl of last-minute preparations. I banged out several stories about Chou En-lai's coming trip to New Delhi to see Nehru, and did the rounds of the embassies asking whether anybody wanted things from Hongkong. All the diplomats did this as a matter of course before travelling south. One had brought me back some film, and I thought I should reciprocate. Knowing I would have to pay duty on gifts, they all thanked me and refused, saying it was quite easy for them to have things shipped up. Just before the end of February, I flew south. The eight-hour air trip was smooth, and I arrived in Canton humming all the dance tunes I was forgetting in Peking. The reunion with Audrey was only days away. "Hongkong, here I come!" I thought as I picked up my gear and thanked the air hostess who was waiting by the step ladder fingering her beautifully plaited pigtails.

Was I pleased to see Canton—dirty old Canton! Near the airfield peasants were already planting early spring rice. The China Travel people had sent a quiet and charming interpreter named Fung, not one of their loud-mouthed propagandists, who

told me I would be staying at the hotel for overseas Chinese. It
was new, but very crowded. Chinese from Indonesia were coming
back to their homeland, Fung explained. Our car drew up at the
hotel, quite near the Pearl River bridge, at the same time as a
busload of these young Chinese, all smiling and happy and well-
dressed. Blue-garbed comrades pumped their hands as they jumped
from the bus. In those early months of 1960 the Communists
were receiving their countrymen from overseas with great
ceremony. Each week they arrived in Canton in their hundreds.
Never before had diehard capitalists been so warmly greeted by
dedicated Communists. The overseas Chinese from Indonesia
were Asia's glamour migrants with Peking sending dozens of
ships to Indonesia to pick them up, and when they reached China
the refugees were met by lion dancers, song and dance troupes
and special reception teams led by some of the Party's top boys.
They were taken in special trains to the cities where they would
settle and were again met on the railway stations by hundreds
sounding off with firecrackers, cymbals, drums and gongs. At
Canton, Chankiang, Swatow, Hoihow and other southern ports,
the overseas Chinese whom Indonesia did not want were treated
like heroes returning from the wars. One of China's aims in
making such a fuss was to cushion the impact of a very sudden
change from a free enterprise society (no matter how disorderly)
in Indonesia to a Communist society. From one day to the next
the returnees must realize that from now on the State would make
most of the important decisions for them. All they needed to do
themselves was to work at the tasks set for them by the State,
and this was usually quite a jump from haggling with a customer
about the price of a pound of potatoes.

Intent on impressing the returnees with their achievements,
the Communists were housing them in Canton's newest and most
modern hotel. They were adding a spacious new wing, but in
the meantime the ten-storey hotel was so crowded that lounges
had been turned into dormitories, with long lines of canvas
stretchers.

I had a room to myself on the sixth floor, complete with
mosquito net and bathroom. I showered, changed and went to
the ground-floor dining-room. When my Chinese meal came I
realised I was the only person in a room crowded with Chinese
who was using chopsticks. All around me were repatriates from
Indonesia, many of them very well dressed, eating European

food with knives and forks. They fed their small children rice, heaped high on spoons.

It was obvious also in the dining-room that the local Communist authorities were going out of their way to make the newcomers feel at home. There was much laughter, back slapping and drinking, a gayer atmosphere generally than farther up north where dinner-table merriment was restricted to high days and holidays. How incongruous the overseas Chinese in their immaculately-cut tropical suits looked next to Communists, dressed as usual in faded, high-buttoned uniforms.

"Where do all the overseas Chinese settling in Canton live?" I asked Fung, when he knocked at my door next morning.

"We have built a new suburb for them," he said. "The New Village for Overseas Chinese."

He took me to see it. It was about a quarter of an hour from the hotel by car, and the modern apartment buildings, painted in pastels, stood out from the general drabness of Canton's grey streets. More than a hundred apartment buildings had gone up, and Fung said the authorities would keep adding to the village as the need arose. The physical problems of absorbing these repatriates were in fact small compared to the larger national headaches. Tens or hundreds of thousands, maybe several million people, could enter China over a few years without seriously disrupting the national economy. What I and other foreigners felt was wrong was the Communist claim that China suffered from a shortage of people. It verged on the criminal to say this when women and children stood for many hours in food queues hoping to buy a pound of biscuits or perhaps a small bag of half-rotten, unexportable fruit. In Canton there were food queues everywhere. Once I let the cab stand for a time, to walk with Fung down several side streets. We were just passing a queue when a thin old man with odd, burning eyes called to us at the top of his voice in good English, "Here you see a city of hunger." I would have loved to have spoken with him, but decided against it. For one thing I felt sorry for Fung, who had walked on without blinking, pretending he had heard nothing. It wasn't his fault that the Cantonese were hungry. And had I talked with the old man, both he and Fung would have been in serious trouble. Fung explained the food queues away by saying people were waiting for their turn to get into community dining halls where they received cheap but ample meals.

As an old Peking resident, the Canton pedicab stations were for me, personally, what the Chinese might have termed an "excellent technical innovation". The pedicab terminals consisted of a small shelter and a pedicab controller. There was a large board listing the fare to virtually any spot in the city. The passenger paid his fare first, then climbed into the pedicab to be pedalled to his destination. Peking's pedicab men were, in my time, about the only residents of the national capital who regularly and quite unscrupulously cheated their foreign clients. A Chinese knows the fare, of course, but not so the foreigner. In Canton it is impossible to pick up a pedicab on the street. You must queue up at a pedicab station. But in Peking you can hail a pedicab man anywhere, and he will take you anywhere—and then charge you any price. As an experiment, I have handed pedicab men half a yuan, one yuan, two yuan and five yuan for the same trip. All took the money, and pretended they had no change. I decided the Peking gentleman about to pocket five yuan (about fifteen-shillings) for hauling me less than a mile was expecting too much. I got some change from a nearby shop and gave him one yuan. He grinned and accepted it.

Whenever I could during my few days in Canton I suggested to Fung that he take a breather, partly so that I could be alone. At such times I usually strolled along the waterfront, by the Pearl River. Long ago some Cantonese must have named the city's river by night. It glistened then like a black pearl, and its slow-flowing waters reflected the lights of the riverboats. In the darkness it was very beautiful, and occasionally from mid-river came the faint splash of oars. But even in the dawn's first light the black, lustrous water changes its colour and becomes a muddy brown. The mysterious lights that glide gently downstream disappear, and suddenly the Pearl River is alive with junks and sampans and barges. Ferries and tugboats take advantage of the current, and race by with surprising speed. Black-clad boatmen propel their simple wooden barges with grace and rhythm, slowly pushing and pulling their long oars, until their little vessels fade into the morning haze. Rhythmically, without haste, a mother washes her children's clothes in the yellow-brown water. Occasionally, as if jealous of its own nocturnal shimmer, the daytime river gives the visitor brief glimpses of colour and brilliance. The sun comes out from behind a cloud, to form a golden path across the brown surface;

and through this gloss moves a Chinese junk, its sails black against the sky. Or a bright, white river ferry crosses quickly from the far shore, spews out its passengers, and hurries back for more—little red flags flying fore and aft. But come down from your tenth-storey hotel lookout; peer at the river and its people more closely. Now the river is ugly, and the poverty of those who live on it grips your throat.

It was a constant wonder to me how some of the ramshackle junks and sampans—which are, in fact, family dwellings—remain afloat. Often they are nothing more than a few planks of rotting wood held together by rusty nails and pieces of wire and rope. On the long, narrow jetties, decorated with potted plants, children romp and hide and skip; mothers dally to gossip; an old woman sits silently near the stern of a sampan mending faded blue cotton trousers. At night families make open fires inside their narrow floating homes, or cook on oil lamps. What percentage of these river dwellers, I wondered, would willingly exchange their precarious, tumble-down sampans for a couple of rooms in a brick apartment? Is a Cantonese junk a more congenial home than a factory dormitory, where sometimes six or eight girl machinists sleep in two-tiered bunks in a single room?

These river people have a variety of jobs, loading and unloading the barges and larger river boats that ply the Pearl, and transporting small cargoes. Others are bricklayers and labourers, now busy erecting wharf sheds and jetties along the slushy shores of the Pearl; many spend their working lives dragging carts. The waterfolk of Canton give the city a special character. The Communists claim that the sixty thousand river dwellers are much better off today than in the past when Canton's land-lubbers would look on them contemptuously because their only home was a boat. Not only along the river, but in the downtown streets with their tall European-style buildings, the life of Canton seems miserably poor. People peer out at the day from dark, dingy, tiny rooms. Thin-faced girls, small hollow-eyed mothers of the future, walk along aimlessly with their younger sisters on their back. These Chinese babies, who spend much of their first year wrapped in a piece of cloth strapped to their mothers' or elder sisters' backs, sleep unconcernedly, heads lolling, despite the constant movement and the chatter of the crowd.

The sun is very hot, and you wonder how all those people feel whom you see harnessed to carts like animals; the women pushing from behind so often look too thin and very old; yet they don't seem very tired; sometimes they even smile and laugh. Often they are still there at night, still tugging and straining. Canton's streets empty slowly as night falls, far more unwillingly than the thoroughfares of Peking. Many people stay near the river hoping for a cool breeze from the water. Others sit in the park under the stars. Mr. Fung once took me to a first-rate acrobatic show given by a troupe from Manchuria. One Chinese clown, who must have studied funny French films, painting his face until he looked like a Mexican Charlie Chaplin, had the audience in fits. The programme finished with a shapely Chinese girl aerialist in a golden bikini whirling around below the big top. It looked a dangerous act, but the show people were not asked to take any chances. The golden girl, and all other performers who did difficult aerial acts, were secured by a safety rope in case of accidents. This didn't bother the spectators. They were completely taken by the clowns, the flying female in her scant gold outfit, the bright-eyed young boys who engaged in boxing matches balancing on top of large wooden balls and the men on the flying trapeze. At the end of the evening the Cantonese gave the Manchurians a standing ovation. Outside, enfolded by the warm summer night, young couples rode happily on a ferris wheel, while in an open-air theatre an audience hooted about the grimaces of a Peking opera actor. Canton, even under the Communists, was nice, I thought. For Canton, despite the Communists, was normal.

Mr. Fung dropped me at the hotel. I went upstairs to my room, washed and changed into threadbare trousers, then caught the lift to the lobby again. Fortunately, Mr. Fung had gone. The night was the only time I could become one of the mob without attracting attention. From the hotel I had heard a constant muffled roar, and walked towards it to find myself outside one of Canton's powerhouses. The noise came from the generators. The street outside the plant was brighter than elsewhere. And then I saw why. A ghostly procession of men were carrying coal into the power plant. They walked through the night jerkily, like puppets, hobbling across the road by the Pearl River, black figures silhouetted against the glare of arc lamps. For a long time I stood and watched the shuffling shapes, and listened to strange rhymes they called to each other to help lighten their burden. From barges filled with coal they struggled up a wooden gangplank with heavy baskets, crossed the street with Chinese drivers hooting sharply at them, and disappeared into the powerhouse which provided light for Canton. In an age where nations are already using the atom to give them more electricity, it was bizarre to see this endless procession of straining men feeding the hungry city powerhouse completely by hand.

One of the greatest Communist achievements in mass psychology has been to convince the Chinese masses of the virtue of hard, physical labour. Nobody in China is ashamed of his job today. Except, I have heard, the people who work in factories producing contraceptives, for birth control is still an idea alien to the Chinese mind. Perhaps the new generation of Chinese can be taught that the nation must limit its numbers if it is to grow strong, and if individual people wish to become richer. But, in the meantime, to have persuaded the meanest peasant that his contribution to the national wealth is a valuable one, is already a tremendous, awe-inspiring feat in mass thought control. In thus courting the masses, Peking has employed some extremely cunning propaganda. *China Pictorial* once ran a big two-page spread about Shih Chuan-hsiang, a night-soil collector. He attended the Conference of Labour Heroes, held while I was in Peking, and the magazine story showed how this man's lot had been improved in recent years. Shih Chuan-hsiang had been a model night-soil carter, and for this he was rewarded. He was given charge of one of the most modern trucks in Peking. The story and photographs showed him attending the Worker Heroes Meeting, and one picture had him shaking hands with Liu Shao-chi, China's Head of State. I wondered, on reading it, whether any president of any nation had ever been photographed in a national magazine shaking hands with a night-soil carter.

Shih Chuan-hsiang, unlike the men who must do this kind of unpleasant job in Western nations, does not feel his job to be an inferior one in the eyes of his neighbours. He can show them the large photograph of Chairman Liu, smiling broadly, presenting him with the *Selected Works of Mao Tse-tung*, which came with the hero's medal he was awarded for his labours.

These psychological methods as used by the Chinese Communists are highly significant. Admittedly, they are possible only in such a land as China where a great majority of the people have the simple minds of children. But there they are effective, and so is Peking's technical innovations campaign which is designed to take the fear out of machines. The average Chinese was terrified of mechanics, and to combat this the Communists encouraged people to "invent" simple gadgets. People who did well in this Chinese industrial revolution were given fine titles like "famed innovator, young pace-setter, outstanding worker, labour hero and worker-promoted-technician." Peking once announced that in a year 3,600,000 workers distinguished themselves in technical innovation campaigns across China. During these drives some of the most ludicrous equipment appeared, and I met many foreigners who could only sneer at the Communists for making a fuss over nothing. But no matter how distasteful the Westerner finds Chinese Communism, if he is honest, he must admit that the Peking government is trying to replace the void in people's minds with a glimmer of knowledge. For the first time, labourers and peasants are being urged to work things out by themselves, and not always to let others do the thinking for them. Unfortunately this does not apply to politics, but in time, after one or two generations, it almost certainly will.

* * *

I spent my last night in Canton by the river, and when I left early in the morning faithful Fung was at the train to see me off to Shumchun. There was no trouble at all at the border. I gave the Customs people an undeveloped roll of film just to see what would happen to it, giving as my permanent address the Hsin Chiao Hotel. Taking undeveloped film out of China was a breach of the law. I received it in Peking from Mr. Hsu, the interpreter, six weeks later. Other rolls I had shot I mailed to myself in Peking from Canton post office. They would keep.

After the dreadful drabness of China, the colour, the lights, the life and the hustle of Hongkong were a great relief. I couldn't have enough of the rainbow neons and the little stalls piled high with fruit, orange, yellow, green, red. And nobody in blue. Never before had I realised how much colour affects the mind. In China, especially in the cities, there is little colour since most buildings are left unpainted. Even the blue dress of the workers loses its blueness through constant repetition. There are attempts being made to avoid the dead, dull look of cities. But paint costs money. Instead the party is putting up huge hoardings and propaganda posters depicting advances in industrial production and hopes for a greater harvest. Here the colour value is also lost because these advertisements say, in picture form, what people read in the newspapers and hear over the radio all day long. Walking through Hongkong's streets, lit up each night as brightly as Peking is only on a few festival days of the year, I understood why so many Chinese preferred being very poor and free to the comparative security they had in China. In there they were harnessed to the Communist chariot. In Hongkong they could do as they wished.

The following day Audrey flew in with the children. She stepped off the plane looking so pretty and pleased—and desperately hot in a blue-grey tweed suit she had bought for Peking. The children wore their woollen overcoats—so they wouldn't have to carry them. In Sydney, where they had been on a last-minute visit to my parents, it was still late winter. By comparison, Hongkong was scorching.

After we had all enjoyed a few wonderfully relaxing days in Repulse Bay, the China Travel Service telephoned to say they had sent Audrey's passport to Canton to be stamped, and expected to have her visa ready soon. The three weeks in Hongkong passed all too rapidly. Over our hotel dinners I assured Audrey that she would enjoy her time in Peking. She said everyone had urged her not to come, and begged her in particular not to take the children into China. Even my father, who professed admiration for the way the Chinese Communists were tackling important developmental projects, suggested that she leave the children behind and go into China alone.

Audrey spent her days buying canned food and other provisions, while I shopped around for a suitable car and some office equipment. We left for Peking late in March. Bill Stevenson, the *Globe and Mail*'s Hongkong correspondent, took Audrey and the children to Blake Pier in his car while I brought some bags in a cab.

"Here's our wallah-wallah," Kim yelled. He had turned eight the previous month, and was the one child who truly appreciated the adventurous nature of our journey. We had promised the children that their journey to China would begin with a ride across the harbour in a launch. We waved Bill goodbye, and as we bobbed up and down in the waves, four terribly excited children giggled and sang and put their hands into the spray that splashed on to the deck. The heaviest of the cases and several big trunks had already been moved by the China Travel Service. On Kowloon side we boarded the green train to the border, and the brief trip with the wide-eyed, hungry, thirsty jabbering children was much more fun than when I went into China alone the year before.

Only for a few moments, as we were walking toward the steel bridge, did my stomach muscles sound a faint warning. No other Western correspondent had ever taken his wife and four children into Communist China. Had I been wise to do it?

16

PEKING—THAT OTHER PLANET

The twins walked across the border into China with their baby pink and sky-blue toy carricots. Each cot contained two dolls. Michelle and Nicole, who were five, had nestled the pig-tailed Chinese dolls I had sent from Peking next to blonde Australians. All four were girl dolls—which was perhaps just as well. To have mixed the sexes might have been carrying peaceful co-existence with the puritans of new China a little too far. The Customs men were delighted, took one look at the twins, settling first a black-haired, then a blue-eyed "daughter" down to sleep on the table where our cases were being examined, and passed our twenty-odd pieces with amazing speed. On the train to Canton the children munched chicken sandwiches and apples, I fished a huge tin of powdered coffee out of my briefcase, and using up about half of my twenty-word Mandarin vocabulary persuaded the train attendant to exchange the Thermos flask of Chinese tea for boiling water. We seemed to reach Canton in next to no time, spending one night there before flying on to Peking in a new Russian-built turbo-prop which carried us smoothly to the capital in three hours flat, a strange contrast with my leisurely flight to Manchuria.

From Canton's summer weather the flight north brought us into the late winter of Peking. From the air we had watched the plane leaving behind the lush greens of the south. In Peking there were no green shoots, either in the fields or on the trees. The faces of the people at the airport were wintry too, rigid, disciplined, unemotional faces. A Chinese group, meeting a Communist delegation arriving on our plane, first smiled at the visitors but as soon as a newspaper photographer began taking pictures their eyes and mouths grew hard and stiff. A good Communist has to look tough in China.

Audrey was flabbergasted at the startling difference between Canton and Peking. We had not been on the ground ten minutes when she whispered to me, "Good Heavens. It's just like being on another planet. What's the matter with the people here?" The people of Peking, and especially the officials, are too close to the core of the new régime which controls more human beings than any other single Government has done in the history of the world. This has evidently had an extraordinary psychological effect on government officials, party leaders and others whose duty it is to see that Communist orders are carried out unquestioningly. They become, after a time, Communist automatons, very efficient robots who mechanically obey every command issued by the supreme councils of the State. Naturally enough, their faces acquire mechanical expressions as well.

The combination of bedroom, office and lounge into which I ushered Audrey with great pride when we reached the Hsin Chiao was a corner room the hotel liked to reserve for special guests. Even before I knew definitely that the family would be coming, I kept telling the management that I wanted one of these larger rooms, and finally I got it. The room was cold, but airy and very light. There were three large picture windows. The two beds could be curtained off, and though the coarse brown drapes were not particularly handsome, they served their purpose when Shane, our youngest boy who celebrated his third birthday in Peking, wanted his afternoon sleep while the other three were making a hell of a din playing Peking Opera around the corner in our second room. The four children had to make do with a smaller space. The hotel owned only huge metal bedsteads, and with three next to each other they virtually filled the children's room. The management could not provide a cot for Shane, even though we knew there was a whole nursery full of children in a staff crèche located, of all places, in the hotel basement. He slept on two armchairs placed against each other.

In the big room we had one large sofa, two armchairs, and a long low table. Apart from the desk in the background, the one half of the room resembled every single one of the reception halls at factories and offices I had sat in so many times. It gave me great satisfaction to manœuvre any Chinese who came into the room to the sofa, sit myself next to him, and motion Audrey and the interpreter to the armchairs opposite. Then I would order Chinese tea from the room boys. I don't know whether my attempts to copy this Chinese Communist brand of hospitality made my Communist visitors feel at home.

High school students taking a break at a construction project in Tientsin.

U Ching-sung, who conducted the tour of an experimental commune in Shanghai. The girl in the cardigan is the former Miss Garbage, of Chapter 19.

A few days after the family reached Peking we took the children to the Sacred Heart Convent school, which is under the direction of the Franciscan Missionaries of Mary, and though the nuns are not exactly up to date in their teaching methods, most Western and Asian foreigners send their children to the time-worn, forbidding building behind its high iron gate. The nuns provide the only schooling available to non-Communist children in China and have about two hundred pupils. As far as I know, the convent is the only Catholic establishment left in China outside the grip of the pro-Communist National Catholic Patriotic Association which runs the Chinese Catholic Church. The Indians can take credit for its survival. The convent lies right in the centre of Peking, only a few hundred yards from Tien An Men, and was a thorn in the Communists' side so they decided to close it. But the Indians persuaded Premier Chou En-lai to let the convent remain. The nuns were minding their own business, the Indians and other Asian diplomats said, so why bother them? The convent provided the only education which the children of diplomats could get without resorting to private tutors for each embassy. The Sacred Heart Convent was a religious island in a vast sea of atheism. The nuns still hold church services in a tiny, very beautiful chapel, and occasionally they find an unofficial anti-Communist priest to say Mass for them.

The day after we had talked with the Mother Superior of the convent, we took the children to their Peking school by cab, and drew up outside the gates among a strange variety of vehicles including sleek diplomatic limousines, jeeps which some of the embassies used as buses, and box-like pedicabs painted blue and built specially to carry about six children. They were pedalled by a long-suffering Chinese whose duty it was to see that the children got to school on time and then home again safely. Our children had missed a great deal of schooling, and except for Shane, who had never been to school in Australia, they were looking forward to going to the "English school" in Peking. In fact, most children were not European at all, but Indians, Indonesians, Pakistanis, Ceylonese, Burmese, and a few Chinese. The nuns ruled the children with a rod of iron, and despite the cosmopolitan nature of the classes all the pupils at the convent were beautifully behaved. The boys would bow and shake hands when introduced to adults, and the girls curtsied.

All lessons were taught in English. Neither in their conversation nor their teaching did the nuns ever mention the Chinese Communists. They did their work as quietly and unobtrusively as possible. Audrey often wondered why the children brought back verbal messages—which became very garbled on occasions. Later she decided the nuns either could not or would not use the Chinese mails to send out school circulars.

With Audrey and the children in the hotel, life became more hectic and far more enjoyable. For one thing, the Chinese themselves were much friendlier and more relaxed toward me. We had a load of fun with the room boys. Audrey realised that to converse with them she had to speak thick accented English. When she heard me speaking to the boys, she said, "What a monstrous language," and couldn't stop laughing whenever a boy came into the room. After a few days she found they didn't understand her because she spoke normally. When ordering meals in the room, we had hilarious guessing games on what would turn up. The moment Audrey hit the Hsin Chiao I got her to take over all those wretched chores I had been grappling with for the past half-year. Food, laundry, purchase of soap, toothpaste, shoe polish—all those niggling little things that had been done half-heartedly by me were thrown into her lap, including the room orders. I would listen as she said slowly, "One piece toast, one hot milk, one egg and bacon. O.K.?" Then following closely the brief training I had given her, she asked the room boy to repeat the order. Counting on his fingers he said, "One piece toast, one glass milk, one eggy bacon."

"Hot milk—one hot milk," Audrey said very slowly.

The boy disappeared down the corridor beaming. It took anything up to half an hour, sometimes forty-five minutes, to get your meal. Back he came with a piece of bread, a glass of cold milk, and a plate of ham. The simplest method of ensuring that you got what you wanted was to tell the boy, "A plate of sandwiches, please." This they all knew.

Our two-room home would have been impossible on a long-term basis. But the hotel bureau was not intended to be permanent. The *Globe and Mail* had given me a handsome allowance with which to furnish a Peking apartment. Before the trip to Hongkong I had been interviewed by a Mr. Liu, an official of the Service Bureau for Diplomatic Personnel just down the street from the hotel, who assured me he would do his best to find us suitable accommodation not long after the family's arrival. He mentioned May, "or June at the latest". Now, in April, the room at the Hsin Chiao was as cold as charity because the central heating had been turned off. I tried to contact Liu but could not reach him. Bernard Ullmann suggested I take his interpreter along to talk again with Liu. But I knew it wasn't a matter of interpreters. If the Foreign Ministry wanted us to have accommodation, we would get it; if they didn't, we wouldn't. It was a simple problem. Here was an example of the persistent and insidious pressures the Chinese used against their own people who would not toe the official line. Since the government controlled everything from housing to food, it was impossible to live happily and normally unless you were prepared to agree with them.

The authorities thought this kind of tactics might succeed if applied against Westerners. In some cases Western diplomatic missions had moved out of their fine old compounds under pressure, but the Chinese were sometimes beaten at their own game. The Swiss still occupy beautiful buildings in a select area of Peking, yet were told long ago they would have to move to new quarters. They replied they didn't feel like moving, and would not do so until they had an embassy and residential quarters which met with their approval. When the Chinese applied more pressure, the Swiss retaliated. "It would be unfortunate if we had to move into quarters we don't like," they told the Chinese. "This might mean we would withdraw our mission from Peking, in which case it might be necessary to ask the Chinese Government to withdraw its mission to Switzerland. I think it would be a pity if we had to move now." The Swiss have not had another squeak out of the Chinese since.

Unfortunately, the *Globe and Mail* could not use this kind of counter measure. All I did was to write more letters—to the Chinese asking whether my application for an apartment would be granted, and to my newspaper to say I hoped the costly hotel bills would not go on indefinitely. Four youngsters with healthy appetites meant the hotel bill was going way up.

Several Communist correspondents assured me they had lived in hotel rooms with families for many months, in some cases years, before getting an apartment. The foreign Communists showed their dislike for the Chinese, and their annoyance at Chinese arrogance toward foreigners, by going out of their way to be pleasant toward us Western reporters. We were so badly outnumbered, there was no point in being hoity-toity. Nor were they. Many of the Russian reporters were as unhappy about Peking as we were. There were Poles and Czechs who longed for the more leisurely life of Warsaw and Prague. Hungarians and East Germans dreamed of a gay night out in the clubs of Budapest and Berlin. They were, after all, also of the West as regards race and habits, though their political affiliations forced them to report only positively and uncritically about Chinese Communist efforts. But behind the backs of their dedicated hosts, the Eastern European Communists joked about the unsmiling stiffness of Peking's officials and their extreme dogmatism just as bitterly as any of us. At diplomatic functions they never attempted to stay within their own camp. Sometimes Communist correspondents even snubbed the Chinese in order to maintain the solidarity of the foreign Press corps. Once the correspondent of the Yugoslav news agency Tanjug, Branko Bogunovic, invited most of the correspondents to a party at his home. The Chinese got to hear of it, and arranged a film night at the International Club for the same evening. Most of the correspondents ignored the Chinese invitation and went to Branko's party. Bogunovic, after three years in Peking, was tired and frustrated. Peking's hate campaign toward Tito extended right down the Communist ladder, and Branko was cold-shouldered more often by the Chinese than Western correspondents. A sore point with the foreign Communists was the refusal of the Chinese to issue invitations to their wives. Correspondents were virtually given diplomatic privileges but they did not include bringing your better half to the many formal functions held in Peking. Audrey, too, became rather huffy when I kept going off to receptions alone. Some of the women had themselves accredited to a variety of little-known Communist journals so they wouldn't be left out of things.

I would have liked Audrey to see the National People's Congress Hall during one of the glittering banquets the Communists turned on for visitors. She wouldn't believe me when I told her of the lavish hospitality in a land where most people did not get enough to eat. I used to watch the faithful Communists stuffing themselves at tables overflowing with heaped dishes of pork, beef, duck, chicken, fish, fruits and sweets. All manner of delicacies, including caviare and champagne, disappeared in a twinkling. These sumptuous banquets were among the advantages of being a high-ranking party member. Sometimes the Chinese celebrated one or two banquets a week, and on special occasions one each night. "How can they turn on these feasts when their own people are hungry?" Audrey asked me. "Surely it can't make a very good impression on the visiting delegations?" I didn't think so either.

It was amusing to study the psychology of the seating arrangements for correspondents. At less important functions there was a touch of co-existence when Farquhar, Ullmann and I would be allowed to sit among Communists, but at the very grand banquets the division was most rigid. Top Chinese officials of the Information Department sat with the Russians, Hungarians, East Germans and Albanians. On second-grade tables came slightly lesser lights in the Foreign Ministry who entertained Czechs, Poles, Roumanians and Bulgarians. Next in line were fellow-travelling Westerners working for Communist papers, published mostly in Europe. On the last table, almost empty, sat Farquhar, Ullmann, Bogunovic and I. At several functions Suwito, correspondent of the Indonesian news agency Antara, would be lumped in with us four scoundrels. I guessed the Chinese figured that the unfortunate Suwito, being neither fish nor fowl, should not be allowed to dine with the élite at the most pukka of the banquets. His table position varied according to how the see-sawing relations between Peking and Djakarta were going.

Perhaps, when preparing the seating, the Information Department's bureaucrats consulted a thin booklet they issued to correspondents. It listed the names of some forty reporters living in Peking, obviously mentioned in order of importance. Heading the group were three *Pravda* men. Then came the three correspondents of Tass, the Soviet news agency, then *Izvestia* and *Komsomol Pravda*. There followed correspondents from North Korea and Hanio, from East Berlin, Prague, Warsaw, Budapest and Bucharest. Toward the end came the names of such men as Alan Winnington, of the London *Daily Worker*, Michael Shapiro who appeared to be working for some journal called *World News*, Israel Epstein who wrote for the *National Guardian* in New York and a gentleman with the name of Fairfax-Cholmeley who was employed by the *New World Review*. There was an Italian from *Unita*, Sarzi Amade. *L'Humanité*, the French Communist paper, was represented by a soft-spoken man named Vidal. Even tiny

Austria had its Communist correspondent in Peking, a typical Viennese named Harry Sichrovsky, not overjoyed but philosophical about life in Peking. He was interested in Asia, and China to him was an assignment with a difference. The Canadian *Tribune* was represented first by a diehard Communist named Sydney Gordon, but during my term a much gentler character, Bert Whyte, took over. Tailing the list were two correspondents from Yugoslavia and the three Western imperialists. Branko Bogunovic was placed fourth last, before us three. Ronnie Farquhar, of Reuters, was next, followed by Bernard Ullmann. I was distinctly honoured. My name was the very last in the book. Everything was beginning to point to the fact that I was not very popular in Peking.

In April the Chinese handshakes I received at Government and Communist Party functions became noticeably flabbier. Obviously the Chinese were tiring of the *Globe and Mail*. Certain Americans did not like us either. I had been wondering how *Time* would handle the interview I had given to one of its representatives in Hongkong. My airmail copy of the magazine came as I was growing increasingly conscious that officials in Peking were becoming cooler toward me.

I had not been too happy about the fact that *Time* had been chasing me for a story, because relations between my paper and the magazine had never been the best. The *Time* boss, Henry R. Luce, is one of Peking's greatest detractors in the U.S. He sees Chinese Communism as the most evil social system ever created. Because the *Globe* had set up a North American news bureau in Peking, *Time* decided to attack us. In its Press section, under the heading "How To Get Along", *Time* wrote in April 1960:

"Last October, after Peking granted a temporary visa to Frederick C. Nossal of the Toronto *Globe and Mail* (circ. 226,000). Nossal joined a corps of foreign correspondents distinguished mainly for partisan reporting. Indeed, of Peking's twenty-five man complement of visiting newsmen, only two others—both wire-service men, one from Agence France-Presse and one from Reuters, Ltd.—are of the non-Communist press. After reading thousands of words of Nossal's copy, his hosts expressed themselves as more than satisfied with the new visitor. Conferring on him the distinction of being the Western Hemisphere's first Red China-based newsman, they extended Nossal's visa another six months—and even let him bring in a car.

"From Peking's point of view, such courtesies to the *Globe* and the *Globe*'s Nossal were no more than reciprocal. In Red China's longstanding suit for admission to the United Nations, the Toronto *Globe* is a warm Canadian ally. 'To refuse to recognise the real, effective Chinese government is bad enough,' said the *Globe* in an editorial last August. 'But to pretend that a rump régime, decaying on a small island, is the true government of China is sheer folly.'

"During his first six months in Peking, Austrian-born Correspondent Nossal, 33, has done little to impair the *Globe*'s diplomatic relations with Red China. Bland, approving copy has flowed westward, uncensored, on Red China officialdom ('gracious and courteous'), babies ('cute and chubby and cuddlesome'), the sights in the capital ('Peking is almost ready for the tourists; it has little to be ashamed of and much to be proud of'), Premier Chou En-lai ('vibrant personality'), and industry ('The organization of China's industrial enterprises is excellent'). Sometimes his stories have sounded as if they were translated from the original Red Chinese: 'The West must come to China, even if it involves the loss of Formosa. The world has reached a stage where most nations would probably admire the U.S. for withdrawal from Formosa.'

"Critical copy has been rare and mild. To Nossal, 'gentle' was the word for Red Chinese thought control. In another dispatch he wrote: 'Here in China, if the weaklings (or rightists or anyone who isn't for the ruling circles) make too much noise, they are silenced smartly.'

"Then he added: 'Any Western commentators who suggest that the masters of Peking do away with their critics are talking utter nonsense.'

"Nossal's uncritical reporting from Red China can be explained partly in terms of Red China's low tolerance for any other kind, partly because he went to Peking under orders from the *Globe* to stick to features and to avoid antagonizing his hosts. In any event, it hardly seems worth the expense."*

When the *Time* attack on the Peking operation reached me, I had lived under Chinese Communism for more than six

*Courtesy *Time*; copyright Time Inc. 1960.

months, and had by now changed my mind about Formosa. The piece *Time* quoted was written after I had been in China only some weeks, and on the surface it did not then look as if the Chinese were suffering very greatly under Communism. But when the realisation came to me that China's physical progress had been achieved at the cost of freedoms which are fundamental to the advancement of humanity, I knew why the U.S. could never willy-nilly throw ten million people on Formosa to the winds. Yet I still believe that the Western powers must approach China more realistically if they wish to achieve peace in the Far East. But, just as everyone else who has studied the Formosan problem carefully, I still do not know how this question can be resolved in the near future. Pearl Buck, the veteran writer on China, suggests that if left to themselves the Communists and Nationalists would find a solution. I am afraid this is an over-simplification of the problem, since negotiations between Peking and Taipei would degenerate into a rather one-sided business once Washington indicated that American forces are no longer willing to protect Formosa. Chinese Communist armies would launch massive attacks from the mainland, sooner or later, and would quickly seize control of the island.

The weakness of the *Time* article lay in its complete one-sidedness. But obviously it was aimed not at those people who had read my China reports but at anyone who had not. A *Globe and Mail* headline on one of my articles had said, "Thought Control in China Gentle But Frightening". I was trying to show that Chinese methods of indoctrination were non-violent and therefore all the more insidious and terrifying. *Time* had conveniently picked out the adjective "gentle", and had deleted every other word in the article which ran to about two full columns of print. There were clearly great gaps in the *Time* piece which talked about the car but omitted to mention that Audrey and the four children had now joined me in what was a fairly unusual family venture. At first I was very angry because I couldn't see what possible purpose such a one-sided report could have. Later on, in Hongkong, one of their men in the Far East, asked me why I hadn't written a sizzling letter to *Time*, and apologised for the report.

Audrey agreed that I shouldn't write to *Time* from Peking.

"Why don't you send it to Miss Chen at the Foreign Ministry?" she smiled.

"Because I want to show it to her—personally. I'd like to see her face when she reads it."

Only a few days passed before I was summoned by the Information Department. I had tried vainly for some weeks to obtain a travel permit for Tientsin where the car was waiting to be collected. My application met with blank silence. The interpreters at the Hsin Chiao made a serious faux pas one day when they bought my Tientsin rail ticket without authority. This had to be given back, and—after much protest—I had to meet the cancellation fee.

"You may come to the Information Department tomorrow," I was told by phone. My appointment at the Foreign Ministry was for 11 a.m. on April 26. The Embassy people had thought it most unusual that a permit to Tientsin, which was almost invariably granted with only a few questions asked, had been refused.

I walked along Chungwenmen Tachieh to the Wai Chiao Pu next day feeling sure the interview would hold some surprises. I was there sharp at eleven and was kept cooling my heels for several minutes. Today there was no Hsu Huang. Nor had the other Deputy Director, Kang Mao-chao, turned up. I no longer ranked as a correspondent who deserved to be received by Madame Kung Peng's deputies. Only Miss Chen and an assistant were there to see me.

"Would you explain the main purpose of your journey to Tientsin," Miss Chen began. The wretched city was only two hours away by train, but anybody would think I had asked them to shoot me up to the moon. I had given the reason for the Tientsin trip during several phone conversations, and had applied in writing for the permit, telling the Foreign Ministry why I wanted to go. Now I began all over again.

"On the advice of the Department of Trade I have imported a car, and have obtained an import licence," I said. "The car is waiting to be collected from Tientsin. I could have it shipped up by rail which would cost 250 yuan. By travelling to Tientsin myself, I can have the car driven back to Peking by a Chinese chauffeur at a considerable saving. Mr. Ullmann of Agence France-Presse is willing to lend me his chauffeur for a day."

"Yes," said Miss Chen, "that will be perfectly all right." Then she added in a most casual manner, "Of course, you know that we are not prepared to extend your present visa. Is it worth your while having the car in Peking for only one month?"

I had told Audrey before leaving the hotel that we had only about six more weeks in those two cramped rooms, so she wasn't to worry any more. It was said in jest, of course, but now I was sufficiently prepared to reply very quietly: "No, Miss Chen, as a matter of fact I didn't know, but since you've told me, what's the position of my newspaper? I am merely one reporter. What about the Peking Bureau of the *Globe and Mail?*"

She said that the paper could make a further visa application for another man but had not yet done so. I definitely could not stay. I asked her the reasons for the refusal. She said the Chinese Chargé d'Affaires' office in London had informed a member of the *Globe and Mail*'s London staff that the Foreign Ministry would not extend my personal visa. "We feel our reasons have been made perfectly clear in London," she said. In order not to affect my reporting of China, which had lately become far more critical, my editors in Toronto had only hinted vaguely that I might have to leave Peking. They had hoped, as we had done, that by allowing my whole family to come in, the Chinese authorities were indicating they would be prepared to grant an extension. Everything— including advice to me late in February that I could bring in the car, office furniture and a refrigerator—seemed to point to the permanent nature of the operation.

I pulled the *Time* clipping out of my pocket and stuck it under Miss Chen's nose. "The Americans think I'm China's best friend," I said. She glanced at it briefly. The situation was really rather funny. Not a flicker of amusement passed over her face. Her eyes gave not the slightest hint of what she was thinking. "What date was it printed?" she asked. "I'm not quite sure. April 18, I think," I told her and added, "It seems I can't please either side. I would like to make one point. Quite apart from the fact that it has cost my newspaper a considerable sum to bring me and my family, with many of our possessions to China, I have incurred personal expenses, and a great deal of personal inconvenience. I realised all along that you could refuse to extend my visa at any time, but I think in view of the circumstances you could at least tell me personally the reasons for the Foreign Ministry's decision."

Miss Chen stuck closely to her instruction. "We feel the matter has been made perfectly clear already in London," she repeated. "And as regards the authorities allowing your family to come to China, we did this as a personal favour to you. We have gone to the trouble of informing you of our decision now, weeks before your visa expires, to give you an opportunity to make all the necessary arrangements for your departure."

I thanked her for this because, of course, they needn't have done so. I have heard of people trying vainly to find out a week, sometimes days, before the expiry of their visas whether or not it would be extended. Often visitors have had to leave in a great hurry.

The whole interview took only half an hour. Before I left I requested for the third time a reason for my banishment. Miss Chen, for the third time, repeated her statement that the Foreign Ministry felt this had been clarified already.

The *Globe's* man in London, George Bain, told me later no specific charges against me had been made by the Chinese Chargé d'Affaires. There were vague conversations about some of my articles, and suggestions by the Chinese that I shouldn't express my own opinions. In a subsequent announcement the *Globe and Mail* told its readers the Chinese had said my reports "had not been, in all respects, accurate". The editor and publisher, Oakley Dalgleish, said in a front-page statement that he had decided to close the Peking Bureau, and had refused to nominate another correspondent to replace me because no specific inaccuracies were listed by the Foreign Ministry.

"Our intention," Dalgleish said, "was that the *Globe and Mail's* representative in Peking would report the news and the background to the news honestly and objectively without favour or rancour."

Time magazine naturally had to have another crack at us. Their first piece was completely discounted by the Chinese decision to throw me out. *Time* felt it had to print an explanation. Accordingly the *Time* editors in New York wrote:

"Waiting in Hongkong for the visa that would permit him to enter Red China, Correspondent Frederick C. Nossal of the Toronto *Globe and Mail* was upset by a series of frustrating delays. Why were Peking's masters keeping him out? 'I can't understand it,' complained Nossal, 'when I can do them so much good.' Peking finally got Nossal's point, granted him a temporary visa last October, later extended it for six months and thereby made him the Western Hemisphere's only China-based newspaperman. In his eight months on the job, Nossal gave his hosts scant cause for offense, generally depicted Red

Chinese life in the most glowing terms (*Time*, April 18). But even that was not enough: last week the *Globe and Mail* announced that the Chinese Communists, accusing Nossal of inaccuracy, had ordered him to leave. Correspondent Nossal could not understand why—and neither could anyone else who had read his effulgent dispatches."*

Presumably *Time* kept a better record of my various conversations in Hongkong during the last days of September 1959 than I did, because I certainly can't remember venturing the opinion that a little-known newspaper reporter could do the Peking régime a lot of good. The "series of frustrating delays" in Hongkong were a matter of a few days. My passport shows I arrived in Hongkong by air from Australia on September 26, 1959—and crossed into China on September 30.

The *Globe and Mail* considered this a good opportunity to break its silence about the *Time* attacks. It reprinted the comment in an editorial "for the attention of our readers who have read Mr. Nossal's dispatches". The editorial went on: "It must be assumed that this *Time* report is as factual as any other article in what is supposed to be the successful man's guide to world affairs. Certainly it is typical of the reporting with which Canadians are insulted every week in the four pages that *Time* considers are enough to constitute a 'Canada Edition'."

I don't think the *Time* pieces harmed me. "You needn't be very concerned," a British diplomat said. "You can start worrying when *Time* says something good about you!"

*Courtesy *Time*; copyright Time Inc. 1960.

17

CHILD TOILERS AND RED SCARVES

Back at the Hsin Chiao Audrey was unpacking one of our big trunks when I burst in. "You can put all that stuff back again," I grinned. "In six weeks we're on our way." I cabled the *Globe and Mail* stressing that I would make a further application for an extension, although I didn't think we had a hope. Then I began mapping out my last weeks in Peking. There would be no immediate difficulty with my work in Hongkong, for I had a great deal of unpublished material gathered in China which had not yet been worked up into articles for the *Globe*. But illustrating this would be more of a problem, and I decided accordingly to take during those last weeks as many pictures as possible; pictures of virtually anything—bazaars, building sites, old men, little boys, Audrey and the family in pedicabs, food queues, hotels, buses, Chinese baby cars. And I got many photographs of Chinese children; children working on the roads, girls planting trees, schoolboys marching. The children of China hold the key to the Asia of tomorrow. There was one good shot of a youngster directing a party of boys across the street. He could not have been much older than ten. He was small and thin, and around his neck he wore his scarlet scarf. He pushed and shoved the others in his troop, among them boys much bigger than he was, and they followed his commands meekly. He was the leader, the young activist, the top-dog in this group of diligent, solid youngsters. The bossy boy was no longer a child, not in the Western sense. He was the Communist of tomorrow. In China, children are children for only such a short time, and then they become young Communists. They grow out of childhood too rapidly, so much so that many Chinese children are today less child-like than their uneducated parents. In the schools and in the streets it is obvious that the Communists have placed all their future hopes on the children, who are better dressed, better fed, often better housed than the parents; when parents are too disinterested in Communism, the State funnels its propaganda through the children.

It was little wonder that Chinese schoolchildren I saw were serious. As soon as they left the toddling stage, they were taught their Communism—morning, noon and night. They, too, studied and toiled, along with the rest of the nation.

The Communist State has no time for childhood as such, not once a child learns to use his hands and his brain. Childhood, for the Communists, is the time when the mind is young and pliant, when it can be moulded more easily into the conformist pattern, when it is prepared to absorb any kind of knowledge pumped into it without asking too many embarrassing questions. Childhood consists of years of learning the simplest yet most important fact of Communist life—that it is a holy thing to be allowed to work for the State. I saw for myself on many occasions children making roads, digging earth, breaking rock, pulling carts, watering trees, cleaning streets, and washing windows. These youngsters, whom the Communists had convinced so completely, made the Western school pupils seem like young beachcombers with too much time on their hands. Our children were taught that work was a part of life, an important part, certainly, but that there were other aspects to life also. The Chinese child is being told that life is work and work is life. The teachers I was allowed to interview were convinced Marxists so far as I could make out. During a series I did on Chinese education I visited schools catering for all ages, although for some unexplained reason I was not permitted to go to Peking University. But Yen gladly took me to Wong Tsi Ma Lane, a five-minute cab ride from the Hsin Chiao, to a kindergarten with two hundred children aged between three and seven. Half lived in the kindergarten all week except Sunday, when they went home. The other half were returned to their parents every evening. The director of the kindergarten was Chin Hsu-tsin, a small and gentle woman with a soft smile. To make sure of her facts she kept referring to a little red diary she had with her.

"Before 1959 most of the children lived at home with their parents," she explained, "but when the parents became rather busy during the 'big leap forward' we took a hundred of the children as boarders."

She claimed that with nourishing cooking, the weights of ninety per cent of the children had increased, and certainly all the ones I saw there looked in the best of health.

"Through games we teach them collective ideas," she went on.

"We try to create an enthusiasm for labour in the minds of the children. They play at being a driver or bus conductor, a zoo-keeper or a cook. It helps them to improve their language. We also teach them to look after their own clothes. When one child is lying on the ground playing, others will come up and say, 'Don't make your clothes dirty like this because the teacher will have to wash them.' We cultivate in them a love for the leaders of the country. We say, 'Why do you think you can have such a fine kindergarten?' And then we tell them it is because of our great leaders. We tell them stories about Chairman Mao Tse-tung, and sometimes we may compose a poem eulogising some of the leaders. One mother has written to us to say the kindergarten is giving the children more love than their own mothers could. Though we have scored some achievements, there is still consider-able opportunity to improve our work."

My next visit was to a co-educational primary school with six grades. There were thirty-one teachers for the 900 students (aged from seven to fourteen). Like most buildings in the old parts of Peking, the school was hidden from the street by a high, grey wall. Tang Hsi-hsung, the principal, took me into different classes, and after a brief greeting the lessons would continue. Children's eyes were glued either to the blackboard or to the teacher's face. They must have been warned about my visit, and yet their real interest in the work was evident. Since there was no uniform (apart from the red Young Pioneers' scarf) the schoolchildren wore anything, making them far more colour-ful in their dress than their parents. Their exemplary be-haviour and wordless obedience fitted into the pattern of a disciplined society. Of the 900 children, 110 were boarders who went home only on Sundays. Parents of another 350 children had applied for them to be boarders but there wasn't room. Out in the yard, the children were having a morning break from class, doing physical jerks in the playground and shouting in unison, "Train yourself to be healthy—so you can defend your motherland and world peace!" We went into the dormitories each of which had fourteen beds and on the cobbled floor underneath every bed stood two tin washbasins—one for the face, the other for the feet, Mr. Tang explained.

"The trend in China is toward boarding schools," he told me. "We have proved that the children who are boarders do better work, and more homework than the others. We get the best results with our boarders. The whole purpose of the training they get is to teach them discipline, and make them completely self-reliant."

As we returned to his office, we saw in one of the school courtyards a low, home-made ping-pong table. I wondered why the Chinese were so crazy about table tennis, which in their schools was treated as a serious sport, on a par with baseball in the United States, ice hockey in Canada and cricket in Britain. Some eighteen months later I learned the reason for the nation-wide campaign to find China's best ping-pong players. In April 1961 the 26th table tennis world championships were held in Peking— with China taking first place in the men's team championship, the men's singles, and the women's singles. The Chinese gained second place in the women's team championship, the women's doubles and the mixed doubles. I suppose they were planning this sporting scoop in the days I was inspecting Peking's schools.

I would not be surprised if the Chinese were hoping to take part in the 1964 Tokyo Olympics. Sports played included volley ball, basketball, football, even baseball. Schools, factories and communes had their own swimming and rowing teams. Many of the youngsters longed to join sports institutes and regular teams because Chinese sportsmen invariably got more and better food. For those interested in their material well-being, it was important to be among the favoured few in China, particularly in times of food shortages. Tang said parachuting was also classed as a school sport.

"But the children don't jump from planes surely?"

"Most of the boys and girls jump from towers, but among the older ones a few selected students have jumped from planes," he said. "Not from this school of course, but when they get older."

At my next port of call, Peking's senior high school No. 65, principal Chou Kwan wasn't very interested in parachuting. Politics was his speciality. It was, he said, one of the most vital subjects taught at the school. Every one of the 845 students, boys and girls from sixteen to eighteen was taught politics.

"What form of politics?" I asked.

"During the political course, students are taught the fundamental theories of Marxism, and learn about China's political economy," he said, listing the courses taught as Chinese language, mathematics (which included geometry and algebra), physics,

176

The riverfront at Shanghai, with ancient junks sailing down the Whang Poo River.

A typical young beauty of Communist China, wearing a white working shirt over her printed cotton jacket, and—China's latest status symbol—a wristwatch.

One of the lanes in Tsang's Alleyway, the experimental commune in Shanghai.

Seamstress Ne Hsua-tsen in one of the unsuccessful urban communes. She is mentioned in Chapter 19.

chemistry, biology, history, geography, foreign languages, athletics, politics and physical labour (which took in such matters as a visit to a factory). For one week in the year, students helped peasants gather the harvest. School hours were from eight till noon, and from 2.30 to 5.30 p.m. Chou said some students went home for lunch, others stayed at school. It depended on how far away they lived.

"In many of our schools," I said, "different religions are taught regularly. Do Chinese schools teach religion?" Many times I asked questions just to see Chinese reactions.

"No," said Chou. "Religion is not taught at school, but pupils are free to practise their religion. If they wish they can go to church on Sundays. At school we train students to help them get the right cultural and socialist ideas into their minds." It surprised me to find children had to sit for an examination in athletics. Those who failed only in athletics could graduate, but if they missed in another subject like Chinese language or politics they had to repeat the final class.

"What foreign languages do you teach here?"

"English and Russian are the most popular."

"In that order?"

"More students take Russian than English."

"What percentage fail when it comes to graduation time?"

Chou Kwan didn't tell me. Instead he said that usually ninety-eight per cent of students, often more, passed their final exams.

"That's a very high percentage. We don't do nearly as well back in Canada."

Chou put on his Communist Party face. The tape recorder inside his head began turning.

"The reason for the good results here is the correct leadership by the Communist Party. The party follows the correct policies, and this leads to greater efforts both by the teachers and by the students. That's why so many pass." Obviously a highly-educated society would not be satisfied with such pat, dull answers given by everyone in the land, from Cabinet Ministers to farm labourers. The Chinese Communists are fully aware of the dangers of education to their particular social system, and to ensure their masses will not be enlightened too rapidly, or too well, dreamed up a plan which many educators—both in and out of China—considered a step back.

Peking decreed that children must not merely be educated. Physical labour was every bit as important as study. Toil by schoolchildren was one of the dogmas Mao has grafted to Marxism. Education for education's sake would never do. It was necessary to follow the mass line, and since the masses worked, children had to work also. And yet, considering the vast problems, the achievements in education have been considerable. Taking education to the masses has meant that Communist teaching now reaches virtually everyone in the land. Schools are run by the State, by people's communes, by offices and industrial plants, by mines. School broadcasts follow peasants into the fields. On the trains I suffered regularly while travellers were taught by radio how to speak correct Chinese. There was never silence in China. The brain, the eyes, the ears— the whole being in fact, had to be fully occupied all the time. This was Peking's psychological defence against anti-Communist thought. Educate people in Communism, and do not give them the chance or the time to question such education.

One story I cabled from Peking dealt with a report by the Education Minister Yang Hsie-feng, who had announced that in the past decade China had established about a million schools and other educational institutions of various types. In these, 200,000,000 people had received education.

"In the overwhelming majority of areas," said Yang, "almost every production brigade in the people's communes has its own kindergarten and primary school, every people's commune its own junior middle (high or secondary) school, and every county its own senior school. Every administrative region has its own secondary technical schools and junior colleges, and every province, municipality and autonomous region various types of institutes of higher education."

A round-up of education statistics claimed that in 1958 educational enrolments showed eighty-five per cent of school-age children in China were attending school. In that year 31,000,000 children received pre-school education, 86,000,000 went to primary schools, 10,520,000 to middle schools, and 660,000 to colleges and universities.

Peking claimed that compared with 1949, three and a half times more pupils attended primary school, four times as many went to colleges and universities and that there were six and a half times as many secondary school students. At the time these statistics were released the biggest educational revolution had been in the pre-school age group. In 1959, said the Chinese, 238 times more children went to kindergartens than before the Communists took office. According to more recent figures, middle school enrolment is now 12,000,000, and the present proportion of children attending school has risen from eighty-five to eighty-seven per cent.

At the April session of the National People's Congress in 1960, the Chinese Communist Party made sure everyone knew that manual labour for schoolchildren was now a nation-wide policy. While outside the congress hall, under grey afternoon skies, children practised marching in Tien An Men Square to prepare for the May Day celebrations, Vice-Premier Lu Ting-yi said China was planning a new education system lasting ten years which would reduce by two years the present primary and secondary schooling, each of which lasted six years. Despite this he wanted educational standards raised and more participation in physical labour by children. The plan sounded crazy.

"With primary and secondary education taking up too long a time it is difficult to popularise education and to raise its quality," Lu said. This was meant to explain away the two lost years.

"He claims the less study, the better the education," I said to Farquhar. Ronnie grimaced. None of us could make out what the Chinese were getting at. We spent the evening trying to work out how educators could get better results and reach higher standards by having children spend less hours in class, fewer years at school—and on top of this making them do more manual labour.

A few days after Lu Ting-yi's speech I was talking about the new schooling system with Yen, the interpreter. I said I felt it was not a bad thing for children to do some work provided it did not interfere with their studies. We were trundling by car through what was obviously a newly-established urban commune, and saw a party of young school-children helping to widen a road. They were gathering bits of stone from one side of the road, filling baskets and carting them across to the other side where they dumped them to make a new foundation. It was not terribly heavy work, and the children looked as if they were having a thoroughly good time. It was with the older children that the more ominous results of this educational system began to appear. After the Communist officials, it was the children of about twelve to eighteen who seemed least friendly towards foreigners. These hard-eyed teenagers had their heads so full with Communist talk of the greatness of China, they had no time for people from other lands. With the Communist régime in China over a decade old, most of the teenagers had forgotten how life was before. They knew only Communism. And for the most part they seemed to like it. Children are often happiest when they are told firmly what to do by someone they respect. I didn't much care for the Chinese teenagers. What a difference there was between them and the carefree, fun-loving youngsters of the West who too often are ignorant of the dangers they will have to face in the future.

The youth of China is, on the whole, convinced that both Communism and hard work will help their country. This conviction is written all over their faces. I heard it in their speech, saw it in their assured walk and confident posture, and no wonder! A vast, powerful, ambitious nation was coming to birth before their eyes, and they wanted to play a part both in its trials and tribulations, and in its progress.

That young people believed the Communist creed was shown by the lack of juvenile crime. Not once did I see the Chinese equivalent of a beatnik or a teddy-boy. There was no evidence of teenage delinquents. It is safer to walk the streets at night in Peking than in most of the world's capitals. There are no hoodlums, no thugs and only a few thieves. The general honesty of the Chinese people is one of the most remarkable victories the Peking régime has scored. Although there is lying and repression on the national level, as regards individual morality, the Communists have made China into one of the most honest nations on earth. This, of course, became less marked during the food crisis when men and women who were either cold or hungry or often both, stole more readily than before. And it would be silly to pretend that just because newspapers don't print crime stories as a rule, the country had no criminals. But for a nation in which corruption and cheating had before been fully accepted by all spheres of society, from the richest to the poorest, China is an excellent example of what a disciplined society can accomplish in detecting and suppressing crime. Nobody believes the Communists have succeeded in changing human nature so drastically that the Chinese nation has suddenly decided, to a man, never to steal again. Stealing no longer pays; the thief has realised that in this rigidly policed state he can be caught too easily.

Often it was hard in China to distinguish good from evil. The dividing line was dangerously thin. The national vices of the Communist system, for example, were hidden behind a screen of praiseworthy self-denial by millions of individuals. This superficial morality had a shattering effect on those visitors who called into Peking briefly, or who were given the red carpet treatment as they were whirled around China by the Communists. On the surface, you get the definite impression that China today is so clean, so holy, so good, so hard-working. Beneath it all lies the unpardonable crime of the Peking régime in depriving individuals of their free will, a gruesome nation-wide sin not apparent to the foreigner unless he lives there for some time, because the new China is a completely closed society.

18

"MEET CHINA'S LAST EMPEROR!"

I was cabling several stories a week toward the end of my stay in China, filing them mainly via Hongkong where Bill Stevenson would retransmit the material to Toronto. In this way we took advantage of the British Commonwealth penny-a-word rate for Press cables, and saved quite a lot, since direct cables from Peking were prohibitively expensive. Not only China, but many Asian countries try to boost their foreign exchange earnings by charging excessively high cable rates. "Won't the *Globe* think you're spending too much on cables?" Audrey wanted to know all the same about mid-May. "They won't have the Peking dateline for much longer," I told her. "They'll scream if they want me to stop." Having that little word Peking at the top of your story gave it a kind of magic. The Chinese knew this. At most functions, Information Department officials had reminded Farquhar, Ullmann and myself what a unique opportunity we had in reporting directly from Peking. With me almost out of the running, there would soon be only the two news agency boys again. Hsu Huang told us there were whole drawers of letters from correspondents and newspapers asking for permission to enter China. The Chinese now allowed me no further interviews, but there were quite a few good news stories to be found. Premier Chou En-lai returned from his abortive Delhi talks with Nehru on Tuesday, May 17, 1960, and the diplomatic corps, and foreign correspondents waited at the airport to meet him. Moments before Chou's plane touched down, a breathless Tass man arrived on the tarmac with whispers about about the Summit collapse in Paris. Michael Stewart, the British Minister, could not confirm the story that the meeting was over. He said he had heard something over the short-wave radio during the night, but the news was vague. Some of the Chinese spread stories that Khrushchev and his delegation were already back in Moscow. Their glee was a few days premature, but the news which came crackling over my short-wave radio that evening was grim. The turn of world events in Paris had a shattering impact on the foreigners in Peking. Most of the diplomats who met Chou had been sad and silent when they heard that the Paris Summit was crumbling over the U.2 spy plane affair. The global crisis completely overshadowed the failure of Chou's main mission to New Delhi, which had been aimed at patching things up with India over the Himalayan frontier quarrel.

As rumours of Khrushchev's actions in Paris ran like wild-fire along the line of diplomats waiting to greet the Chinese Premier, even Soviet Ambassador S. V. Chervonenko looked anxious. Only the Chinese seemed pleased. Their attitude was, "We told you so. The West doesn't want to talk peace with anyone." The Peking régime could now say with renewed confidence that their constant warnings about "U.S. war preparations behind a screen of peace" had proved correct. The moment Peking had confirmation from Paris that the Summit was over before it had started, they organised their mightiest anti-U.S. rally yet. More than three million Chinese crowded into Tien An Men Square and along Changan Boulevard for several miles to scream abuse at Washington.

A few days after Chou's arrival we were back at the airport to meet Lord Montgomery, arriving for the first of his two recent visits to Communist China as the guest of Mao Tse-tung. The Communists had sent one of their latest glamour planes, a Russian-built Ilyushin 18 prop jet, to Canton just to fetch Monty, and the huge aircraft had flown north virtually empty. Monty said he wanted to talk to the Chinese leaders and ask them about their stand toward the West. He spent hours with Chou En-lai in Peking and later met Mao Tse-tung in Shanghai. The Chinese thought Monty might be useful in channelling the official Peking line to Western newspapers, and they were right, since on his return he wrote a series of positive articles which ignored the harsher aspects of the régime. Over lunch with Michael Stewart, Montgomery wondered about attracting Chou En-lai to Britain. "I've already invited him and I'm asking him again when we next meet," he went on. "Do you think he'll come?" Present at the British Minister's luncheon party were Ronnie Farquhar, Richard Harris, of the London *Times*, and I. Stewart, who was host, said he thought Chou would not visit

Britain unless he was officially invited by Prime Minister Mac-
millan. But Monty didn't see it that way. "He could come as
my private guest. On his own. Well, I suppose he would
have to bring an interpreter." None of us was sure whether
the Field Marshal was serious or not. Personally, I think he
was fooling.

The Chinese whirled Montgomery around Peking at high
speed, showing him factories and communes, fêting him at
banquets each night of his brief stay. The oddest function he
attended was the Peking banquet given him by Chou En-lai just
before he flew south to meet Mao. It was a fantastic affair, and a
stranger collection of guests was rarely seen at an official Communist function. Monty, enjoying himself immensely, met
generals who were friends of Chiang Kai-shek, wealthy Chinese
capitalists who were co-operating with the Peking régime and
former war criminals whom the Communists had pardoned.
Chou En-lai took Monty's elbow and led him to a meek, middle-
aged man dressed in a faded, ill-fitting boiler suit. "Meet China's
last emperor!" said Chou.

Henry Pu Yi, now 55, had been the last emperor of the Manchu
Dynasty which ended in 1912. Until 1945 he sat on the throne as
the Japanese-appointed emperor of the puppet state of Manchukuo
in Manchuria. Pu Yi shook Monty by the hand. "I'm a new man
—the new Pu Yi," he muttered. "He's a very good gardener, the
new Pu Yi," someone told Monty laughingly. The former
emperor was now working in a botanical garden.

Montgomery was having a grand time. He passed to former
Kuomintang General Tu Yu-ming. "He fought against Chen
Yi," said the Premier. Marshal Chen Yi, who was also in the
group doing the rounds of the guests, guffawed. He stepped forward and shook his one-time adversary by the hand. Monty asked
General Tu how Chen Yi had managed to defeat his army of one
million men. Tu grinned. "All my men went over to the other
side," he said.

The Chinese were obviously trying to impress Montgomery
with the democracy of Communism. He seemed convinced that
the nation's leaders were most reasonable people, very willing to
be good friends with the West, and left China less than a week
after his arrival. One of his remarks kept the dour Communists
grinning for weeks later. He was being shepherded around an
industrial plant in Peking when the party came across a large

painting of a man whose face was almost hidden by a mass of hair and a bushy beard.

"Who's that?" asked Monty, with soldierly distaste.

"Karl Marx, sir," whispered a British aide.

Monty grunted, and turned to his Chinese hosts.

"Marx needs a haircut," he announced and moved on.

*   *   *

Towards the end of my visit it became clear that China's food troubles were worsening. One Vice-Premier, Tan Chen-lin, who, by the way, was not mentioned as being present at the 1962 National People's Congress, announced in a speech in April 1960 that four hundred million people were eating in community dining-rooms in China, but that this number wasn't enough. The nation's communal eating habits had to be expanded, he said. In the same speech Tan reprieved millions of birds which had escaped the anti-sparrow campaign. The Communists had issued a top-level party directive about pest extermination which said, "In twelve years beginning 1956, rats, sparrows, flies and mosquitoes should be practically wiped out wherever possible," which meant people had pursued sparrows mercilessly. Zealous Communists caught sparrows in nets and ate them. Boys killed them with catapults. Soldiers shot them dead. In the cities and towns people beat drums day and night, never allowing the sparrows to settle for a moment's rest. The poor birds fluttered helplessly until they fell to the street completely spent, and were killed. Soon commune chiefs noted a sharp increase in insect pests. There were now too few sparrows. Grasshopper plagues ruined crops. Beetles and worms attacked fruit. The sparrow campaign came to a sudden halt. Tan Chen-lin told the peasants something they could have proved to him years before. "Sparrows are the natural enemies of insect pests which harm orchards and other trees," he said. "We should stop killing sparrows from now on." But what about the pest extermination directive, people asked. Tan had this worked out. Among China's four pests, bedbugs would replace sparrows. Article 27 of the National Programme for Agricultural Development now reads: "In twelve years beginning 1956, rats, bedbugs, flies and mosquitoes should be practically wiped out wherever possible." Chinese bedbugs were hopping mad about the amendment.

The most important local story in mid-1960 was the formation of the urban communes, the first detailed references being given at the April session of the National People's Congress. A few city communes had been conducted on an experimental basis ever since 1958. The Peking régime wanted all Chinese, and not merely the 500 million peasants, to join communes. For several weeks during May there was obvious commotion in several of Peking's suburbs. People marched about carrying flags and placards. Yen and the other interpreter would not tell me where urban communes had been formed, but Audrey and I came across one for ourselves during our tour of the city. A group of people were sewing great lengths of cloth in the middle of the street. Near-by footpaths were cluttered with piles of scrap metal. Housewives sat around plates of steel hammering away briskly. There was an interminable noise and bustle in the areas where communes had recently been formed. I was not allowed to enter or inspect any Peking commune officially, though we sneaked away in a taxi several times without an interpreter to take pictures.

We spent our last days in Peking saying good-bye to the few real friends we had made in China—Kaare and Liv Holum, Pete and Marit Metselaar, Joseph Kallukaren, of the Indian Embassy, our doctor Alec Petigura and his sparkling Chinese wife, Winnie, Derek and Mabel Houghton and, of course, Ronnie Farquhar, who agreed to come to all our farewell dinners at the Hsin Chiao only when I threatened to smuggle the hotel's recipe for chicken Stroganoff—the one dish he liked—out of the country for good. The Ullmanns gave us a party to which they invited several of the Eastern European Communist correspondents. Why hadn't I spent more time with them, the Communists wanted to know. They claimed I was being thrown out because I had not studied "the Communist point of view" sufficiently well. Also departing about the same time was Alan Winnington, the London *Daily Worker* correspondent, who had evidently had his fill of Peking. He was being transferred to East Berlin.

We did not know until the evening before we left whether we would be allowed to travel south via Shanghai. The following morning, the Shanghai travel permit stuck in my passport, we were off, with Hsu announcing proudly that the hotel manager had granted us the use of his personal car for our final drive through Peking. Ronnie Farquhar and Richard

Harris, the London *Times* man who left China a few days later helped us pile our suitcases and children into the back of the huge maroon Mercédès, and waved farewell from the steps of the Hsin Chiao Hotel. At the airport for once we did not have too long to wait until take-off. Six heavily-laden outcasts (we finally had to tell the children they were leaving China again so soon because the Chinese did not like what their father was writing) marched to the small plane. We were horribly overweight, and even little Shane had two plastic airline bags slung over his shoulder, with his favourite teddy-bear clutched in his hands as he climbed into the cabin of the two-engined aircraft.

Soon we were bouncing along the runway, and off into the air. We didn't stop bouncing for six hours, all the way to Shanghai. The aircraft was far too light, and popped through the sky like a ping-pong ball. The entire plane-load of passengers, including about ten children, went a variety of colours from grey to blue. The plane wasn't pressurised and there must have been a lack of oxygen inside the cabin. After an hour of extreme discomfort, Michelle went into a fitful sleep. Her breathing became so light Audrey and I were really worried. Behind us a Chinese child had lost consciousness. The air-hostess, young and boiler-suited, told passengers not to worry, that everything would be fine. She looked rather white herself.

"Let's go on to Canton by train," Audrey suggested in the plane after one particularly unpleasant lurch. But the moment we limped into the semi-circular airport building at Shanghai and dropped our gear on comfortable leather couches, all was well again.

Western-trained architects must have designed Shanghai airport. It had large bright tourist posters, placards advertising Shanghai-made goods, and shops selling fizzy drink, postcards, novelties, sweets and food. It was completely unlike the arid Peking air terminal with its self-conscious, pompous architecture. Who has ever heard of a modern airport with several dozen steps leading to the place where baggage is weighed? But paying commuters were unimportant in China. The wide steps at Peking airport gave the terminal building an imposing air. It was designed not for the ordinary traveller but for the VIP—who doesn't carry his own bags anyhow. Shanghai's architects had built their terminal before the Communists arrived. It was geared to take a much larger flow of passengers, and though far older than the recently-completed Peking airport, was incomparably more modern.

Two taxis took us to the Huping Hotel at the corner of Nanking Road and the Bund. Huang Fen, our interpreter, was a cordial fellow. He was rather quiet, and soft-pedalled on the propaganda. He had mapped out a full programme for us, which was carefully written into a little black book he carried; much of it had to be jettisoned for lack of time, but I agreed to take a trip to Ming Hang, a new satellite city Shanghai had built, if he would find me an urban commune. I had seen several of Peking's urban communes, I told him, and wanted to compare them with Shanghai's. Huang said a car would be waiting for me downstairs at 9 a.m.

*   *   *

We were having breakfast in the roof-top dining-room of the hotel when Huang Fen joined us. From our table we had a clear view of the Bund and the Whang Poo river. Ferries were ploughing back and forth. "When we're through with our programme, Mr. Huang, we might take the children for a ferry ride." I hadn't realised this would wipe Huang's good-morning smile off his face so fast. He consulted his diary and found it was not on the plan.

"Do you think there will be time?"

"Sure! We'll do it after lunch one day," I said. "Before an afternoon appointment. We can have a quick meal if we're short of time. Or we could take some sandwiches along on the ferry."

"Oh, no. Your family must take lunch. But do you know whether the ferries run in the afternoon?"

"If you don't know, I certainly wouldn't. They seem to be running all day. People are getting on and off just a few hundred yards from the hotel. Go to the window and have a look."

Huang was thoughtful. "Why do you want to go on the ferry?" he asked.

"Children like ferry rides, and I'll be able to shoot some good pictures of the Bund from the river."

"I shall make enquiries, and will let you know."

After breakfast Audrey and the children went off to look at the shops while Huang escorted me to the Shanghai Foreign Affairs Bureau where I wanted to pay Foreign Ministry officials my respects. I couldn't catch the name of the man who received me. He asked how long I had been in China, and had I travelled? He was a gracious, courteous Communist, and I wished he had been in Peking. Where had he been before the new government took office, I asked. He had served in the Red Army in the liberated areas from the time he was a teenager. Huang must have told him of my wish to visit an urban commune. He began a long dialogue about the total absence of urban communes in Shanghai. Since the idea was to form urban communes gradually, and step by step, he said, Shanghai had not yet begun its commune campaign. But in one district people were conducting an experiment, with an embryo urban commune, and if I were interested in going there they would be happy to receive me. I said, "Yes, of course, I would love to visit the experimental commune," and with this the interview closed.

Our first major engagement was to inspect the satellite city. It took the cab an hour, along a fair road, to reach the Ming Hang Hotel, where we were met by Mr. Pang Hsioa-wei, a puny hook-nosed fellow who either had too much work on his hands or had just bought a new timepiece. As we talked he looked at his watch at least once every two minutes. He wore a small pair of Chinese slippers on his wee feet which were jiggling nervously as he spoke. Before 1949, he said, Ming Hang was a bankrupt village. "The life of the working people was very poor. They didn't have enough to eat or to wear."

I settled back for the "brief introduction" having at least been allowed first to walk along a broad tree-lined boulevard sweeping through Ming Hang's centre, past highly modern buildings so I could take pictures while the afternoon sun was still out. Poor Pang was very worried about my camera, though I wasn't taking offensive pictures. I showed the black cars of party bosses outside the Ming Hang Hotel, a miniature car which had been built in a Shanghai motor plant, a child carrying some shopping home to mother, a factory girl posing for her boy friend's camera next to a new bicycle, girl road workers with wide-brimmed sunhats eating their lunch, and the general street scene which was airy and bright. After our stroll Pang, in between slurping his tea noisily, told how the village had changed.

The former population of 5,000 had grown to 70,000. Eleven big buildings in the main street had gone up in seventy-eight days, he said, and within three months all construction along the street was finished. Houses in Ming Hang were built to nine architectural designs, and there were five colours—white, pink, grey, pastel yellow and cream. They were pleasant in appearance from the outside, said Mr. Pang, and inside each apartment had a lavatory, bathroom, kitchen and balcony, as well as cupboards and built-in wardrobes.

Wringing his timid little hands, Mr. Pang repeated the well-worn phrases: "While carrying out the socialist line of construction, the Communist Party has paid great attention and shown much concern for the living standards of the people. The masses have deeply realised that they are now the masters of their country, and their initiative and creativeness have become so high that they are quickly building up their country." More furtive glances at the watch. Mr. Pang was scratching his ear, I scribbled into my notebook, and had begun jiggling his fingers as well as tapping his little feet. A nervous breakdown seemed imminent.

"There are thirty-one stores in the satellite city. Divided into five categories. The first are department stores catering for children's and ladies' needs, furniture, clothing, clocks and radios. Secondly, there are food shops, restaurants (including Islamic restaurants), snack bars and shops which sell iced drinks and fruit. Next are the service centres where you can have your laundry done, buy photographic equipment, and take baths. These service centres include barber shops and flower shops as well as community dining-halls. In the fourth category are bookshops, post offices, banks and pharmacies. Lastly there are the markets where people go for a variety of food, meat, vegetables and coal." Mr. Pang did not mention the ration tickets people needed to buy goods, nor did he explain what banks and pharmacies had in common. But he had swotted hard, and was now reciting his homework. "In this nice suburb, all school-age children go to school." My pencil moved mechanically across the page. I envied those visitors who could use this time for a mental snooze. "As regards culture, we have a workers' club, a cinema, a theatre, a cultural centre and libraries. Then there is health and hygiene. Ming Hang has two hospitals with 440 beds. Every school and factory has its own clinic. We have opened a small park here recently. Because of socialist construction, Ming Hang has undergone a fundamental change. From a former village has sprung a satellite city."

After going to all the trouble and expense of building this showplace, I thought, why in the hell don't the Communists have competent men to advertise it instead of employing this human gramophone record? "Under the leadership of Chairman Mao Tse-tung, we have grown very strong and we are prospering under socialist construction." I'd also had eight months of indoctrination, and at least could listen to this twaddle without going slowly crazy. It flooded into my ears and out again.

"How much do people earn?" I asked Pang. "We have mostly young workers here, and they would average seventy yuan a month. With two people in the family working, you could save quite a lot. The monthly rent for a small three-room apartment is ten yuan." For a brief instant, his eyes had a spark of life about them, but now the mental tape played on. "The tuition fees at our schools are very cheap. . . ."

It was my turn to look at the time. Mr. Pang paused for breath. There was a moment's silence, at which I clutched eagerly. "Would you kindly tell the gentleman that we have another appointment this evening," I said to Huang. "It's already getting dark and we'll have to take a meal at the hotel first. Thank him for giving us his time." I pointed meaningfully to Mr. Pang's watch.

On the return journey Huang told me that a visit had been arranged to an experimental urban commune. I hoped it would be more rewarding than Mr. Pang's satellite city.

19

SHANGHAI, THE FIRST URBAN COMMUNE

As we drove out to the Shanghai urban commune, I reflected how, some weeks earlier, I had been watching Mao Tse-tung on the brilliantly-lit stage of the National People's Congress Hall, when Vice-Premier Li Fu-chun, the bookish, grey-haired chairman of the State Planning Commission, told the 1,063 deputies present that "all the cities are now setting up people's communes in a big way". Mao, appearing for the first time at an important public function since the 1959 October celebrations, sat busily writing as Li read his ten thousand word speech.

Nobody was very clear initially what the urban communes were supposed to achieve, whether people would be re-housed and how many city communes would be formed. After the Congress was over, several of these questions were answered, mainly by the Chinese Press. Neighbourhood industries in urban communes would feed the large State-owned industrial enterprises, and would help to dispose of waste matter from the big plants. Urban commune members gathered scrap metal to be melted down, chemical waste which could be turned into fertiliser, and waste paper to be pulped. Small commune factories produced everything from insecticides, clothing and kitchenware for consumers to machine parts for the big plants around which the communes were originally formed.

The party thought that by herding city dwellers into the mess halls set up by the urban communes, they might reduce food consumption. The Peking leadership felt it had learned enough lessons from the mistakes committed in the rural communes to give urban communisation a mighty push along. By July 1960 the Communists claimed fifty-five million people were living in over a thousand urban communes with populations in each varying from several tens of thousands to almost half a million.

The citizens who evidently showed least interest in joining urban communes were the Shanghaiese. By the time Shanghai's few communes were mentioned publicly early in 1961, the entire communisation movement in the cities had virtually slowed to a halt. Shanghai's tardiness must have been very embarrassing for Tsao Ti-chiu, secretary of the city's Municipal Communist Party Committee. He had submitted to the 1960 National People's Congress a joint statement together with colleagues from Peking, Tientsin, Wuhan and Canton which said the five cities would set up urban communes. But there was a loophole. The statement said no attempt should be made to enroll everyone in the communes at the same time. People with doubts about urban commune life should not be persuaded to join. The Chinese Communists would most probably use the same excuse today if asked why urban communisation did not go ahead rapidly after its inception throughout China. Expansion of city commune organisation was, as far as one could tell, largely abandoned during the economic crisis. Throughout 1961 the Chinese press ignored city communes altogether.

"What does an embryo urban commune look like?" I asked Huang as we set off from the Bund. "You will see. The experimental urban commune you are visiting is called Tsang's Family Alleyway." The last commune I had inspected at length, although then I was unable to talk with people, had been in Peking, near the north-western corner of the inner city, on the road leading to the Great Wall and the Ming Tombs. I had been there with Audrey and the children on the Monday before we flew south to Shanghai. Long lines of boys and girls, just out from school, were snaking along the street on a fly-killing campaign. Each child carried its own fly-swatter. Other youngsters were sweeping pavements. Women, their hair covered with dirty towels wound into turbans, were crouching in lanes, welding and hammering at iron bedsteads and throwing bits of scrap metal on piles. The din had been unbelievable. One small workshop was making fur animals. Looking through doorways into courtyards we had seen carpenters' shops, shoe mending stands and outdoor repair stations for bicycles, pedicabs and cart wheels. From every mean little window came the noise of work. Finished or half-finished articles had been dumped on the street awaiting collection. Compared with the Peking urban commune, Tsang's Family Alleyway was well camouflaged. There was no appearance of special activity from the main street, as the cab stopped outside a narrow lane. At first, it looked a delightful place; none of the dingy, dusty lanes we had seen at the Peking commune. Here, the principal alleyway was festooned with red and white slogans, and bright murals were painted on the newly whitewashed walls of the houses. In the courtyard of a crèche tiny tots tumbled into each other, plump, laughing youngsters without a care in the world. On the surface it seemed a normal, happy place. The Communist who showed me around was a drably-dressed giant named U Ching-sung, who with a big shock of black hair was not unlike a handsome young version of Mao Tse-tung. He repeated the bit about the "embryo urban commune". The experiment at Tsang's Family Alleyway was succeeding, he said, leading the way as usual straight into the Communist sanctum complete with the photographs of China's Big Four—Mao, Head of State Liu Shao-chi, Chou En-lai and Chu Teh, the rugged soldier who roamed through China's countryside as Mao's general for decades. Chu Teh is now chairman of the Standing Committee of the National People's Congress.

U Ching-sung began the inescapable account of how awful things had been before Communism came. Tsang's Alleyway was ruled over by the underworld, he said, and gangsters were in control. There was blackmail, and much seducing of women. The homes now occupied by faithful Communist toilers were brothels, gambling houses and opium dens. He couldn't leave the U.S. forces out of his tale. "During 1946 the U.S. imperialists occupied Shanghai and their soldiers came to the brothels here in jeeps, dashing through the alleyway. Women were frightened to come out of doors. Many were seduced and beaten and cheated by the Americans."

Sometimes during these accounts I found it hard to keep a straight face, but the smiling foreigner doesn't deter a dedicated activist. The story merely becomes more lurid. Dutifully, I took down all the commune man said. My notebook became dotted with those two most common abbreviations, B.L. and A.L., for "before" and "after liberation".

"Before liberation the alleyway had only thirty university students," said U Ching-sung. "After liberation there were five-hundred. Before liberation, the Kuomintang régime did not care whether people were dead or alive. After liberation, our sinister life had gone forever."

Since most of the workers in Tsang's Family Alleyway (so

named because several thousand of the residents had the same sur-
name of Tsang) were women, three females in blue trousers sat in
on the talk. One of them, Li Mio-tsin, told me she used to be
called Miss Garbage at school in the olden days because her father
was a sweeper. Miss Garbage, now married with three children,
had a job in an alleyway nursery.

Though Chinese Communist statistics are deadly dull, it was
interesting to see how the bosses of Tsang's Family Alleyway had
succeeded in pressing the great majority of housewives into
joining the communal work. There were 1,245 able-bodied
housewives among the population. Of these 1,197 were working.

"Only a few dozen are not helping in socialist construction,"
U Ching-sung told me. "The city people have seen how peasants
in the rural people's communes have improved their living
standards and progressed in agricultural production. So we,
too, in the cities, wish to join communes and work in the same
way."

Tsang's Family Alleyway had twenty-four community dining
halls, where nearly 8,000 people were eating. Evidently 5,000 or
more preferred to take meals in private. There were fifteen
nurseries with a total population of 1,300 children. The average
person spent ten yuan a month on food at the community dining
halls, although it cost between twelve and thirteen yuan if they
wished to take better meals. Most of the dining halls had a
service right around the clock to cater for night workers. House-
cleaning was done on the basis of eighty cents a day if the housewife wanted help all day long. She paid ten cents for a person to
come and clean her home for two hours. What struck me as odd
was that a seamstress who earned twenty yuan per month could
pay twenty-four yuan a month to a cleaning woman to tidy her
home. On top of this came her meals and other costs like laundry
and clothing. I have read several reports, by the way, about
communes providing members with clothes but never came
across this practice myself. In the various rural communes I
visited, workers invariably bought their own clothes from their
wages.

When it looked as if U Ching-sung would never stop talking I
suggested we should begin our tour. Whole houses in the experimental commune had been converted into miniature factories.
In each room, sitting grim-faced and silent, women worked
ceaselessly assembling telephones, cutting material and sewing,

either by hand or on machines allegedly donated to the commune. Trying to talk to them was useless because not only Huang but the women activists and U Ching-sung were listening and taking notes. I took a picture of one woman sitting at her sewing machine with a stubborn, almost angry twist on her lips. When I asked her name she attempted a half-hearted smile. Ne Hsua-tsen was a mother of four who worked six days. "How much do you earn each month?" I asked. "Twenty yuan, but these days remuneration doesn't matter. We are building socialism." Rates of pay were virtually impossible to establish, especially on an hourly basis. The Communists encouraged people not to worry about money, and the number of man-hours the State was handed by Chinese who "volunteered" for spare-time labour during the "great leap forward" years reached staggering proportions. Hourly rates could not be assessed accurately since workers on set wages might be allowed to study during working hours. Or they could attend political meetings. Eric Chou, a Chinese newspaperman said that before he had come to Hongkong he spent many months in a school set up to "remould" the thinking of intellectuals. During this time he was paid his full salary by his Communist bosses. Cold cash, to the Communists, hardly mattered. What they dearly wanted, and what many could not give, was the fullest support for their policies. Incidentally, some weeks after telling me in the autumn of 1961 that he could never go along whole-heartedly with Communist policies, Eric Chou, an editor of the Hongkong Communist newspaper *Ta Kung Po* finally broke with Peking for good, and fled to London.

In Tsang's Alleyway most of the women obviously had no love for their new chores. I looked around the room at the seamstresses and scribbled into my notebook, "None look happy." We went into one of the mess halls. The sight of the rice or millet mash always depressed me. Here at least there was some variety. A menu, stuck up on the wall, gave a choice of about twenty dishes. U Ching-sung said people could spend anything from a few cents to several yuan for a meal, depending on their means. The place was crowded. Some fifty people, most of them women and old men, sat at primitive tables eating their lunch. Several children had saucepans which they held over the serving counter to be filled up. They paid and walked home to have a family meal in private.

From the diplomats in Peking I had heard that the city communes they visited had appalled them, and I must say the Shanghai experimental commune shattered me. The rural communes had not been nearly as grim. Peasants took their time, leaning on their spades or gathering the harvest by slow, age-old methods. The pressure did not seem to weigh them down. Provided there was enough food, they were content. But in Shanghai, along those whitewashed alleyways, the tyranny of Communism did exist. It was in the eyes of the old men who spent their day taking staples out of magazines, and in the voice of the peasant woman who was wiring up receivers in the telephone workshop. I had asked her how the women felt about having their children at a kindergarten during the week while they worked. Her grumbled answer was never translated. Huang said, "She speaks a dialect nobody can understand." Tsang's Alleyway was one of my most depressing experiences in China. I was glad to leave there. I think it had given Huang quite a start, too.

*   *   *

In my urban commune folder I had gathered a great pile of Communist propaganda about the new city organisations. Audrey had taken the children for a walk, and in the free hour before the 1 p.m. rendezvous I had arranged with her in the Huping dining-room I looked through the glowing Communist newspaper reports from different parts of China. The women of Chengchow, capital of Honan Province, were seemingly vastly different creatures from the glum workers I had met at Tsang's Alleyway. This is how the New China News Agency correspondent stationed there pictured the new life in a commune. "Early every day," he wrote, "flocks of women in the north-east corner of Chengchow city go chatting and laughing on their way to their neighbourhood factories to begin a new, busy and joyous day. In the past these women had to do a daily round of shopping, cooking, cleaning and minding their children. Their round of chores ended at bed-time to begin again the next day at dawn."

Without bothering to mention that in the greater part of the world most women still go about these daily chores reasonably contented with their lot, the report said that now everything in Chengchow had changed, "including the lives of the former housewives". There was a description of how the urban com-

197

mune was born. Kai Hsiu-jung, secretary of a local Communist
Party branch in Chengchow and the chairman of the local Community Committee, suggested to some interested housewives that
they "might start a neighbourhood production team". That was
in May 1958. "Women of about a dozen households immediately
took to the idea and set to work. Being unskilled and lacking
initial funds, they began making simple things like cloth shoesoles,
paper bags and other small articles for a department store which
supplied the raw material." Kai Hsiu-jung helped them to establish
links with the store. Soon they "found the merits of working
collectively" and their skill improved quickly by pooling their
ideas. The women's team got a reputation for its good work,
more orders came in, more housewives joined and the group split
up into sub-teams.

"With the increase in steady work," the New China News
Agency report continued, "the question of providing regular care
for children and preparing meals came up. Chia Hsiu-ying, one of
the housewives, said, 'Oh, if we could have a dining-room and a
nursery like the factories do!' Another woman picked up the idea
and said, 'Why don't we set them up ourselves?' Before she
could finish, the other women started agreeing. One of them
offered a kitchen knife, and others pots and pans and other
utensils. Tu Hsiu-chen, known for her good cooking, volunteered to take over the kitchen and another woman said she
would take responsibility for the nursery. The twenty-one
households making up the teams pulled down the walls separating
their courtyards so that they could come and go more easily, and
called it a big socialist compound. Freed from household worries,
they now all could work eight hours a day. Labour efficiency was
doubled. Their success rapidly caught on among other housewives in the vicinity who flocked to visit their socialist compound." And so on. This particular report, and scores of others
that were identical, went on interminably about how successful
the early urban communes had proved.

Another story in the *People's Daily* gave detailed descriptions of
an urban commune in Harbin's Hsiangfang district which had
established a network of community dining-rooms, nurseries,
kindergartens and service centres. Household work formerly
done by ten thousand housewives, said the paper, was now being
handled by 3,100 members of the commune service centres.
"When the workers go off to work," the Harbin story went on,

"these members come to tidy up the homes and do all the household chores entrusted to them with enthusiasm and care. They have the confidence of all the families. With the development of collective amenities, the working women can now go to spare-time schools in their free time, and fifty-one schools of various levels have been set up by the commune to meet their needs." The commune, established around Harbin's giant bearings plant, took in eighteen State-owned factories, twenty-nine foundry, machine-building and other plants which were merged from hundreds of small workshops. The Chinese claimed that a survey of 8,330 households in one street of the Hsiangfang commune showed that in 1959 family earnings rose by 28.6 per cent over 1958. Harbin, one of China's experimental cities in urban community living, established its first commune late in 1958. Then nobody breathed a word about it. While in Harbin, I must have driven through dozens of commune streets, but none of the Chinese told me a thing. Perhaps they didn't know themselves that communes had been formed!

By trying to organise city dwellers' lives to such a staggering degree that even visitors from other Communist nations were thunder-struck, the Communists hoped to raise not only production but also people's income. The party was asking citizens to trade individual freedoms for the sake of national progress. In many urban communes, householders were told to hand the keys of their homes or rooms to commune service centres on leaving for work. It is plain that the Communists wanted the city housewife to disappear altogether since they considered looking after a family was not sufficiently productive. Women who were housewives and nothing else were accused of "backwardness". Normal family tasks like cooking, cleaning, mending and washing could be handed over to "service stations". The daily family meals could be eaten in a communal mess hall with other members of the collective. The Communists promised urban commune members they could own personal belongings like clothing, household goods, furniture, and even houses and bank deposits. But private ownership of anything in China, the way things were moving, seemed useless. What was the point of owning a house if the State, using its Communist activists, made things unbearable for the owner until he was forced to rent out a large portion of it, naturally at a rental suggested by the authorities? Why worry about furniture and household goods if you knew that each day several commune members would examine your room? The urban commune service stations did everything for the commune member except scratch his back. They put new soles on his shoes, repaired his bicycle, washed his underwear, scrubbed kitchens, dusted floors, bought train tickets, booked seats for the theatre, tailored the blue boiler suits to measure. Most of all, the Communists wanted citizens to sit down together in the collective canteen. This need not be as difficult for them to achieve as it seems. In a society organised by the State, the authorities can make food easily available in canteens and impossible to buy in shops. Or they can merely close a local food store and set up a community dining-room in its place. Nothing could be simpler!

It must be pointed out that the Chinese claim that peasants and city dwellers formed their communes in a burst of spontaneous community activity is utter poppycock. In China, the Communist Party leads and all others follow. Up to a point, of course, the Communist activists need public support. Or at least they cannot act in the face of passive peasant resistance. But nobody pretends that during the formation of the rural communes the peasants willingly gave back the land they had been handed by the régime several years before. It was the pressure of a dissatisfied population which forced the Chinese Communist Party to embark on its drastic programme of modifications in 1960 and 1961. On New Year's Day of 1962 the *People's Daily*, the most widely read mouthpiece of the Chinese Communist Party, promised "that if an average crop harvest is reaped this year and the adjustment in industry made more effectively, we can provide a more solid foundation for a leap forward in the future and, after a long period of work, build our country into a mighty socialist power with modern industry, modern agriculture, and modern sciences and culture".

But there were not many other promises in that editorial which admitted, once again, that large numbers of people had to be transferred from cities and towns back to the countryside to help grow food. "Only by recovery and expansion of agricultural production," warned the *People's Daily*, "can the supply of most of the raw materials for light industry be reliably ensured, the living standards of the people further improved and a solid foundation of heavy industry provided."

Peking had moved from the elated exaggerations of several years ago to the "blood, sweat and tears" propaganda it falls back on whenever there is a crisis of any kind. With the emphasis placed on the rural areas, the urban communes were shelved, and their future is as nebulous as the future of their rural counterparts, and indeed of orthodox Communism in an ever-changing world. Three years after their birth in 1958 the rural communes were no longer recognisable. Peasants, in 1961, were tilling private land again. Free enterprise in rural areas was a new vogue. Threatened with increasing hunger due to physical inertia and spiritual stagnation among farmers (which reached its lowest point during the two winters after we left China) Peking adopted realistic, but for Communists, drastic measures. Peasants were given the right to trade their own farm produce and handicrafts, produced in their own time, at rural fairs specifically organised for this purpose. Even the Communists realised that this kind of free enterprise was a sure-fire method of raising production. The moderates in the party were accused of resorting to capitalism by the extreme left-wing. "One step back, two forward," the leaders reminded the critics. "We'll start communising again when we're ready." In the light of things to come, the urban commune newspaper stories I filed away in April and May grossly overstated the success of the city experiment just as U Ching-sung had exaggerated to an unbelievable degree the "communal joys" of Tsang's Family Alleyway.

Although Huang's ambitious programme was never completed, he did arrange several other visits to a children's club, a Buddhist temple, and a "pleasure house" which in the bad old days had been a brothel and now was a people's theatre. On the last evening, he shepherded us along Nanking Road with its giant Technicolor hoardings of steelworkers, peasants and professors to the eighteen-storied Cathay Mansions. We stood in the strong wind on the roof of the skyscraper to get a bird's-eye view of Shanghai. Directly below was the Soochow Creek crowded with hundreds of moored junks and sampans. Well-loaded barges passed beneath the Garden Bridge into the Whang Poo River.

"The people do not have to sleep and eat on the sampans as they did before liberation," Huang was saying. "Now many of them live in the 170 people's rural communes around Shanghai. They have a far better life than before."

From the roof we had a superb peep into the grounds of the British Consulate, just at the end of the Bund. The British had preserved their large downtown grounds, and the trim Consulate lawns looked ready for a Test match. They were an emerald island in a leaden sea of grey roofs and streets. "I wonder when they played the last game of cricket in Shanghai?" I said to Audrey. It was no use asking Huang. He would have been too young to know. But he did point out a park just opposite the British Consulate which in the olden days displayed a notice: "Dogs and Chinamen not allowed."

The clock in the Customs House just down the road from the hotel struck six as we approached the Huping. The chimes must have been modelled on London's Big Ben.

Last thing, I went to the river to watch the junks. Tattered, patched sails gradually changed colour from a dirty white to the copper red of dusk. The sun was setting over Shanghai, marking the death of the day.

20

GOODBYE, HAUNTING FLAGS

We were flying south-west. For me it was the close of the assignment, the end of those brief eight months that had taught me more about China and Communism than eight years of studies on the outside could have done. Already there were the memories. I saw Farquhar's bright blue eyes twinkling at me through horn-rimmed glasses as we sat listening to translations at a rally of a speech by some automaton attacking for the umpteenth time "the man-eating, cannibalistic system of capitalist imperialism". I wondered whether Chinese children think U.S. millionaires feast on human flesh? Memories of the sad, forced gaiety at the British Club dances, with everyone trying so desperately to enjoy the evening; of pretty Marit Metselaar extricating herself from the clutches of a visiting businessman who was rolling around the dance floor with one too many under his belt; of the roly-poly Chinese women in their drab winter padding. The only females who hadn't looked ludicrous in the winter were the tall girls, like the air hostess on our plane. She was walking toward me offering passengers miniature bananas three inches long. No sophistication for her. No lipstick or powder, no slender nyloned calves blossoming below a trim, knee-high skirt. Like the pilot and the other passengers, she wore a boiler suit. But she had a friendly smile like the girls I had seen at the Hsin Chiao dances, with a brass band playing "After-the-ball-was-over" music. I remembered the Chinese soldiers dancing with each other at the National People's Congress Hall, after a banquet, wheeling around the highly-polished floor rigidly, like large marionettes. The air hostess would have made a far better partner.

Kaleidoscopic reminiscences came and went on that last flight. The boy three seats in front of me could have been the little chap with coal-black shining eyes whose picture I had taken at Peking Zoo. He was balancing precariously on the back of an enormous tiger. A fearsome beast. Stuffed. The twins had thought it so life-like they wouldn't go near it. Imperialists were paper tigers, Mao Tse-tung had said. The Chinese Communists called the U.S. forces on Taiwan paper tigers, but they weren't game to prove it. They merely shouted about it at the anti-U.S. rallies. One rally had featured pig-tailed girl soldiers. Quite cute some of the female warriors were. They sat on the ground, in their lap neither the head of a lover with pleading eyes nor a baby sure of a kiss. In their lap rested a rifle. "Not loaded, I hope," I said to one rather beautiful soldier as I took her picture. She didn't understand. Nobody seemed to speak English. Why should they? The air hostess had just a few words. Now there was a typical Chinese girl. Not as beautiful as that one girl soldier. Just average. But genial and refreshing.

She reminded me of the chattering young bus conductresses in Peking who nattered on incessantly. "What in heaven's name is she saying?" I had once asked Richard Harris when we were on a bus together. "I've yet to get on a bus with a silent conductress."

He had laughed. "I'll give you a literal translation. She's saying, 'Have foreign guests aboard. Are there any seats?' She's asking for volunteers to get up for us."

But what about the other times, I asked him. He explained it was the usual public education campaign, don't spit, move down the aisle, form queues at bus stops, don't heave garbage out of windows, make way for mothers with children, keep the bus clean.

The Chinese Communists were dedicated people, I'll give them that. Their fanaticism frightened me, but I also admired them for it. In their one-track Marxist minds they were fighting for much more than a few hundred or, for that matter, a few million, dollars. God, what a life it must have been for party men. A dull, arid neverness with no laughter, no love. The only permissible passion was work. And, of course, the party. Once you were in the party there was hope. The black chauffeur-driven cars, curtained with white lace for added privacy, were a few years nearer. The party could mean power, and power was even better than money. Party men, in spite of regular rectification, purification and correction campaigns, in the end were infinitely better off than most. They got special rations. And how they had enjoyed those Peking banquets, which, by the way, were later cut back from a dozen and more courses to only four or six because of the bad impression the huge meals made on foreign visitors to the Chinese capital.

The plane landed at Nanchang, capital of Kiangsi Province. While we taxied off the main runway, three jets moving in formation wooshed into the air, as if hinting at China's growing armed strength. Most of the military attachés in Peking thought the Communists hoped to build the nation into a great nuclear power. When it came to defence, China was the biggest mystery on the map. All we really knew was that she had vast land armies, many millions strong, with several hundred millions, from young children to middle-aged women, in the militia.

No outsiders can follow China's progress in the world arms race. Her isolation helps rather than hinders her military preparations. While the West talks openly about the location of missile bases, military security in China is so tight foreigners have been arrested for taking photographs of privates ambling through a park. Diplomats in Peking admitted they knew nothing about China's real military strength. The territory is immense, the Press rigidly controlled, the people well disciplined. Nothing short of nation-wide revolt can prevent China from emerging as the best-armed Asian power. Russia has given the Chinese at least one nuclear research reactor, now operating since 1958, which has led some scientists to say the Chinese will explode their first atom bomb by 1963. Lately estimates have put the date further into the future because Russian pressure against Peking must have been accompanied by a withdrawal of Soviet experts from nuclear installations, and therefore China's atomic potential is anybody's guess. With or without the bomb, disarmament is the mightiest weapon China holds in her fight to gain more recognition. A world disarmament pact without China's participation would be about as futile as a cart minus its wheels.

In the Nanchang air terminal, a small, squarish brick building, we waited patiently until a smiling Chinese came up, and said in faultless English, with just a trace of an American accent, "There's too much cloud over Canton, but they hope it'll clear before long." We got talking. He was in his early thirties and had worked for American Airlines in New York and elsewhere before coming to China soon after 1949. He had been a pilot in the Chinese Air Force, but said he was forced to quit because he was putting on too much weight.

"Don't you find it strange living here?" I asked.

"You get used to it." He was unusually frank. "People forget how poor the Chinese were. Security is important to people here. You can't be fired like I was in the States when the airline no longer needed me. You always know that tomorrow you'll eat again."

Security, yes, but look at the price. "Why must everybody agree with the Communists? You've got to praise the party to get on. Doesn't it get tiring?"

"You grow used to it. You know there's work. That means a great deal. It's better than being sacked." He had a big chip on his shoulder about that American Airlines job.

We took off soon after. Below were soft greens, endless canals criss-crossing the fields, and on the brown water minute, toy-like barges. Two hours out of Nanchang we banked down over the hills near Canton, above the lush square lots of young rice and the blue pools of flooded paddy fields. They must have known the Nossals were coming. Our hand luggage was taken from the plane to a waiting station wagon by trolley. By 4 a.m. we were in the Ai-chun (or Love of the Masses) Hotel, a depressingly dark place with one compensation—its magnificent view over the Pearl River.

That evening we took the children to a puppet show with marionettes the size of a two-year-old, but we turned in fairly early since our interpreter, a grumpy, pimply-faced girl of about twenty-five, insisted we must be ready to leave the hotel next morning by 6.30 a.m.

Canton was already stirring when we drove to the station. I couldn't help feeling again that the Cantonese must hate Communism, and were constantly punished by Peking for adopting a lackadaisical attitude toward their political masters. Canton sported no red flags, no wall posters of Mao. The "couldn't-care-less" atmosphere was most marked. People lounged around, just as the coolies did in Hongkong when it was too hot to work. Apart from the queues outside mess halls, even at that early time of morning, I had seen hardly any communal activity in Canton. A few hopeful souls were tending cabbages and spinach they had planted right next to the concrete footpath. The Communists called this "suburban or neighbourhood farming". Around Peking's diplomatic quarters, where the Chinese road builders had left plenty of space for nature strips, wheat instead of grass was growing because food was so scarce.

Our spotty girl guide saw us safely into the airy observation car at the end of the train.

"I hope you will come again to China," she said as we shook hands.

"I'm sorry we couldn't stay longer this time. No sooner had my family arrived than we were forced to leave."

Her face fell. I did not go into details. "Goodbye, and thanks for your help."

The brief journey to the border was comfortable. The children were well rested and in good spirits. The observation car was empty except for us and a small party of Indonesians being escorted to Shumchun by their Chinese hosts. We got to the border at nine-thirty in the morning, and there was the inevitable Mr. Fung, lanky and, as usual, fluttering about nervously. It was my fourth encounter with Fung. He urged us to get out of the train quickly so that we might make the early connection into Hongkong. Good old Fung had not changed. Always rushing people. "With four children I'm not hurrying for anybody, Mr. Fung," I warned him. We took our time as we marched along the platform, filled out the Customs declarations, and waited for the baggage examination. In all we had twenty-two pieces, including the twins' toy carricots. The Chinese Customs men opened, one after the other, about fifteen suitcases. They went through my files, reading stories and letters, carefully scrutinising negatives. But we seemed to be doing fairly well, and Fung still wore a vaguely optimistic smile. They then found the prints I had bought from a Chinese photo agency on Wang Fu Ching. There were scores of them. The Customs man peered at each one, handing them on to a girl assistant, who passed them on to a third party. When a soldier appeared on a photo it was laid aside pointedly.

"Where did you get these pictures?" the boss of the Customs people asked.

"I bought them in Peking. The Foreign Ministry told me where to get them."

They glared at me suspiciously. By now there were at least half a dozen Customs and other officials swarming round our baggage. How could such secret defence information as a grinning Chinese soldier holding up a large cabbage be issued by an official agency of the People's Republic? The soldier photographs fell into two categories. There were pictures of army manœuvres—nine small Chinese tanks, with six soldiers clinging precariously to the sides of each vehicle, rolling through hilly countryside, some officers studying a newspaper, army landing craft with machine-guns mounted on small gun carriages making for a beach, naval torpedo boats in action, a dozen Chinese jets flying in formation over a military airport. Even these pictures didn't say much, but the Customs boys were equally worried about the second category, of the Chinese Army at work; a young soldier in a Mao Tse-tung cap with the giant cabbage, another examining a field of spinach. Three soldiers in fur caps and padded uniforms swung picks at a dry patch of earth. Four grinning soldiers peered at four snuffling hogs. A single soldier wearing an Army cap working among a group of canal-diggers had been plucked out with the others by the zealous protectors of China's defence secrets. The hour they spent studying the pictures lengthened into two. Time for lunch came. We could eat up-stairs, Fung said, in a special foreigners' dining-room, and the examination of our luggage would continue later. Fung seemed very hurt. We had ruined his day.

About 1 p.m. Audrey and I held a conference on strategy. Up till lunch we had kept the children fairly quiet, but now action was needed. The twins laid out their dolls on the tables where the cases were being examined. Shane was put to sleep on the only sofa in the Customs room. Kim was examining the three National Geographic maps which the Customs girl studied with a colleague, telling them where I had been in China. I began scribbling notes, and Audrey kept Fung running with requests for hot water to make coffee.

By one-thirty the row in the Customs became unbearable. Shane had woken up and was crying and so was Michelle whom Kim had punched. Nicole had broken one of the toys we had bought in Canton to keep the children quiet on the final journey, and was badgering people to fix it. I was typing away as noisily as possible. The distraught Customs men conceded defeat, and withdrew their troops into an adjoining room from which we heard them shouting into phones. I guessed they were ringing Canton, possibly even Peking to check whether my story about the photographs was true.

The Customs chief came rushing into the turmoil of the tired, grumbling children. It was 2.15 p.m.

"Who was with you when you ordered these pictures?" He spoke excellent English.

"Well, naturally I took my interpreter. As you know I can't speak Chinese. I picked the photographs I wanted, and he helped me to fill out the order forms. He dictated the picture captions and I typed them, right in that place."

"Where was this shop? Was it near the big department store?" I drew a little map for him, and he nodded.

An Army officer arrived to view the dozen-odd photographs showing soldiers, and dismissed each one as harmless. Still the Customs people were not convinced, and in the adjoining room made more phone calls. By 3 p.m. I was getting uneasy. Four large packing cases which had been nailed up in our room in Peking were still unopened.

It was my turn to haunt Mr. Fung. He was walking up and down the platform, a badly shattered Fung, obviously embarrassed that a few innocuous photographs could cause such havoc.

"We never caught that first train," I grinned at him. "The second and third trains have gone too. How much longer will they be, do you think?" He had such a helpless, hang-dog look on his face I felt sorry for him.

"They will let you know the answer soon," he mumbled weakly.

At three-thirty I marched up to the man in charge of the Customs Office and said very firmly: "We have now waited here for six and a half hours. If you are prepared to release some of the cases, containing clothing, I think my family should be allowed to cross the border into Hongkong. I will stay behind."

The Customs people agreed to this immediately. I kept one small attaché case, a toothbrush, tinned coffee, several plastic mugs, a spoon, a jar of sugar, a tin of cream, paper and the typewriter. The children led the way to the bridge, I walked with Audrey, and Fung brought up the rear. Possibly he thought I might try to skip across into Hongkong with the family.

I squeezed Audrey's hand. "Don't worry. Go straight to the hotel. I'll be there tomorrow." She said goodbye to Fung. "If you don't let my husband go by tomorrow, we're coming back to fetch him—the five of us, howling children and all." Fung's long face was pathetic. The children glared at him across the wooden barrier. "That won't be necessary, Mrs. Nossal, I am sure." I waved to Audrey and went back to the Customs room with him. All the luggage, except for the wooden crates,

had gone with Audrey. The situation was now distinctly unpleasant. In twenty-five minutes, at 4 p.m., the border between
Hongkong and China would be closed. I thanked my lucky stars
that I had given myself an extra day. It was Thursday, June 2.
My visa to China would not expire until tomorrow. What with
uncertain air travel and the Communist mentality I had decided a
day up my sleeve might be useful.

If they wanted to be difficult they could spend a good day
looking through the four packing cases. Two of them contained
my desk which was crammed with papers. If they were really
slow, the examination of the packing cases might last beyond
tomorrow, and on Saturday I would be stuck in China without a
visa. People had been arrested for less.

At three forty-five the top Customs man walked up. His
uniform looked rumpled after the day of crisis. He spoke in
clipped tones. "Here are your photographs. We are releasing
every one of them."

"Good," I said. "Thank you. What about my three maps?"

"Yes, the maps." He unfolded them. They were National
Geographic Magazine maps of the Far East, the China coast
from the Korean border down to North Vietnam, and of the
Chinese mainland. "You will notice one of these maps was
printed in Washington in 1945, before the People's Republic was
established. This map is all right." He pointed to the other two.
They were dated Washington, September 1952 and October 1953.
"These maps call the Chinese capital Peiping. As everybody
knows, our capital has been renamed Peking. Nevertheless, it has
been decided to release the three maps to you. But we wish to let
you know that we consider this an unfriendly act against the
People's Republic of China."

I had to smile. I tried to stop myself but couldn't. "Let me
assure you it was not intended as an unfriendly act by me personally. They happen to be excellent maps which my newspaper
mailed to me. The *Globe and Mail*, in its stories, calls the city
Peking, never Peiping. Now what about the packing cases?
Will you have time to start on them this afternoon?" I walked
outside the room where the crates had been left. They had
vanished.

"We are releasing the packing cases."

I could not believe my ears. The wooden crates held more than
our 20-odd leather cases and air bags combined.

"I take it the crates contain nothing of a controversial nature, no more of these pictures?" What in the hell did he expect me to say, with the border closing in a few minutes?

"No, no more pictures," I said. There weren't any, either. They might have confiscated a few more Chinese newspapers. They had taken all my Peking papers except copies of the *People's Daily*. Export of other Communist papers was now forbidden because of the growing food crisis. Papers were giving peasants advice on where to find edible herbs, leaves, grasses and roots.

"If you have nothing more to declare, then the Customs examination is over. You may proceed to Hongkong." It was 3.54 p.m. by my watch—six minutes to go.

"The packing cases are now being transported across the border," said Fung breathlessly. "We must hurry."

I picked up the typewriter and attaché case and began to walk. Fung, with his long legs, was urging me to get a move on. He was always a few steps in front.

From the platform to the bridge was a distance of a couple of hundred yards. Finally Fung snatched my typewriter and ran. He beat me to the border by a good twenty yards. I still had three minutes, shook a very relieved Mr. Fung by the hand, and crossed into British territory.

"You just made it," said the bulky British police officer. The last of several barbed wire barriers blocking the bridge was put into place. I looked for Audrey and the children, but they had already left by an earlier train. I turned back for a moment. Above the railway station and the frontier guard house, the flags of China were limp, still. Half an hour later, on the train into Kowloon, the scarlet Chinese flags were haunting me, as they had often done in my room at the Hsin Chiao during the first five months, before Audrey came. Always in Peking there were the red flags, during the October celebrations, at the political rallies, huge red banners flying from the gate of Tien An Men, flags inside factories and communes and on the high earthen dams which millions of Chinese peasant hands had raised from nothing. Red flags and singing peasants. Such sad singing. And the laughter I had marvelled at early in my stay. Later I realised it was laughter mingled with tears. During many drives to the outskirts of Peking I heard the peasants singing as they toiled. They sang with neither a smile in their eyes nor joy in their voices, but because it made the work easier.

Once I stopped to watch teams of singing men and women pounding the earth of a newly-dug canal. Eight men were competing against a dozen girls near by. Each group worked around a huge flat stone. They lifted the weight with ropes, keeping time with the song, then let it drop to the ground. They moved slowly along the embankment compacting the soft earth, back and forth, while other peasants deepened the canal. Again, by the new canal, were the red flags. At times I came back from such lone outings bewildered and puzzled. China had so many, many people like the dead-eyed peasants, who all had to be fed and clothed and housed. I would scurry into my room and try to shut out China, to forget Communism and the Chinese people and their countless problems. But the sad singing of the peasants had followed me into the room, and when I closed my eyes I was dragged back into their midst, engulfed by millions of men in blue. And all around, the red, blood-red flags.

EPILOGUE

No feeling of surging relief swept through me as the train rolled away from China. I was glad I hadn't been forced to overstay my visa, yes, but if anything I felt disappointed. The Peking job, despite the drabness and the frustrations of daily life, had been a challenge. I had watched the continuing revolution in a nation of seven-hundred million poverty-stricken people. I was sorry that a small but important experiment in peaceful co-existence attempted by my newspaper had failed. The *Globe and Mail* had been scrupulously fair in presentation of reports, publishing both the positive stories and the criticism. To penetrate the bamboo curtain had meant a great deal of preparatory work—including a trip to China—by the editors of the paper. Getting their own man into Peking on a semi-permanent basis was a triumph yet never once had I been urged from Toronto to tone down my more critical material. In his front-page explanation on the closure of the Peking bureau, the editor and publisher, Oakley Dalgleish, made no apologies. "Our intention," he said, "was that the *Globe and Mail*'s representative in Peking would report the news, and the background to the news, honestly and objectively, without favour or rancour." He advised the Chinese Foreign Minister, Marshal Chen Yi, that the *Globe and Mail* felt I had been honest and fair, and that in the absence of specific charges against me the paper could not consider naming a replacement. The courage of their convictions had forced the *Globe and Mail* to abandon the Peking dateline, considered in many newspaper circles as the most glamorous in the world.

Why this yearning by news organisations to have a man stationed in Peking? Isn't it just a capital like any other? No, far from it. Peking is the political centre of an astounding experiment taking in almost a quarter of humanity, the capital of a hard new world being reborn in an ancient environment. It is a region that must be explored for, even in an age of incredibly rapid communications, when men are travelling into space and preparing for visits to the moon, Peking remains isolated from the rest of the globe. Editors realise that the China of today is the most remote and mysterious of the great nations, her hinterlands more impenetrable than the jungles of New Guinea, her Communist rulers as arrogant and inaccessible to most as the monarchs of the Celestial Empire were in the past. China, one of the fountainheads of human civilisation, has become the enigma of the atomic world. Nobody could predict what she would do next, though it was a little easier to make guesses from Peking than from the outside. Covering China from Hongkong is dull by comparison to working inside. Those who say one can assess and observe the Chinese scene more accurately beyond its borders are talking nonsense. It is an absurd claim, for in spite of all the restrictions, once across that short steel bridge that leads into China you are in another realm.

It is little wonder that Peking's policies—both internal and international—seem quite undecipherable to most foreign governments. The old poverty and the newborn power, the timeless face of the peasant, the burning eyes of the Communist, the mud hovels on the land and the extravagant Communist palaces thrown up in Peking—all these contrasts were China as she is today. It is vastly important that more Western political leaders, scientists, educators, businessmen and reporters should try to batter down the many barriers that keep the West out of Peking. Even a glimpse of China, such as mine was, made it possible to gain a more balanced impression of a nation whose leaders are determined to outwork and outbreed us. The overruling phenomenon I saw there was the pounding rhythm, now slower than for some years because of disillusionment and food shortages. But the Chinese Communists are doing their utmost to mend their breach of contract with their people. At the top there remains an urgent, and for the West, an ominous striving. The Chinese masses are engaged in a frantic race for the global supremacy of Communism. Peking's party chiefs want to remould not only the thinking of the population to suit Marxist policies but to change the whole character of the people.

For thousands of years the Chinese people have been human reeds, bending with the winds of time. Their passivity and submissiveness had made them both gentle and slow. The Chinese culture that blossomed through centuries of dynasties was wilting long before Mao came on the scene. The Communists want to enliven the nation once again, to transform the resigned peasant into a fiery crusader. There comes, of course, the acute contradiction between this goal and the other Communist aim— blind obedience and national discipline. Communism is trying to lift the Chinese people out of their enslavement to poverty only to subject them to absolute servility to the State. In 1960 and 1961, as food rations dwindled, the meagre ration of liberty allowed to the Chinese was raised slightly. The Party was thrown into confusion by tidal waves of doubt flooding through even the simplest Chinese minds. The splendid placards of abundant harvests and the magazine photographs of bright new cities were all very well, for a time. Too many Chinese began asking themselves the same questions. "When is it my turn for more food and a better home? When can I relax?"

Yet there is no denying that Communism has done much for China. The Peking government has cleaned the land of corruption, of filth in the streets, of warlords and bandit hordes. It has been ruthless in stamping out organised prostitution and gambling. Organised vice cannot exist side by side with the Chinese brand of Communism. The Communists give children and their parents schooling, Marxist education admittedly, but better than nothing. The labour armies mobilized by Peking are turning out goods ranging from tractors and trolley buses to pins and needles; they are building cars, locomotives, refrigerators and television sets; they are launching tugs and trawlers, freighters and submarines; they are harnessing rivers to provide electricity and water for irrigation.

But weigh against these benefits the losses, to the individual, the family, to human dignity. Since Chinese citizens are supposed to belong to one seven-hundred-million-member family fathered by the State, the home life of people is made to seem unimportant. Children are encouraged to reserve their energies for the State, and the contacts with their parents are growing looser. Worse by far has been the suffering of the intellectuals and the educated middle class. They face two choices—compliance with Communist commands or social extinction. Temporary relaxations in Party dominance and control do not alter Communism's fundamental dogmas, and therefore the non-conformists have no hope of swimming against the current. Every so often, as in

1961 and 1962, the reins that harness the nation to the Party's chariot will be eased slightly. But the top men in Peking cannot afford to be too pliant for long. Liberalism, to the Chinese, is a form of Marxist revisionism, a twisting of the dogmas that Mao Tse-tung has pronounced as pure and universal truths. While they live and strive, the Party's leaders must believe implicitly in the orthodox Communist faith they have studied, preached and practised for nearly forty years. If they also had doubts, it would be nothing less than an admission that their materialistic religion is a pipedream, a utopian rainbow they will never reach. In the history of man, their cause is hopeless, and will not survive. The gradual death of feudalism, colonialism and rampant capitalism must be followed eventually by the disintegration of orthodox Communism. Any religion that makes Party politicians and the people under them into the greater and lesser gods of an earthly heaven cannot endure the test of centuries. Communism can and will, however, have drastic repercussions in the immediate future. It is an atheistic religion that will find favour and continue to spread in a materialistic world.

Peking's Communists have realised this, and are using the Marxist foundation to build China into an industrial giant. If they succeed, even by the end of this century, the world's economic and political picture will undergo a change far more revolutionary than that caused by the Kremlin's Marxists. Industrialisation in Japan and Hongkong has already caused upheavals in the economies of Western nations. But China has seven times more people than Japan and two hundred and twenty times as many people as Hongkong. The potential alliance of Chinese manpower with Japanese technical know-how is the main reason why not only Western nations but the Soviet Union are courting Japan, and coming to her with trade pacts and extravagant promises of lasting friendship.

Western hate for Chinese Communist methods does not minimise their eventual effect on our economy. We must face up to the fact that Communism is not as unpopular as we might wish. Admittedly, in highly-developed communities the Marxism of the Soviet Union or the more dogmatic Communism of China would find it almost impossible to take root. We make the mistake of blindly damning all aspects of Communism, in any part of the world, as essentially evil. The Chinese are not as foolish. "We will take from the Western way of life anything that is good," Chinese Communists used to tell me, "and reject what is bad." They were prepared to study our social system, picking and choosing as they wished, and avoiding the mistakes we made. But men like the late Senator Joseph McCarthy struck such fear of Communism into American hearts that people developed a mental curtain which slammed shut the moment the word was mentioned. Yes, Communism is an alien, arid doctrine. But it is not all bad. It has some excellent points—socially, economically and internationally. These aspects of Communism we of the West should be studying. If people knew more about Communism, they would be less afraid of it, and we would be in a better position in the struggle between the two systems.

The need of the West today is a common cause. Western global policies are beset by a tragic aimlessness. People in our nations, where science has pushed living standards to an all-time high, are searching for a meaning to life. In the Communist bloc and in the underdeveloped lands this quest presents no problem. The Communist countries have their common goal—to communise the globe—and the poorer nations will be kept busy for decades seeking national unity and a better life for their peoples. To Asians and Africans the people of the West are, even when taken on the average basis, incredibly wealthy. The energy of Western free enterprise has given to millions houses that stay warm the year round, roads as smooth as glass, automobiles so simple a child could drive them, a vast variety of food and consumer goods. Workers have been handed docile, push-button machines, and have been granted a shorter working week. To keep highly-paid staffs working (and therefore buying the goods we make) our industrial plants are campaigning for planned obsolescence. Consumer goods are at times made with one express purpose—to ensure the owner won't keep them for too long. We have come to accept the easy life as a matter of course, and we push aside serious thought about people and nations who have not yet reached our standards. Unless our children are taught in their schools that the advancement and well-being of the poorer lands is the responsibility of the wealthier nations, the West is set on a collision course with disaster.

In any contest for supremacy, education is the key to final success. If the Communist propaganda machine can indoctrinate the populations of nations within its sphere of influence thoroughly enough for several generations to follow governmental directives unquestioningly, Communism might well grow to frightening proportions. The time the West has to halt the creeping Communism which threatens the world's balance of power is growing short. Only a massive educational programme can achieve rapid results. In nations embracing well over 1,000 million people, the principal subject taught in countless schools is the materialistic religion of Communism.

Western schools teach mathematics, sciences, languages and some give social or religious instruction. But there is no longer any common bond, no single faith that holds Western culture together as Christianity did in the past. In societies satiated with material wealth, Christianity is losing its crusading spirit. Although we like to think of ourselves as a Christian community, the overwhelming majority of Western peoples do not practise Christianity. Most church-goers consider it sufficient if their Christianity is a once-weekly affair. In the Communist bloc, on the other hand, the Marxist dogmas are not only taught but must be obeyed daily. The idea that paradise on earth will come when the Communist missionaries have converted the globe is drummed day and night into people of all ages in lands stretching from North Korea westward as far as East Germany. Our loose, unconnected social and religious teachings in the West may be a poor match against Communist cultural offensives in the coming years. To beat Marxist teachings, mere anti-Communism is a hopelessly feeble weapon. The free nations must produce a higher, more stimulating social order to give the billions of poor people on earth hope for tomorrow.

Unless a revitalised, unified Christian church can meet this challenge—and this is dubious in an age moving too rapidly toward materialism—the West must find another common target at which to aim. The idealistic slogan of a better world for all should be transformed from a figure of speech into action. Few people, and fewer children, are given the opportunity to study the complexities and jealousies existing between the rich and the poor nations of the world. Because we lack the necessary education from an early age, most of us can't understand the issues involved. Education must help people in the West to identify themselves personally with the battle against poverty, disease and hunger being waged in Asia, Africa and Latin

America. It is not enough for governments to tell taxpayers: "We're raising our foreign aid grants which means your taxes are going up again!" This is the easy way out and it won't work. Just as Communist children are being taught to build a Communist world, our schoolchildren must learn that it is their duty and privilege to create a new order where men of all colours and creeds will help each other to grow wealthier in a climate of freedom.

Idealistic education must be mixed with realism. The giving of money and food to the poor is not enough either. The West must recruit its own vast force of space-age missionaries who are prepared to leave their homelands, as did the Christian crusaders of old, to spread education and knowledge among illiterate populations. More technicians, doctors, nurses, engineers and architects, farmers and economists must go from the rich world into the poor to preach and to teach. Western helpers in their millions should be prepared to sacrifice several years of the easy life at home if our aid programmes abroad are to assume some meaning in our own as well as in less privileged societies. The most common traveller in Asia is the American and European tourist, and it is hard to imagine a worse representative of Western culture. If millions of people can afford to float around the world aimlessly, for the sheer fun of it, why can't Western governments organise a massive migration of trained men and women whose basic mission it would be to show new nations how to help themselves? Several organisations such as the United Nations, the Colombo Plan, other political and cultural alliances and wealthy private enterprises have already pioneered such schemes. But these are only a drop in the ocean if we are to shoulder the task realistically. President Kennedy's plan for a peace corps is fine. But how much greater would be the impact if the West as a whole initiated an international education campaign with the sole purpose of elevating the underdeveloped nations to our living standards. Such a scheme can be conducted on the world-wide scale needed only if we realise that this is our one powerful counter against the dedicated Communists operating in most uncommitted countries as well as within the western alliance.

Nuclear armies will contain Communism up to a point. Western educators, bringing with them not guns or bombs but knowledge and help would prove far more effective. Above all, there must be unity of purpose among the so-called Christian nations of the West. Already a beginning has been made. A much wider, more ambitious global crusade to lift two-thirds of mankind out of hunger and poverty would breathe fresh life into our education, and would bring new meaning to a Western culture groping selfishly and smugly toward the third millennium after Christ.

INDEX